'Through concepts like psychological safety, people will thrive, value will be created, and the human condition will improve in concert with technology. *People Before Tech* is your essential guidebook to a human-centric approach.'

Heather McGowan, keynote speaker and author of
The Adaptation Advantage

'Unoptimized and disenfranchised teams will be your new norm unless you take action. In *People Before Tech*, Duena Blomstrom shows you how to create Psychological Safety and change lives. A must read.'

Karen Ferris, change management expert,
keynote speaker and author

'What Duena has done has not only thrust the human back into the heart of HR but also extends this deep into organizational psychology and the nature of productivity, teamwork, and workplace culture. A recommended read for leaders who want to change and transform their business and how they engage their workforce for the better.'

Theo Priestley, futurist and co-author of
The Future Starts Now

'Duena and I connected over our passion for psychological safety and making the workspace human again. Or as Duena puts it: "getting rid of our human debt". This book shows why psychological safety is a need-to-have and not just a nice-to-have if you want a successful company today and in the future.'

Gitte Klitgaard, Agile coach and keynote speaker

'The world faces great uncertainty in respect to increasing automation and the role humans will play in the future of business and the role work will play in our lives. *People Before Tech* tackles this issue head on as the culture of companies changes to digital-first and humans second. Duena provides us with a plan to keep humans engaged and differentiated during this global transformation.'

Brett King, bestselling author of Bank 4.0 *and*
The Rise of Technosocialism

PEOPLE BEFORE TECH

The Importance of Psychological Safety and Teamwork in the Digital Age

Duena Blomstrom

BLOOMSBURY BUSINESS

LONDON · OXFORD · NEW YORK · NEW DELHI · SYDNEY

BLOOMSBURY BUSINESS
Bloomsbury Publishing Plc
50 Bedford Square, London, WC1B 3DP, UK
29 Earlsfort Terrace, Dublin 2, Ireland

BLOOMSBURY, BLOOMSBURY BUSINESS and the Diana logo are trademarks
of Bloomsbury Publishing Plc

First published in Great Britain 2021

A catalogue record for this book is available from the British Library

Library of Congress Cataloguing-in-Publication data has been applied for

ISBN: 978-1-4729-8545-3; eBook: 978-1-4729-8546-0

2 4 6 8 10 9 7 5 3 1

Typeset by Deanta Global Publishing Services, Chennai, India
Printed and bound in Great Britain by CPI Group (UK) Ltd, Croydon CR0 4YY

To find out more about our authors and books visit www.bloomsbury.com
and sign up for our newsletters

To Dara, my 10-year-old son, who doesn't even need to be as amazing as he is to be making me want to wake up earlier and earlier, and put in the work to build a better reality, so it awaits him when he grows up.

Contents

Foreword
by Prof. Dr Amy Edmondson

I am delighted to write a foreword for Duena Blomstrom's terrific new book. I have gotten to know Duena and her work well over the past year or so, during which we have had many conversations to share ideas, explore the challenges of teamwork in organizational life, and brainstorm solutions. In these generative conversations across an ocean – well before COVID-19 made such meetings ubiquitous – I was consistently impressed by Duena's nuanced grasp of the concept of psychological safety, as well as by her appreciation of why it matters so very much in today's organizations. More importantly, I discovered – and learned from – her passionate, practical approach to making a difference.

I also came to admire Duena's productivity (this book seems to me to have been written with astonishing speed) – as well as her confidence that she could contribute to an already overactive conversation about psychological safety in the management press. The result is an engaging and practical book, full of insightful examples and practical tools. Duena is equally fluent in conveying the psychological challenges faced by human beings trying to bring their best selves to work as she is in designing tools and technologies that can help.

This book is a resource for leaders and managers in all kinds of organizations, private and public sector, small and large. Although the culture of business is prone to viewing psychological safety as something 'soft' or 'nice to have' if you can afford it, Duena explains why psychological safety is, in fact, at the very foundation of a functional organization in today's volatile, uncertain, complex, ambiguous

(VUCA) world. Psychological safety is 'hard' – not soft – in that it goes against our spontaneous self-protective instincts. It's necessary because all work today is knowledge work – and inescapably collaborative.

You may find yourselves bemoaning meetings as a waste of time and groups as places where good ideas go to die, but increasingly the truth of our profound dependence on each other for ideas, observations, questions, and concerns is overwhelming. This is why the success of any organization today is dependent on people's willingness to speak up. And speaking up is dependent on psychological safety. Without it, the behaviours that underlie effective collaboration, innovation, and even effective risk management are rare, and in some work environments all but impossible. To get anything accomplished in a technologically complex society requires the input of information and process sophistication from many fields. This does not happen without psychological safety.

These issues have become all the more important as the world becomes more complex and multicultural, making diversity an increasingly salient feature of organizational life. Engaging and integrating the insights of people from diverse backgrounds to produce new understanding and creative solutions requires psychological safety.

This book's emphasis is on people *and* technology – despite Duena's provocative term *PeopleNotTech*. It patiently explains how every aspect of our lives and organizations has been affected by technology, and argues that our humanity can be reaffirmed rather than lost amidst the many changes introduced by the rapid pace of digitalization and other technological changes.

Duena's work is dedicated to changing lives – by 'making people happy and highly productive at work'. A generation ago, that statement might have seemed an oxymoron. 'Happy' and 'highly productive' were simply seen to be at odds. The former might have implied doing what you want, perhaps at a relaxed pace, while the latter was achieved by a nose-to-the-grindstone approach, tolerating the hardship of work to get through the day and find happiness elsewhere. Today, in the knowledge economy, when we are so very dependent on ingenuity and collaboration to get challenging, interdependent, novel work accomplished, we are most productive when we feel good about who we are, what we bring, and how we work together with others. Happiness comes from meaningful engagement, not from work avoidance. And engagement happens best in an environment of psychological safety.

Psychological safety is here to stay. Enjoy learning more about it.

Amy C. Edmondson

Preface

'Human Debt™' is a term I coined while working on my first book, *Emotional Banking: Fixing Culture, Leveraging FinTech, and Transforming Retail Banks into Brands*, and it corresponds to an IT concept called 'tech debt', which refers to wrong turns, bad decisions or ignored mistakes made when writing code or architecting a system, which eventually have to be dealt with and cleaned up or the system is not sustainable and will collapse. 'Human Debt™' is the equivalent, which we have created in workplaces where emotional quotient (EQ), human connection and teamwork have been neglected, demoted and shunned. I resolved to find ways to 'do something about it'. To power this work, I had to turn to my own 'why'.

It's a simple and everyday one for me: I want to eradicate the Human Debt and, thanks to new technological innovations, it is much less of a lofty goal than it may seem. The intention is not to point fingers and paint all organizations with the same brush as there are many pockets of greatness, from HR heroes to the agile superheroes, who are true change makers, often lonesome knights valiantly battling the windmills of the organization with all their might. I have met tens – if not hundreds – of such exceptions and I am not ungrateful or oblivious they exist, I am simply being honest about what the size of the remaining Human Debt is, despite their efforts.

Broadly, we have neglected our workforce – we have put their happiness second. We have made empty gestures of respect. We have barely considered their well-being. We have picked up and dropped terms such as 'employee satisfaction', 'engagement', 'morale', 'passion', 'purpose', 'collaboration' and 'team building' and have done precious little for any of them. We have suffocated them with process and made them fearful and weary, often placing them in survival mode. They are acutely stressed, tired, afraid and unmotivated. Their mental health is on the sharp decline and we pretend that's none of our business. We treat them as resources. We employ no true empathy. We value IQ over EQ. We regard anything to do with understanding and helping them as an afterthought or a weakness. We never prioritize and value them. It's a modern-day tragedy and this accumulation of missed opportunities and lack of foresight and courage will eventually prove devastating. Just like 'technical debt' always needs to be paid, the bill for Human Debt has been presented to the vast majority of incumbent organizations and those who will not find a way to pay it off urgently by investing in people practices will see their business strain under the crippling effects of losing key staff and spending a growing percentage of time and resources battling accelerating turnover and lack of productivity.

Here, I will show how Psychological Safety is the only high performance lever we need, and teams are the only unit we must focus on. I will demonstrate how frameworks and methodologies that are meant to help a mythical 'organization' alongside empty rhetoric are harmful and we shouldn't waste our time on them. However, if we get Psychological Safety right, it results in high-performing employees who will also be satisfied and emotionally balanced. Organizations are moving from detailed long-term planning ahead of time to use more loosely defined roadmaps and working in small increments with measurements and indicators for guidance engaging in regular introspection and continuous improvement to produce the right results faster – something known as 'Agile'. I plan to eventually be able to use these Agile Key Performance Indicators (KPIs) to show that, simply because I feel that's Agile's greatest calling, beyond delivering results fast. Humanity has conjured it as a proof of concept of what it is possible to achieve if you shift the focus on humans. That's my why.

Sounds like a lot, but it isn't. It's a simple and deeply needed approach. I share it with the team. We're stupendously lucky, we know. For all of us at PeopleNotTech, which I co-founded, this 'why' is so evident we need no mission pep-talks and no vision reaffirming moments: 'Change lives by making people happy and highly productive at work'. It's so grand and deeply felt that it gets us all out of bed and ready to do hard work, naturally. But of course, for other companies and other people, the 'why' is much harder to find. If you run teams, you have to help them find it. And if you don't, and you only run yourself, you need to find it too.

The name of our company in itself is arguably controversial. Being called 'People Not Tech' when we are designing a software solution at the intersection of research and everyday work raises eyebrows and that is precisely why we chose it. It is a paradox we are more than willing to explore and debate at every given opportunity as it contains the crux of the issue – even if we employ technology to enable chemistry at work and to design and foster the perfect team dynamic and we use all the magic of tech we can muster, and while we firmly believe that real change at scale can never happen in the absence of any software to enable the People Practice, it is still never about the software but always about the people. It keeps us honest every day.

When we arrived at the blessed certainty that to effect great scale change in organizations, we have to do so at the team level, we looked at many theories on networks and team dynamics (from Tuckman to Gersick and even more effective models such as FiroB) and there simply isn't any other lever that correlates more closely to how well a team performs than how safe they feel as a unit. Sadly, for anyone interested in a quick sure-fire fix that ensures people are effective when they are plunged into the new ways of work (WoWs), there is no other factor one can reliably point to. Giving people more money, titles, responsibility or perks, while nice and useful, is not nearly as good as giving them a work environment where they feel heard, supported and can flourish. It's that simple.

Let's face it, the good of the enterprise is too lofty a goal. No one wakes up in the morning and goes to work powered solely by the need to ensure more end customers have access to their product or service. For the most part, even the good of the team is too lofty a goal – previously castrated by process and with few ways to do anything for the good of their people other than show compassion by commiserating over beers once in a blue moon, leaders find it hard to want to effect change. Most people at every level do want change and betterment to happen; they don't scoff at it as an afterthought in their heart of hearts.

I don't believe in business concepts done exclusively in the name of higher moral ground. At the very least some part of the motivation needs to be of a commercial nature, where the business can immediately see the connected value.

Before Psychological Safety, despite the efforts of scholars and specialists who could show the negative impact on turnover or the positive impact on hands-on KPIs of employee satisfaction, the topic of keeping your workforce happy was viewed as something that was 'nice to think of if there's any time and budget left after we do the real stuff'.

Psychological Safety is most commonly defined as 'being able to show and employ one's self without fear of negative consequences of self-image, status or career' at an individual level, in Kahn's definition of 1990, but it has been developed into a solid definition of a group dynamic with the studies of Professor Dr Amy Edmonson, who calls it 'a shared belief that the team is safe for interpersonal risk taking'.

We define a Psychologically Safe team as 'A team that feels like family and moves mountains together. One where it feels like they are making magic together – they are speaking up, open, courageous, flexible, vulnerable, learning, unafraid and are having fun together in their bubble while having a sense of accomplishment about their exceptional performance'.

Despite the immediate sense of relating that anyone reading these definitions feels, they were hardly noticed by the business world until Google resurrected and popularized the concept by placing Psychological Safety as the first element the high-performing teams they studied needed to have at the conclusion of their extensive Aristotle study. We will speak about this in the chapters to come.

Psychological Safety changes the game when it comes to the Human Debt – it has such a clear connection to productivity that for the first time, here's this concept that – incidentally – means employees are happier at work while simultaneously being more productive and useful to the business in being so.

Speaking of said happiness – when it comes to Psychological Safety it isn't a goal but a blessed by-product. In a sense it is not a method to intentionally increase it – instead, an aim to have so that people can be vulnerable, therefore courageous and flexible and therefore resilient, open and therefore connected.

Psychologically Safe teams are happy. Substantially happier than their counterparts. And therefore, they stay and develop, but more importantly, they work faster and smarter. At Google, Amazon and a handful of others, there is a number on Psychological Safety. Not only a number on employee happiness, although that exists too, but also a specific measurement and bottom-line correlation to Psychological Safety. The number is not a public one and, in some cases, not even one that's known to employees, but it exists and it informs more actions and decisions than surprisingly many of the traditional other business KPIs. This is why they do well. This is why they can employ technology to react fast to what the consumer needs and build addictive experiences. This is why they have 'culture' that is envied across the board.

This is their secret sauce.

Years ago, when I first heard of the 'Psychological Safety' construct and had no clue what it meant, I immediately shuddered with the idea of yet another fluffy 'for the good of the employee' concept offered by misguided unions. It immediately evoked images of forced job security at all cost, such as what is at times seen in Scandinavian countries where retaining employees is taken to extremes and combined with the power of the local unions, breeding a climate where performance and effort are superfluous as everyone is a permanent fixture.

These days I remind our team that many other people will feel this doubt at first, until they connect with 'team is family' and with 'teams make magic when they have Psychological Safety', and that we must help them overcome this pre-programed reaction against 'fluffy human topics'. If some will believe it is about automated job security, more still will think it belongs in the same bucket as the mental wellness conversation as it applies to employees. These days the topic of mental health is – thankfully – on everyone's agenda and so that's a natural association to make.

A few others will tell us they've heard about Google's efforts and it's all about trusting your teammates. The fact is, of course, in as far as it is about humans experiencing a healthy environment, there is a connection between all of the above, but none of these is the actual definition and the concept is far more complex and a lot more mercantile once we understand the connection to the high-performing teams of the digital elite. And that makes it all the more important and sustainable.

As an undeniable poetic justice bonus, the new ways of work, designed to showcase the speed of technology, are de facto used to show the evident advantage of having happy people, just as it is admittedly an anomaly that technologists-cum-CTOs-or-CIOs will be the ones to find ways for their people to be a real team before HR or CEOs, but it doesn't ultimately matter how we arrive at this as long as we stop thinking it's fluffy and start showing its numbers.

They say money can't buy you happiness but in the case of your employees, reducing your Human Debt to increase their Psychological Safety in teams and therefore their resilience and happiness can increase both the revenue and lasting success of your business. Psychological Safety is a team dynamic concept. Teams are non-negotiable. Speaking up is the positive behaviour we need to grow, to innovate, to create, to be highly performant and impression management is the collection of fears that does the opposite. Ultimately, becoming truly Agile at heart and reducing your Human Debt through a People Practice with EQ and Psychological Safety at the centre is your only chance to win, like Google and the rest of the digital elite.

CHAPTER ONE

Work Today, Work Tomorrow

- VUCA, Digital Disruption and The Speed of Technology
- The 'Human Debt'
- The Age of Humanity
- The Organization – The Human, The Team
- Get Clarity
- A 'Speak-Up' Culture – Create Real Dialogue for Collaboration
- Get a Real To-Do
- Make HR Great Again
- Permissions
- Focus on Teams
- Become Truly Agile – WoT For WoW

VUCA, Digital Disruption and The Speed of Technology

The age of information has changed everything. Technology has affected the way we live our lives in deeper and more impactful ways than we have yet had the chance to even analyse.

If a generation ago we could so happily live without modern technology, nowadays, we have become reliant on it for nearly everything. From our social lives to our private lives, to the way we work, all have dramatically changed over the past 30–40 years, but the speed of change has accelerated furthermore over the last 10–15 years and to be efficient in this new paradigm, we must spend time understanding what that means for the way we interact with others in a professional environment.

Every aspect of our working lives has now been touched by digital, irrespective of what industry we are in, and there is no sign of stopping this trajectory of change. With every week, a new type of technology springs up and the resulting products and offerings are constantly evolving or transforming. As a result, customer expectations have risen tremendously now that they avail themselves of the effects of digital. The expectation of 'new' and 'better' is growing continuously as consumers develop a clearer understanding of what is possible and instinctively know they can continue to up the ante and ask for more.

When apps first came out, they were a luxury. Mostly designed for entertainment, consumers viewed them as non-essential and had little to no expectation of them. When smartphones became more commonplace, the way people interacted with technology changed, in particular as these applications became tightly interwoven with every moment of our lives. Nowadays, there are very few actions that are 'non-digital' in that they neither happen online nor on our phone, nor are enhanced, aided or enabled by technology and for most people in the western world, a life completely off the grid and devoid of technology feels nigh on impossible.

Driven by market competition, technological advancements have only accelerated and with this increased speed of innovation comes a greater expectation from consumers. Living in a world where we provide, expect and consume, fast technology changes the pace of everything. The fluidity of the situation gave birth to the term of VUCA. VUCA stands for Volatility, Uncertainty, Complexity, Ambiguity and it defines our new world. In fact, if you work in technology, this is the new normal and dreaming of any kind of return to the clarity and stability of the past is useless.

In the work environment, we have leapt from typewriters and paper shuffling to bytes and Zoom meetings within the space of what is practically years. For most professionals, this has involved a serious transformation process which requires a transformed mindset beyond the practical aspects of work. Coming to grips with the continual changes in the way we work hasn't been an easy endeavour – it is made even more difficult by the uncertainty and acceleration which faces us in the future.

Everything is moving faster than we can keep track of – it took airlines 68 years to reach 50 million consumers, while it took Facebook only three. It took Pokémon Go just 19 days to reach 50 million users.

In *Superfast: Lead at Speed* Sophie Devonshire lists example after example of the speeds at which our world is changing. Among them, she describes Google's firm sense of urgency and growth, accredited by their EMEA president Matt Brittin to 'Moonshots' – a groundbreaking innovation project out of California, where they only focus on ambitious, speculative research projects which may not necessarily be profitable but represent tremendous leaps forward. Matt Brittin summarizes them:

> *Look at it this way, if you try and make something 10 per cent better, you're likely to take an incremental approach – start from what you've got and refine it. If you try and make something 10 times better though, you've got to start from scratch – first principles – find a new way. To compete in the age of the Internet that's what you need to do because the rate of change in the digital world is faster than it's ever been.*

It is in this world of speed that we see extreme growth happen. Companies come and go faster than ever before (in 1965, the average tenure of a company in the US was 33 years, by 1990, it had shrunk to 20 and by 2026, it is estimated to reach 14) and these numbers are skewed by meteoric raises to the glory of companies that are natively digital and comfortable with VUCA (Dollar Shave Club sold pre-profit for 1 billion dollars to Unilever in five years and Airbnb's valuation went to $58 billion in the same time frame).

This is the unimaginable speed that renders what we learned in school and what we took years to perfect as utterly irrelevant. This is why the mere notion of skills or training can be seen as useless. This is why our existent ways of measuring risk and preparing for every eventuality are no longer serving us. This is why we ought to rebel whenever we hear the term 'process' and why outdated ways of work should horrify us. This is what makes everything around us unclear, ever-shifting and supremely uncomfortable.

In these times, the only certain elements we can count on, the only useful parts that remain sustainable and relevant are those fundamental human qualities, abilities and skills that help us breathe in what feels like a never-ending crisis response mode, which is arguably what our VUCA world brings. Chief among them are courage, flexibility and resilience. Empathy, purpose, passion. Connection, communication, trust, decency, goodwill, spirit. Emotional intelligence and heart. The essence of our humanity. All virtually untouched and underappreciated in the 'professional' realm.

When a company has been built with people at its core and maintains these values, they stand a good chance of remaining competitive but for most organizations, VUCA and Digital are recent and bedazzling entrants in their business's life so they lack the luxury of a tabula rasa exercise where they can build on these pillars, where their foundations would be laid around the humans in the organization. They cannot very well organize a purist exercise where everyone gets out and only those with the brains and the heart to match what they are building get back in. If only that were possible, they would stand a chance to start reducing their Human Debt and therefore win in this fast-paced digital VUCA world.

The 'Human Debt'

'Technical debt' (also known as 'code debt' or 'design debt') is defined in software development as the cost and effort of rework needed to correct choices made due to taking 'the easy way out' when designing a solution instead of 'doing the right thing' and implementing a better approach if the latter implied more work and effort. In other words, it is what happens when software developers cut corners. As with monetary debt, the technical debt incurs heavy interest as the need for changes is ignored time and again until that's not possible anymore and often leads to a need to completely rebuild the codebase from the ground up.

It occurred to me that, in the same ways in which we incur technical debt, we have also incurred its equivalent at the organizational level, regarding our employees. Hence the term 'Human Debt™', which refers to all the shortcuts we have collectively taken in the professional world when we ignored some of the heavy lifting that would have been needed to ensure our people were happy at work.

'Human Debt' is an umbrella which includes moral concerns of employee well-being, happiness, care and respect. The mere term of 'human resources' is intensely disrespectful and practically sums up the theme of Human Debt – we have collectively treated our people, our humans, our employees as nothing but another resource. In some modern-day enterprises, it has been corrected to 'capital' and that's accurate and welcomed *if* sincere. They are typically the same enterprises that will have a 'chief heart officer', a 'chief purpose officer' or a 'chief happiness officer' before they have a 'chief human resources officer' but of course, this is only important in the instances where this is not a simple rebrand of a title for the sake of PR or trends but a reflection of a true change in mentality. The companies who have undergone this change are far and few between.

Changing the narrative to focus on qualitative elements rather than quantitative has always been challenging. The best example of this is when in 1975, in San Francisco, Tom Peters and Richard Pascale, two well-respected management consultants and strategists, sat down to work out what could be done to change the dire situation of American workers in recession. Both in awe of what the Japanese were doing to turn their loss into an industrial revolution win by work ethics and methodology, they proposed the difference between them and their American counterparts lies in the lack of a higher sense of mission. They are certain that people and tools are no different and the competitive advantage of different processes is the result of one major gain they have: a sense of shared value that runs down the organization to the employees. A mission to match a strong vision.

Both go on to write books but Pascale's book, *The Art of Japanese Management*, is met with reticence and raised eyebrows – what's this talk of mission and shared values? So what if the Japanese went to work for a higher purpose? Peters' *In Search of Excellence: Lessons from America's Best-Run Companies* has a different tone if it touts the same concepts and as a result, lands better popularizing the idea that a company must have values and a real vision and not simply offer jobs.

Nowadays, everyone has a marble plaque in the hallway with the vision carved out and laid bare for all to see and we can debate its effectiveness and *raison d'être* all we like, but having had that introduced back in the day, it has shaped the way we view work and elevated the economy when the focus shifted from employed worker bees to invested partners so it stands as the first example of the idea of 'purpose'.

We have to move past the discomfort and advance to discussing the crux of the issue: How do you make employees genuinely love you? How do you avoid ever mandating it and instead nurture and painstakingly build it within your people until they are all owner-level invested? All in. All heart. All about reducing or better yet, eradicating this Human Debt.

The Age of Humanity

We have known for a long time that we have to ask the hard questions, and examine the true extent of the Human Debt and be willing to take a can of kerosene to the status quo, but it was never clearer than during the 2020 COVID-19 crisis.

With our very lives at stake, humanity had to show its magnificently adaptive nature to survive. We saw the fabric of our day-to-day lives modify as needed to respond to the threat and with it, a beautiful community spirit shining through as examples of deeply human acts came from every part of the world and every walk of life.

In business, with usual practices impossible, the topic of remote and flexible work became an overnight reality, showing beyond doubt that it was entirely possible to let go of at least one of the many fixed ideas we carried around in the world of work – how people must be chained to a desk in a physical office space for a certain amount of time, in a certain location to work together. Once that assumption was successfully proven wrong, many others started to be questioned and, coupled with the newly found appetite for true humanity, a vibrant dialogue on the value of humans in the workplace ensued.

Perhaps we can finally all agree that we need a culture change, respectful and kind working environments, but the answers as to how to arrive there have to be able to dictate a radically different approach to what we value and how we see work, as the health of an organization won't improve discreetly and incrementally as a result of a few workshops and a few office posters but through radical and deep change.

What doesn't work

- Doing what we've been doing – organizing and managing the enterprise as we have in the past with the same hierarchies, the same structures and the same job titles based on the same selection criteria, same definitions of value and same lack of respect and care our humans have been feeling;

- Ignoring the concept of 'team' – it's a neglected structure which incidentally happens to be the only one we can reliably affect in terms of behaviours and practices;
- Theorizing or preaching about the organization and culture as a whole – while potentially all true, it is also ineffective rhetoric which achieves no real change;
- Offering generic 'don't be an a-hole'-type advice – needed as it may be, it won't accomplish anything as, while most people already have good intentions, they don't know how to correct problematic behaviours while caught up in the web of a toxic culture in which defensive, protective attitudes stemming from the lack of Psychological Safety can pervade in their particular team bubble;
- Paying lip service to the 'future of work' concept – talking about a new paradigm in general as an overall concept of ample importance and then consider it sorted with the implementation of the new cycle-to-work scheme or the new office layout;
- Hoping for any 'out-of-the-box' solutions – in particular, adopting any newfangled 'framework' or 'process' some expensive consultancy pushed with no introspection, critical examination or ownership and no intention to further invest in a day-to-day People Practice for all.

What will work

- Question everything in the status quo;
- Understand, beyond a shred of doubt, that fixing the Human Debt is everyone's number one day job and nothing can be seen as a higher priority to continue competing in today's environment;
- Ensure every last one of those in charge of other people is high on Emotional Intelligence and able to understand emotions in themselves and others and is highly empathic;

- Prioritize and protect the Psychological Safety of every team, including the board;
- Show the correlation to the bottom line;
- Break it down into exact and actionable tasks and ensure everyone feels they have the permissions and tools they need for a healthy and sustainable People Practice;
- Change the narrative that used to focus exclusively on hard skills and ignored EQ and group behaviours;
- Redefine values around humanity, not numbers;
- Make everyone feel happy and valued to see them achieve high performance;
- Obsess about the team as a core concept;
- Invest in an Agile mindset change.

The only true mechanism of ensuring we thrive in this VUCA world is to take a leaf from the books of the digital natives and empower ourselves and our employees with emotions and attributes that reduce this Human Debt. Empathy, complex emotions translated to data, shared purpose, passion, goodwill, respect and care.

The Organization – The Human, The Team

Most of us have seen our fair share of outdated organizational structures and know their dark side. Everything from homogenous boards and lack of diversity to rampant politics, misguided incentives, a disregard for new paradigms, lack of authentic vision, fake purpose and no real regard for the importance of technology or interest in repaying any of the Human Debt.

We all have the stories, the eye rolls and the heavy sighs to illustrate the issues. Too many organizations are tired, sick, maybe even terminally ill. 'Organizational design', 'organizational psychology', 'cultural change', 'breaking silos' and 'banishing toxic workplace politics' – these are all immensely important goals that make or break success stories but, before we could define them as pivotal levers such as Psychological Safety and Emotional Intelligence, they remained nebulous and theoretic. And these levers happen at the two next levels – the team and the human.

So, is there anything to be done at an organizational level as well? Yes, there is.

- Get clarity;
- Instil a 'speak-up' culture;
- Get a real to-do;
- Make HR great again;
- Focus on the team;
- Permissions;
- Become truly Agile.

Get Clarity

Many organizations seem to be stuck in a pattern of confusing capital topic for mere 'fluff': this forms the basis of their Human Debt, where despite the best intentions in the world and with a mandate to do well and change the culture, they still float between big themes like 'AI', 'future of work', 'well-being', 'engagement', 'group systems thinking', 'servant leadership', 'trust', 'passion', 'purpose', etc and resolve or make serious headway in improving none. It's a carousel of meaningful topics hidden between inconsequential terms and tinged with hundreds of proprietary frameworks and acronyms as left behind by valiant Don Quixote types who tried to battle the Human Debt before.

For anything to move and progress, they'll have to shake away the redundant terms and concepts, free themselves of proprietary frameworks and instead rethink and rearrange everything around the true levers of change – the individual and the bubble (AKA the team) by digging deep into the basics of the language and the very nature of the concepts.

The importance of clarity cannot be overestimated, achieving it is the cornerstone to any type of successful endeavour and its importance has only risen directly proportional to the increased difficulty of VUCA as an antidote to paralyzing confusion.

It is only when we start becoming razor-focused on the core concepts and the important values that we start wondering what the specific parts are that we have to diagnose to better each of those elements. What are the practical methods to breed change? What can we hope for? How does it all fit in the overall vision/trend/etc? What are the things that work for us? What matters the most? How do we build a genuine obsession with humanity and reclaim it as a USP?

A 'Speak Up' Culture – Create Real Dialogue for Collaboration

This one is the biggest one of all, the crux of the issue. Speaking up, with its intrinsic daring and good-willed nature, offering constant and honest feedback and opinion with no fear of repercussion is the fundamental behaviour that builds Psychological Safety and therefore high-performing teams.

We think we are talking to each other at work. We think we're opening up and communicating and to a degree, we believe we have a genuine dialogue, but the reality is that moments of real communication are few and far between in our work environments, buried under a mountain of stress, fear and impression management and covered by acronyms and consulting speak.

Some of the initial signatories behind the Agile Manifesto (the document that spelt out the importance of humans above anything else in software development) are true champions for humanity. Some would argue that they have done more for employees in the workplace by demonstrating value than most HR departments have, and they firmly place the ability to really communicate at the centre of it all.

Take this Twitter dialogue between two such giants. When GeePaw Hill, a reputable Agile software coach, says 'Collaboration – frequent focused direct human dialog between people who experience each other as trusted equals – is at the heart of my agility, and it is the single most radical and revolutionary behaviour we can engage in', he gets Kent Beck – one of the initial signatories of the Agile Manifesto and the father of test driven development – to react by saying 'I'm not crying. Okay, yeah, I'm crying. This is indeed the beating heart of it!' What this essentially speaks to is that, to do any of the work, in particular, the innovative, involved, intelligent, non-sequential, EQed, flexible, empathic kind needed by today's VUCA environment of technology and customer expectation, you need to find a path to true collaboration.

While it starts with courage, collaboration requires real, raw, regular and honest dialogue. To obtain it, you need to have a team that bravely communicates all the time – openly, in plain English/own language, fearlessly, with radical candour, empathy and good intentions towards getting the job done and that is the essence of a Psychologically Safe and therefore highly performant team.

Psychological Safety is what makes a team a team. A family. A unit. An organism. Not a collection of disparate people, personalities and reclusive styles. The latter just can't engage in any dialogue or collaborate so why would we ever allow it? To achieve this utterly open dialogue, we must become 'Speak Up', goal-oriented and focused on our People Practice, both at an organizational level and a team level.

Get A Real To-Do

For leadership, their company-wide People Practice has to include a vast piece of transformational work to make a dent in the 'Human

Debt'. It cannot remain at an aspirational level, nor can it stay largely implicit at best. Instead, it needs to urgently become intentional and explicit.

If we were to be working in an Agile way (and who can afford not to nowadays?), if the 'Future of Work' Epic (which is the overall 'goal' or 'strategic objective' or overarching story that describes a piece of work in Agile) is *'Create end products and experiences our customers will love through the use of technology and remain competitive and highly performant in our digital VUCA world'* then the Sprint (the unit of work used in most Agile methodologies defined by a short duration – usually a week or two – and a defined set of tasks that have been collaboratively chosen from the team from the backlog) could be to *'Achieve an Agile mindset with people at the centre'*. Then every card should be about building a minimum viable product (MVP) around growing EQ and Human Permissions for the team leader and increasing Psychological Safety in every team they have. So they can communicate. So they can collaborate. So they do care. So they perform. So they work. So they are human.

Every true leader should have a board; a real one not (only) in their minds and hearts but in some modern project management software such as Trello or Jira (or even physically on an office wall if one still exists for their company!) where everyone else in the team sees their to-do list in terms of steering the ship and what they are currently working on.

We have to get back to the drawing board and wonder what makes the organization efficient, flexible, reliable and above all, simple and solid.

We have to ask what makes people willing to share knowledge, lend a helping hand, collaborate truly, be themselves, dare, care, have the drive, work hard, invest, apply themselves, bring others along, embrace change, trust, learn, burn with some type of inner fire and move at a pace that makes it all possible.

The organization's return on investment (ROI) will, from here on, only come from a place where we have tackled this big epic and have started making a dent in the Human Debt to get real workplace chemistry and magic and serendipitous cultural alignment à la the likes of Apple or Google.

Make HR Great Again

According to Gartner, 'Seventy per cent of CEOs expect the chief human resources officer (CHRO) to be a key player in enterprise strategy, but only 55 per cent say CHROs are meeting this expectation. Even fewer CFOs agree (30 per cent).'

The above stat is a very loaded one. For one thing it shows that, in most cases, HR is more of a cost than an asset and in the past few years, this perception has become more and more clear to those who look at the objective reality of the hard numbers such as the chief financial officers (CFOs). For another, it shows that there is a clear appetite from the top leadership of taking their employees into account when shaping the strategy, so they are jonesing after valuable insight in this area.

If you ask the CFOs, they are clearly not getting that. Some say HR as a function has pushed itself to the edges of the business – just go to LinkedIn and search for forums such as DisruptHR or the HackingHR franchise to see this – and that they've done so by taking on operational and compliance tasks that are so easily replaceable by technology and that ironically, they will be one of the first traditional business functions to disappear due to automation, potentially before call centres or other operational business units.

Let me tell you what HR does in most organizations today: PR/Internal Communication and Admin. Loads and loads of admin and this admin may be labelled as talent-connected tasks, but without true investment in these, it is still purely admin. Even recruitment and selection are a series of process-driven tasks, devoid of passion and with little to no input from good old-fashioned intuition. The same goes for retention, talent management and performance, which are often antiquated exercises in paper-pushing with no understanding of the market context that is designed to meet a quota and have no expected transformative results. Lastly, leadership development efforts are seldom a profiling and bettering honest exercise but mostly ticking a box or at best, a recreational activity, etc. In essence, they do what a future version of Sage or Xerox or any other accounting and operations system will very soon accomplish with little to no human intervention. On top of that, they often blame keyword matching and their lack of intimate understanding of the task on the speed of technology. Since new technologies and ways of work come out every week, how are they expected to keep up with what the current definition of talent even is at any given point? But that's a supreme cop-out as we see in examples of best practice and yet another symptom of the overall lack of curiosity about people they exhibit at times.

One of the voices that most advocates for the importance of HR and describes ways in which the function can once more be elevated to the olden days' desideratum of true 'business partner' is Patty McCord, author of *Powerful: Building a Culture of Freedom and Responsibility* and the executive behind Netflix's 'people first' culture. She describes how for Netflix HR is the cornerstone of the business and how they take their talent scout role extremely seriously.

In one instance she describes how HR saved a deal they were negotiating with Nintendo. With a tight deadline for a crucial delivery for Nintendo Wii, they were in a position where they simply lacked any team with the necessary technical skills so they needed to form a new one. Bethany Brodsky, a dedicated recruiter, went the extra mile for the company and spent enormous amounts of time familiarizing herself with the most minute technical intricacies of the project and comprehending the task. Armed with insider knowledge of the level that would have made her a valiant team leader for this team, she was then able to build the perfect team which eventually launched the promised product on time. That is the level of above-and-beyond that HR needs. The willingness and passion of this specific employee made the project possible from a human perspective.

Patty has gone on to emphasize that HR needs deep reform and that they need to treat people like adults, ask them questions often and empower them to ensure they are enthusiastic and invested enough to perform to the best of their abilities.

Now let me tell you what HR *should* be in charge of – the health of the organization and its people. They are the keepers of its soul.

HR leaders who haven't taken on this challenge and haven't seen the depth of the Human Debt have cornered themselves into becoming a disposable resource instead of a value creator. What any senior HR professional should have done a few years back is to look around and see where technology and people are heading and resolve to become the number one trusted advisor for the CEO.

They should have become the real-life Counsellor Deanna Troi from *Star Trek*, a people whisperer ready to steer the team towards a new era where soft skills and emotional intelligence matters. If we look at the stats above, it is clear that leadership is feeling an intense need for that role to be fulfilled. Very few have done so though and most traditional companies of various sizes are left with a human-with-insight-about-humans hole where the chief human resources officer (CHRO) would have been. Enter the chief technology officer (CTO). Or chief information officer (CIO) or digital leader. Or really any leader tasked with using technology or making technology. Anyone who sees first-hand that the tech in itself is secondary. Anyone with a real delivery imperative. Anyone entrusted to usher the company into a new digital era.

A good example is Agile/DevOps leaders who see the value of technology and the fact that its success or failure depends on nothing else but the people employing or building it. The speed and excellence intrinsic to the new ways of work has eliminated the need to eternally seek better process or strive for 'best practice' and has instead opened the gates for altogether more foreign concepts to business to enter.

With clarity on the method and the tools, there is suddenly space to see that it is the chemistry between people in a team, their Psychological Safety and behaviours as a group dynamic, their collective and personal EQ, as well as their individual desire to be open and collaborative and innovative and remain focused on their People Practice that makes the real difference. It is therefore not a sizeable logical leap to assume that in the future, the only leaders tasked with focusing on the human capital are the ones who directly utilize it, the ones closest to the delivery, and that in tech companies in particular and then in those companies where knowledge and digital dictates the customer proposition, HR departments will be gone and the function simply distributed between those who most comprehend it.

In digital, design and Agile native organizations that are customer-obsessed – AKA the examples we all strive to be – the HR function is already very different to most other companies and it is this difference that augments their technology prowess into making them successful.

Google doesn't call it HR but 'People Operations' and beyond the colourful spaces and the nap pods, they are forensic about increasing Psychological Safety and ask their team leaders at every level to firmly plant employee goals into their objectives and key results (OKRs). Amazon has a famous 'People Science' department; Disney has always had it as a motto to treat employees like customers and – in what is the most telling example of the importance they place on human capital, but also a potential signal that they are done with the function in itself as a separate entity and they instead view it as fully integrated in every aspect of their business and part of the day to day – Apple has gone in the opposite direction in dissipating the function and handing the keys to its retail sales to one of their HR leaders, former Vice President of People Deidre O'Brien, with CEO Tim Cook reiterating: 'At Apple, we believe the soul is our people.'

Meanwhile, in most (thankfully not all as there are blessed exceptions) other organizations, HR carries on like it's 1999. While they have their heads down in payroll and diversity policies, they are missing out on deeper analysis and design. While they pore over personnel numbers, they miss collecting and analysing data about their greatest asset. While they negotiate holiday pay with talent chosen by keywords, they miss all the tricks to find those with empathy and curiosity who can succeed in this new business paradigm and ways to make their teams resilient, break their silos and give everyone the Psychological Safety they need to innovate, create and be productive.

Everything is changing around HR and the advent of Artificial Intelligence and the way it could eradicate some functions performed by human employees in their discipline remains a looming threat, yet most of the time, they persist in being in denial and staying the same, performing more and more menial tasks that will see themselves confined to oblivion very soon.

To survive and not be assimilated into smarter functions that truly understand the value of people, HR must stop focusing on irrelevant points such as the 'which keywords' and the 'where' of how we work but instead go back to the 'who' and add the 'why' to regain a seat at the boardroom table before those who are already there and making a significant impact to the growth of the business – the Agile leaders – push out that empty chair and teach everyone else why people are our greatest value and our greatest risk.

There are only two parties that can make HR great again: leadership and HR themselves.

To change, HR must recognize its current position in the team first. Admit they've been benched and are intensely replaceable and go back to their core skills that are impossible to replicate by machines then advocate them to their respective organizations to better the perception of their role. They must enter those boardrooms where the strategic real conversations are happening and announce they have arrived and why they must be there to drive change and keep the soul of the organization. And once they do, the leaders have to pull out a seat at the proverbial table and be grateful they have their own Commander Trois to help them 'boldly go where no one has gone before' – to a Human Debt-free organization of happy employees who can sustainably remain competitive.

And they can. They absolutely can.

The most human-obsessed of the humans we have in the workplace are those we need to become the saviours in this new world of ours and the key to achieving amazing things. Allowing them in earnest to rebuild the organization is wise and necessary if we all want to win.

Permissions

Open any HR magazine and you'll find they still dance like nobody's watching. These are some of the actual verbatim titles and concepts I saw in one of them recently: 'Line manager progression', 'Compensation techniques', 'Why your people mistrust technology', 'Staff training – on the job or off the job?'. And that is what is supposedly being debated and analysed, aside from how the day-to-day revolves almost exclusively around semi-legal and admin tasks that rudimentary software can and will perform better very soon in their stead. Nary a word on the major themes that are reshaping everything we know in the workplace. The new ways of work, the customer expectations, the speed and promise of technology, AI, or the ways the employees perceive all this. Not a lick of mention of what to do to re-program humanity back into the workplace.

In place of beating the dead horses of the useless topics above, this should be the urgent three-step To-Do of HR everywhere with ambitions to last:

- Obtain true permission (AKA 'buy-in') for 'reducing the Human Debt' (by encouraging everyone to focus primarily on a strong day-to-day People Practice based on empathy and EQ and a continuous preoccupation with Psychological Safety) from the business based on demonstrating value;
- Communicate that permission to employees where it is heard and, more importantly – and infinitely harder to achieve – to where it is believed and trusted;
- Help people work on reigniting passion, rediscovering themselves through individual practices from well-being to gratitude and to increasing kindness, empathy and compassion and feel respected and cared for;
- Create an environment of growth and innovation by fostering solid 'permission to fail' where employees feel valued for their courageous and experimental nature and have no reason to fear and impression manage.

These permissions are imperative as there's a disheartening amount of giving up and inertia happening, both at the individual and the organizational level in many places of work. It's an insidiously vicious circle too – the individual can't keep being invested in the mission and stay connected to what makes them perform to the best of their abilities with all their heart and mind into what they do, while the organization doesn't seem to give much of a flying hoot about their well-being beyond sourcing a cheaper gym membership and has long lost touch with what makes the individuals they hired 'capital' not 'resource' since they no longer show their fire and change-makers are few and far between. And then both sides just go through the motions.

You can't mandate organizational change – you have to use your best snooker moves where it becomes the end result. The ball that will start the chain reaction has to be Psychological Safety, with its extreme common sense and appeal to intrinsic human decency, and if we focus on polishing this one and sending it off on the right trajectory, the next one it will touch and set in motion will be the 'permission to be human' and that one is truly the transformational propulsion that the organization needs.

If HR or anyone else wants a poignant example of the importance of the 'permission to fail', they can find it in *The Culture Code: The Secrets of Highly Successful Groups*, where Daniel Coyle tells the story of what made Google what it is today – the way they won a head-to-head innovation battle with what was then an industry giant, Overture, when they were at the time (2002) not far from their very humble startup beginnings. The story of how Larry Page, one of the founders, printed out the essence of the problem the team tasked with this was facing and stuck it to a kitchen cupboard, and how it was seen by a member of a completely unconnected team – Jeff Dean – who then spent his weekend attempting a fix and eventually found one which resulted in the team creating AdWords, which effectively made Google rich overnight (in the year following alone, the company's profits went from $6 to $99 million).

Jeff didn't ask anyone if it was OK if he tried a fix. He didn't ask for permission. He didn't feel he needed approval, he wasn't fearing any ridicule or reprimand. Powered by what he perceived as a Psychologically Safe company-level team where there was camaraderie but also fierce debate, he felt he had clear permission to experiment and therefore implicit permission to fail and so he single-handedly moved the company forward in a giant leap.

What those magazines should do is explore what are the best ways to grow People Practices at a team leader and team member level. Is it by honing in on speaking up? By introducing meditation nooks?

By rewarding a demonstrable gratitude practice? By creating a 'Pay it forward' program? By helping people build healthier mind practices and habits? By reinforcing the importance of personal responsibility? By showing how good leadership means servant leadership that's connected and caring?

One of the things we inbuilt into our team solution's dashboard is a monthly challenge and of the new ones we've introduced, one is aimed at increasing kindness and empathy – a practice snapshot – challenging leaders to ask their guys to try a pre-meeting mantra focused on their teammates – 'Just like me, they too want to have a positive experience, be heard, respected, connected, allowed to learn and grow and be happy' – before each ceremonial meeting. It's a small example but there are hundreds, thousands, of ideas like that waiting to be born once HR gets us those permissions that we so urgently need to evolve.

Focus on Teams

Described in multiple TED Talks and Daniel Coyle's *The Culture Code* alike, the Marshmallow Man experiment created by Peter Skillman asked participants to use uncooked spaghetti, tape, string and a marshmallow to create the tallest freestanding structure. The groups are of four, the teams made up of different segments of people, from designers to architects, entrepreneurs, Fortune 500 leaders and even school-age kids.

To everyone's surprise, the group that did the best and built the tallest structure was the latter. They averaged far higher structures than the lawyers and CEOs and the newly MBA-ed group did the worst. The reason lies in true collaboration. The kindergartners immediately related to each other as a strong team which had the safety to experiment together and were completely devoid of impression management (they had no fear-based behaviour where they were avoiding appearing ignorant, incompetent, negative or disruptive/

intrusive/unprofessional). The kindergartners were a real team and as such, they managed to make team magic. It is one of the most poignant examples of the value of the team concept.

I keep returning to this and in Chapter 3, 'Teams and the Search for High Performance', we take a closer look, but the idea of the team has been severely devalued in the past 10–15 years and we must wonder why and fix this because having it unresolved means a lack of essential focus.

Gone are the days when team building was on the yearly L&D budget or even preoccupation list, vanished are the exercises, foolish as they may have appeared. Few enterprises even talk about the concept internally, much less do they engage with the term as they should, and efforts to build and better teams have all but disappeared. The concept was strong a while ago and then, if we were to look at when it started fading in importance, we see that it slipped out of our collective consciousness in the workplace for one reason or another.

I strongly believe that its lack of true power today is one of the heftiest roots of evils in organizations, in particular in how its absence plays at the leadership level and alongside a bevy of other human behaviours that are less than desirable. While it's not there, we have nary a hope to build and uphold the utterly necessary Psychological Safety we need.

If we cast our minds back to the 1980s and 90s, the idea of 'team' was everywhere and while not as strong as it is for, say, a sports team, it meant a lot. As time went by, the word is still there, but its meaning seems to have diminished more and more over time, to where oftentimes today, it is there, but utterly empty.

Many factors could have contributed to this, from the rise of the hero cult in the workplace and a decline in the overall mental well-being of workers and therefore in their level of true engagement to a general lack of interest in true collaboration and an increased focus on the individualism of society at large. This is evident in all types of stats today, including those that say that despite an apparent increase in communication due to social media we are, overall, more isolated than ever – with surveys such as the one conducted by Cigna Health Insurance in 2019 suggesting that 46 per cent of respondents who were heavy users of social media felt lonely.

For one reason or another, these days the concept of 'team' is at its weakest and at best, refers to the immediate work circle of an employee and it is never wider than that. In a time where we speak about ecosystem and collaboration as the only ways to progress and innovate, we are simultaneously unable to think of the new intersections and groups those demand in an intimate and functional way.

Many of the concepts that we do invest in these days are utterly abstract and unactionable, such as all the variations of 'organization', which is essentially no more real and actionable of a construct than Santa Claus, whereas the concept of 'team' is the only truly leverageable unit in an enterprise and yet we've lost it along the way.

If we were to reinstate the concept of 'team' to its intended – or at least former – glory, we couldn't help but become invested in recognizing and desiring its pattern in every interaction we have. Ad-hoc, cross-functional, natural and momentary team moments happen to all of us every day, whether we define them as such or not, but the lack of definition is what makes them less powerful. To be a team, we don't need a lot. We don't need a name, we don't need a place, we don't need a certain time frame or a plan. Also, we don't need to establish and decide on norms or processes. All we do need is to be willing to call ourselves that, to be available to bring our whole selves and feel like we belong, and we need a common purpose and willingness to get a certain task or set of tasks done.

You and I reading this are a team in thinking about the topic.

All the people attending a conference for the day are a team.

The WhatsApp group where your kid's classmates' parents chat is a team.

As are all of those in the wider monthly Ops meeting, including those guys from Marketing and that woman in Compliance.

What about the leadership team? Maybe the least 'team-y' of them all. Often an impression management fest of fear and impostor syndrome displays, meetings at the top are rarely those of a real team with strong purpose, goals and goodwill. And where there is no team, there can be no Psychological Safety and if there's none of that, there's no hope of staying performant for the long VUCA haul, no matter what we tell ourselves.

I challenge you to spend some time this week thinking of the concept of 'team' – is it as strong as it should be in your life? How many teams are you part of? Are you a team with your friends? Your gym buddies? Your spouse? Are you psychologically safe, free, vulnerable, authentic and truly working together to a purpose in those? What about at work? Who's in your team 'on paper' and who is in your mental collection of minimum viable products? Who has your back and who are you making magic with?

Become Truly Agile – WoT for WoW

Another powerful shortcut for any organization who comprehends the speed of technology, the promise of digital and the challenges of VUCA is to look at Agile/DevOps as a way to gain momentum on paying off the major Human Debt we have acquired.

Agile as a Way of Work (WoW) is gaining in popularity in most industries as it is the best method to achieve solid results at speed. Any project run in an Agile fashion will be undeniably faster and better executed than if it had followed a traditional waterfall methodology of project management.

Aside from the speed and quality of delivery Agile brings a lot more value through how it is, in its essence a new way of seeing things. A change of mentality. A transformation of a linear, sequential, risk-averse thought process and a complete revamp of the mindset we have traditionally had in business. As such, the principles we find in Agile seem to refer to project management or software development in particular, but really, they encompass such a shift at a core value level that they encompass powerful new practices and behaviours around experimentation, communication and leadership. In fact, most of the topics tackled above as firmly on the to-do of any smart organization who wants to remain competitive would be implicitly served by becoming a truly Agile organization that embraces the manifesto from the heart at a DNA level. They would be putting people first, they would have a decentralized, autonomous organization with servant leadership and deep respect for both employees and customers, they would be valuing feedback above all, they would live and breathe experimentation with courage and an appetite for failure at the core and they would be intensely focused on the team and its Psychological Safety to enable them to run fast and deliver better.

Amazon is arguably one of the most Agile companies in the world – even if they do not expressly call themselves that – with their meteoric success being attributed to an ability to be supremely nimble and customer-obsessed. Founder Jeff Bezos is reportedly obsessed with speed and as a result, was very invested in offering firm permission to fail – 'You need to be good at quickly recognizing and correcting bad decisions,' he says. 'If you're good at course-correcting, being wrong may be less costly than you think, whereas being slow is going to be expensive for sure.' This is the same company behind a bevy of innovations that have become staples of our modern-day life despite having been founded a mere 25 years ago; the same company that reinforces utterly Agile mindset pillars such as the customer obsession, the way they communicate, the two-pizza teams and their autonomy, their leaders' sense of ownership and purpose, their preoccupation with the value of data and their clarity and structure, which allow for fast-paced growth. In other words, Agile is so immensely all-encompassing of all the good and the right that we could be asking for at an organizational level, that if brought about as a deep change in the Way of Thinking (WoT), not a mere change in the Way of Work (WoW), it can save the day from all other points of view.

Tools and processes have evolved and the canvas of the organization has stood still, frozen in the 1980s, unwilling and unable to come along on the evolutionary path. Consumer expectations have grown and yet the thinking of how to make our people happy has shrunk. Technology is running at a million miles an hour and organizations crawling along to the tune of the same KPIs and departments.

In most industries, we seem to have let organizations just happen and then simply fester and deteriorate. Except for the digitally native enterprises, organizations are effectively accidental and not by design. Had they been by design, they would have been built without Human Debt. As it stands we can but hope we can reduce it. To do so, we must rethink, re-dream, redesign as best we can by shifting focus from the general overall theme of 'culture' or 'organization' to the lower levels where we can affect change, namely the team and the people, and then demonstrate the missing care and respect in allowing them to be daring, open and Agile. Only then can we see progress and compete.

CHAPTER TWO

Process Versus People – Agile, WoW and WoT

- New Ways of Work and Thinking
- The New Ways of Work Aren't New
- What is Agile?
- What Agile is Not
- Agile by Design or by 'Transformation'
- You Can't Have the WoW (Way of Working) Without the WoT (Way of Thinking)
- Agile and Humans
- Why Agile is Hard
- Agile Superheroes
- Agile, DevOps, WoWs and Reducing Human Debt

New Ways of Work and Thinking

The correlation between Agile and Psychological Safety in teams or really, that between the new ways of work and people topics, is not evident to all and sundry. While there are a handful of us across industries who could supposedly be considered DevOps enthusiasts who intensely comprehend it (and I would urge you to look up, follow and read anything by Gene Kim, Karen Ferris or Gitte Klitgaard), the obvious connection is still relatively obscure and here, this chapter attempts to establish the link as well as the essence of these new ways of thinking and how they relate to employees.

If 'eradicating Human Debt through Psychological Safety' is my biggest life goal, the second one – and one I am prepared to admit is far harder to explain and defend – is the hypothesis that Agile's true calling is that of demonstrating the value of humans at work. It ought to be easy to explain.

Agile is 'about project management', which is not 'that IT thing there' but the way we humans work. Psychological Safety is 'about employees', which is not 'that HR thing there' but the way we humans work. Furthermore, Agile is nothing to do with any methodology, but everything to do with putting humans first. The humans making the things, and the humans using the things.

Psychological Safety is about the humans making the things. Agile shows that for the human using the things, to get the best things fastest, the humans making the things have to have Psychological Safety to make the best things fastest.

To me, the direct connection is absolutely clear. Anyone who knows me is aware I have a self-confessed efficiency fetish. First and foremost, I like things that are done fast, and – ideally – right too, but if not, they can be improved upon fast again. Ad nauseam. I also love the promise of technology, the fact that I know what it can accomplish and with what speed if used 'for the good'. I have no patience, I love experimenting and I'm obsessed with betterment – in myself, what I do, the team and others. I'm built, personality-wise, for the so-called 'New Ways of Work'.

Realistically, the reason why I've been an Agile practitioner in my product work and an Agile 'anthropologist', enthusiast and vocal advocate for the last 10–12 years is that there is something in my intellectual and personality makeup which means I am predisposed to embrace anything that offers a faster path to better things. And that, in essence, is what any of the ways included in the enormous umbrella of 'future of work' brings. Speed, flexibility, a continuous thirst for learning and better results.

Put that way, while it stands to reason it may not 'come as easily' to everybody, it is almost incomprehensible how anyone would be any less in love with the ideas brought forth by these new methods, but despite how they have been around for literally tens of years, they are far from having become the new normal yet despite how most places will have them as a goal, should their business model include digital in any form.

If we start at the definition, we'll notice almost any new methodology that has been proposed as a way to improve project management in the way humans interact in the workplace with a purpose of improving efficiency in the past 40 years is included in this. Some of them have originated in manufacturing, some in software development. Some emphasize changes in particular parts of the processes we employ, some advocate deep and general transformation of a theoretical nature and of entire mindsets. All, whether they are willing to acknowledge it or not, require deep altering of the way we are thinking.

A curious thing about the term is that if you take a closer look at which 'discipline' claims the concept, you will find that both overall strategy/leadership and HR and IT or Project Management think that 'the future of work' is 'theirs'. In other words, different parts of the organization feel they have a claim or even a monopoly over the ideas contained within it.

While this is explainable by the enormous span of the concept, the separation is likely one of the reasons why these topics are still considered avant-garde and they are rarely 'all in' anywhere else but in the new entrants that built with them in mind from the ground up, as the fragmentation of the message makes it harder to demonstrate the value at a helicopter view level. So, what are the new ways of work and why are they still 'new' and not just 'the way we do things' already?

To understand more about the differences, we have to look at the way various projects have been done traditionally in most organizations and we can lump them all under the term 'Waterfall methodologies' as compared to the projects that have been built using 'Agile' or 'Iterative' methods.

In the latter, when we manage a project or iteratively develop software, there is an expectation of a continuous loop based on learnings and user feedback and to obtain it, the work is split into smaller batches, each ideally resulting in a minimal viable prototype – whether of a feature or product – which is then used to obtain said feedback.

This implicitly involves rapid hypothesizing, quick decision making and design, and rapid execution of what is viewed as an experimental result, delivered and deployed solely to collect a data point and enable evolution towards a finished product. The work is therefore sliced in the smallest possible increments that would enable creating such a prototype focusing on current and ever-challenged assumptions and therefore not stumbling at unknowns, and is done collectively and highly collaboratively by teams having a 'no blame' culture that welcomes failure so they can continue creating the next iteration and so forth. Seeing how accurate estimates, stable plans and predictions are often hard to get in the early stages, and confidence in them should be very low, Agile practitioners resolved to reduce the leap of faith needed before any evidence of value can be obtained and replace it with feedback and data points obtained early and regularly instead.

On a practical level and to oversimplify and generalize, keeping in mind multiple methodologies of how to achieve the above exist, this means that teams split a piece of work into smaller components (using terms such as 'epics' to describe the overarching intention to 'user stories' to describe the byte-sized suppositions and then 'tickers' or 'cards' that describe tasks) and then they include all these individual tasks on a list of to-dos commonly known as 'backlog' and in some cases, a 'product owner' or a 'scrum master' prioritizes them, after which the team grabs tasks off it and completes the goal of the respective burst of work, which typically never lasts more than a couple of weeks and is commonly known as a 'sprint'.

Most Agile methodologies include a series of other 'ceremonies' such as 'sprint planning' and 'kick-offs', 'daily stand-ups' and, at the end of the sprint, a 'retro' – short for 'retrospective' – so that they can discuss what they saw happened. All governed by 'experimentation' and 'feedback'. By contrast, waterfall methodologies rely on no such loop expectation as the concept of feedback is not central to their implementation. As a result, the presumption is that upon defining a piece of work, be it about a project or a piece of software, teams ought to take time to meticulously explore and define all requirements then painstakingly design every aspect of the finished product according to the initial research and hypothesis. Then start developing it, oftentimes by centrally assigning tasks to a distributed lower hierarchy.

From a practical standpoint, this typically refers to projects that can take at a minimum, months to plan and years to execute, involving phases such as 'feasibility studies, research and analysis', 'scoping', 'requirements specifications', 'design', 'implementation' 'testing and integration', 'operation and maintenance' – all often governed by 'strategy' and 'roadmap'.

If you wish, one is an active, always-on, continuously evolving implementation of a live product or solution, whereas the other is a rigid, lengthy and fixed path to a defined result. Iterative/non-sequential philosophies assume they know nothing and they must ask a lot, whereas waterfall/sequential thinking assumes it knows everything and shouldn't ever ask, but instead blindly keep to an initial plan. Needless to say, only one of these two methods matches the speed of technology and the ever-higher expectation of the digital consumer.

The New Ways of Work Aren't New

There is, de facto, very little that's truly 'new' about the 'new ways of work'. The first mentions of 'iterative', in terms of a way to perform a piece of work in particular as it pertains to software development, can be traced further back than the commonly presumed 1970s. The very first traceable one probably comes from Walter Shewart of Bell Labs in 1930, as he recommended his 'PDSA' (Plan-Do-Study-Act) methodology – demonstrating that it all boils down to common sense that dates almost as far back as modern software development.

Pinned as a contrast – the opposite of Iterative and adaptive – Waterfall methodologies are sometimes wrongly attributed to a paper in the 1970s written by Winston Royce entitled 'Managing the Development of Large Software Systems', where he describes government contracting work as best governed by a strict sequence of 'requirements analysis', 'design' and 'development' phases. These are described as not only following each other rigidly in a linear fashion but they are also expected to be lengthy and highly structured.

A little-known irony, however, is how history fails to mention that the author recommends the process to be done at least 'twice' and then goes on to describe iterations in the rest of the paper, hence never really advocating for what became the definition of classic waterfall structures in project management and software development after this article. However far back we go and irrespective of whether we understand the origin of the confusion, agree or disagree with the need and genesis for both, the fact remains that over the past 40+ years, the vast majority of projects have been running in a waterfall manner and are therefore manifestations of sequential, long-term and fixed thinking, which represents the very opposite of incremental, experimental and evolutionary software development and project management.

Having done things in a certain way for this long – irrespective how many project corpses have been famously left in the wake of it – means not only has the methodology become ingrained in the common consciousness of the business world, but it has effectively shaped the way entire generations structure their thought patterns. This starts as far back as in schools where, if we examine the educational process today, we see that sequential thinking and lack of experimentation are sadly the norm.

What is Agile?

According to Wikipedia – *'During the 1990s, a number of lightweight software development methods evolved in reaction to the prevailing heavyweight methods (such as waterfall) that critics described as overly regulated, planned, and micro-managed. These included: rapid application development (RAD), from 1991; the unified process (UP) and dynamic systems development method (DSDM), both from 1994; Scrum, from 1995; Crystal Clear and extreme programming (XP), both from 1996; and feature-driven development, from 1997. Although these all originated before the publication of the Agile Manifesto, they are now collectively referred to as agile software development methods. At the same time, similar changes were underway in manufacturing and aerospace'.*

In 2001, 12 software developers, who had been highly proficient in establishing and using some of the above programming methods and new ways of building software, met in Utah and produced this document:

Manifesto for Agile Software Development

We are uncovering better ways of developing software by doing it and helping others do it.

Through this work we have come to value:
- Individuals and interactions over processes and tools
- Working software over comprehensive documentation
- Customer collaboration over contract negotiation
- Responding to change over following a plan

That is, while there is value in the items on the right, we value the items on the left more.

The above document, while written with software development in mind, is to me the best example of a true blueprint for having an Agile outlook on every aspect of one's professional or even personal life. If we simply replace the word 'software' with anything from 'organization' to 'product' or even 'results', we have the clearest declaration of why remaining flexible, change and learning-oriented, open-minded and results driven is the only way to be adaptive and progressive.

Some like to think of Agile and Lean Six Sigma – which is another acclaimed project management method that focuses on performance – as two sides of the iterative, fast and results-driven coin: one in software development and one in entrepreneurship. I think the terminology is unimportant and shouldn't be based on whether one is running a project to build software or a project to build or run a company and that instead of focusing on the differences, we ought to focus on the unifying and defining features and the intersection that firmly exists conceptually in the idea of rapid delivery of evolutionary increments.

Some are married to one or other of these Agile methodologies and serious wars break out between various approaches, with Scrum being considered the most structured and regimented of them (some dub its practitioners as 'Scrumtamentalists', which gives a measure of the strict perception) while 'softer' approaches such as Kanban – a visual workflow management system – found their way in the lives of businesses everywhere as well. Furthermore, almost everyone in the industry, even those utterly sold on a certain verbatim set of practices, has a different definition and is intensely married to it. Which splits us. There's an 'Agile' vs 'Agility' angle (and to avoid that particular distinction, I like to simply lump everything in the '#Agile' umbrella). Then there's the distinction between 'Agile' and 'DevOps' – and then there's the distinction between theoreticians and practitioners, each at times armed with disdain for the other, and of course the multiple 'to Scrum or not to Scrum', 'is SAFe [Scaled Agile Framework] safe or not', 'the only "true" Agile is ... [XP (Extreme Programming), Scrum, FDD (Feature Driven Development), Kanban, Lean, DSDM (Dynamic

Systems Development Method) or even more obscure own flavours such as Crystal Clear to cite only the classics]'.

Despite the inclination to split hairs or insist on terminology, most agilists will agree that the actual approach is secondary and not nearly as important as realizing a change in mentality shift and understanding the transformational basic principles of working from a common backlog that is eternally being examined in light of feedback. So, for all the differences, there is a clear unifying kernel that's well understood and shared at a DNA level by all who have come to understand and love Agile, which is that it demands the best of us, keeps us most flexible, invested and honest, and can only be done right if done from the heart and not by mandate.

What Agile is Not

As I touched on before, in some industries we think of Agile as just another method conveniently confined to IT and the way they make software. In reality, it's immensely far from that.

Agile is not only for IT

In fact, our beloved 'growth' across the board and in every imaginable industry is heavily contingent on agility and the ability to use data and technology to quickly and flexibly respond to new market reactions.

Countless figures support the fact that businesses who use Agile in every type of endeavour set themselves up for being on the right growth path and that is utterly industry agnostic. There is no reason why every project in a bank, an oil&gas or a big pharma, be it regulatory, operational, digital proposition, R&D or the annual BBQ can't be run on a Kanban board. Organizations who can't see that as at least a goal to work towards are not only missing out on the possible results, but containing the practice to only one part of the organization, which is simultaneously a pity and a signal that they think of it in isolation and on a small scale.

Agile is not project management or software development, Agile is a transformative new way of looking at how we do things.

All the things.

Agile is not Reorg

Looking at various 'Agile transformation' projects, one starts to see patterns emerging that may explain their relative lack of success. Invariably, the story is the same. A couple of years ago, the organization has bought into some consultancy's pack and decided to 'become Agile' and within months has let people know they no longer belong to the existent structures such as departments and groups, but are now part of tribes, own products or are all 'engineers' now.

Armed with courses to become Scrum masters, YouTube videos on XP and a Jira corporate licence, armies of people now pray for the daily stand-ups to wrap up already so that they can go back to business as usual.

Agile is not a set of practices

This bit should be immensely self-explanatory considering the Agile manifesto but all too often it isn't. Using the supporting software and practices that Agile uses simply for the sake of ticking a box, in lieu as a means to support a thought pattern, is ludicrous but sadly widely spread. Tools and processes in the absence of a strong purpose foundation are dangerous indeed as they tend to take over and guide how people do their work in all aspects, in an inertia of practice that ultimately accomplishes nothing.

In one bank we worked with that is particularly 'implements-heavy and practice-light', we have had to message around, 'You can be Agile with just pen, paper and goodwill', hoping to reset their people's mindsets.

Ultimately, Agile is a religion

If we stop and break down what the ideas behind these methodologies are, inevitably we find they hinge on people. Collaboration, empathy, goodwill, purpose, they are all in-built in understanding that to make all the intended greatness happen, this is the fastest and most organized way. That principle must be sacrosanct for Agile to work. One must believe strongly in the possibility and desirability of accomplishing things faster by working together, staying alert and responsible, and driving forward with emotional investment.

Organizations that don't actually have that strong belief at their core and implement it as a meaningless fad inevitably fail to see results. Companies that have their people lead teams as an absent-minded second job, those that think of the Agile practice as a hobby or extracurricular activity, while expecting everyone to still function as usual, will have sorely missed out on the promise.

Agile is a way of thinking and a state of mind

One of the things I say to the new people in my team as well as to clients is 'unless you have a Trello board for your house chores, you don't get Agile'.

Having an intensely personally relevant A-ha! moment where the advantages of doing things in this new way are glaringly obvious is a sine qua non condition to making the most of it. Which is why organizations that simply mandate it and do nothing to elicit those moments in every participant end up having massive Agile shadow organizations composed of armies of consultants and coaches to help them go through meaningless motions and wonder why they can't accomplish Google velocity.

In a way, Agile is like Yoga (I recognize this comparison will lose you burly, weight-lifting types, but stick with it) – it doesn't change who you are, it places you in new positions where you take shapes you didn't know you could to access the parts of you that were great to begin with, but have been encumbered with dogma and process. Furthermore, just as Yoga does with timing, breathing and movement, Agile too involves continuous intentionality and affirmation.

To push the comparison even further, doing a spot of Yoga by the sea on the beach of your all-inclusive hotel on holiday while waiting for the others to wake up doesn't mean you have a practice and the flexibility and results that come with having one.

Let's go back to basics. The Agile Manifesto's values are:

Individuals and interactions over processes and tools *AKA 'People First'*

Working software over comprehensive documentation *AKA 'Feedback Artefacts'*

Customer collaboration over contract negotiation *AKA 'Empathy and Purpose'*

Responding to change over following a plan *AKA 'Flexibility and Innovation'*

All the goodness that most organizations have chased for so long: software delivery that supports customer centricity promptly by using the human capital, AKA making things that clients love, fast, by using their people, is contained in this manifesto. And it's not new or risky as it has served everyone from tech giants to big organizations in multiple industries immensely well for years, with mind-blowing results for those who trusted it.

Which brings us to the crux of the issue: TRUST.

Can execs trust Agile to be one of the few silver bullets to give them a shortcut to a competitive consumer proposition that ensures they retain the relationship in a time where they are under attack from other proposition makers, who are nimbler and more willing?

Can execs trust their people to undertake the hardest task given to them in their professional career and send them a message to:

> *Please embrace this, stop waterfalling in your head to pass the time in the stand-up meeting, stop wondering whose departmental P&L this is, throw away what you know of this organization and start taking personal responsibility, act with purpose as if this is your own shop, keep an eye on the helicopter view, you're part of it, rely on others, make things fast, be willing to take risks and fail, believe that you will not be held back or punished for it, have passion for what you make, understand how every item on the backlog translates to real-life goodness for the consumer and above all, keep practising courage?*

More importantly, can their people trust their execs to mean it?

Agile by Design or by 'Transformation'

One of the key reasons why the conversation around Agile practices has heated up is that the results obtained by companies who are truly Agile are undeniable.

Famously, these results were coming exclusively from tech giants out of Silicon Valley but increasingly, other big organizations in far more obscure industries are joining the party. These companies have either created or transformed an internal culture of innovation that sees them ahead of their competitors in vying for the attention of their end consumers chiefly by employing Agile across the board in a way that resonates with almost every employee. Everyone knows their favourite DevOps speed anecdote these days – Google deploys thousands of times a day, Amazon every 11 seconds, while the average bank five times a year, etc:

- 208 times more code deployments;
- 2,604 times faster incident recovery time;
- potential 75 per cent quicker response to strategic opportunity;
- a possible 64 per cent increase in decision cycles speed based on consumer feedback;
- 57 per cent less silos and more interdisciplinary teams;
- 52 per cent more likely in leveraging technology;
- 106 times faster overall velocity.

Those are just some of the numbers that reports brought us over the past 10 years.

These numbers feature in many decks and you might be forgiven for believing such undeniably useful stats are template level for most consultancies who have been responsible for carrying the transformation to everyone else and spreading the good word, hence originating successful Agile transformations. Nonetheless, if we look at the companies doing well while travelling on a path of building a truly Agile organization, we can almost always trace it nearly exclusively to an internal impetus to deeply change and achieve more. Despite how fundamental a shift this is, and despite how traditionally, companies only undertake fundamental shifts if some big strategy house designs them, or at the very least sanctions them with the board, it seems that, for the most part, the organizations succeeding with Agile are a lot more self-made in their desire for transformation than consultancy-led.

As compared to the 'legacy shift' or the 'digital transformation' programs that have been initiated by heavy decks paraded to boards, Agile seems a lot more greenfield in origin. It has come about as a solution to what is effective and works, first in software development in particular and then project management in general, and is now starting to thankfully seep into any other function that requires fast, reiterative, execution and at that, it has spread silently and unofficially, which is a tremendous shift from the model above and consultancies are more running fast to catch a wagon to jump on than driving this train.

This also explains why their attempts at showing they understand Agile 'best practices' are modest and reactionary and reduced to a certain portion of their efforts whereas the majority of buzzword bingo is still firmly hinging on discussing 'digital' in isolation and as a 'cure-all'. Most consultancies insist that 'digital transformation' is the higher concept – the be-all-end-all goal, whereas Agile takes a backseat as the execution piece of that transformation, but can that be right?

Agile as a way of thinking can arguably be seen as the higher concept as it is going to remain long past completed legacy or digital transformations, which are just hygiene for this moment in time. Looking at the frontrunners in Agile – Google, Spotify, GM or Amazon – none of the Big Four consultancies can say '*Yes, that's me, I wrote this magical 50M- strategy-deck as usual, gave these guys the blueprint of how to become Agile to the core, and here they are, they've done it and look at their success story*'. Granted, the vast majority of these Agile success stories are companies who are young enough to have been built as Agile and Digital from the ground up, the so-called 'digitally native' but even then, the building has largely been without any help from any of the consultancies you would have expected would have been part of that journey.

Some claim that the examples of best practices to build Agile organizations at leadership level from the big strategy houses such as McKinsey or BCG or Bain are modest because of the devious commercial motives that can be attached to their reluctance to pull the leader aside to say, 'Look, no one needs to know but let me show you what this is all about, three columns, to do, doing, done, let's spend the day falling in love with Agile – or Scrum, Kanban, DevOps or simply mental flexibility and never being done, OK?' The malevolence would be that, while they haven't designed and conducted the Agile transformation, the consultancies have quickly recognized the transformative potential and the enormous impact the lack of change in mindset will have, and have decided to protect the dysfunction for commercial reasons to be able to keep selling their traditional model of 'bums-on-seats', this time in the armies of agile coaches they provide to each organization.

While when it comes to software development, industries are slowly moving away from the warm bodies consultancy framework and demanding a lot more success-based models, when it comes to cultural change, strategy houses everywhere with few exceptions haven't yet found a formula to work for them. They simply seem oblivious as to how to charge for changing the DNA of an organization to where it becomes intensely open, flexible and human. They don't yet know how to charge for stimulating a company's (or even a leadership team's) sense of purpose, unconventional knowledge, appetite for continuous learning and passion. As a result, they don't know how to charge for making them truly Agile in their heart of hearts. If they won't figure it out fast, chances are the future belongs to organizations who will become Agile with the use of a mirror and a Google show-and-tell, not a consultancy's overpriced strategy deck.

'Agile Transformations'

There are hundreds of thousands of companies out there today struggling with their own version of some Agile or Digital transformation. The problem starts with the very use of the word 'transformation'. It's grandiose, murky, all-encompassing and ultimately meaningless in the grand scheme of things and its monstrosity alone discourages real results. Ironically, in its very essence, preparing for one of these big transformations is the antithesis of any Agile principle as it starts with huge waterfall-type big-bang exercises.

Perhaps we should start replacing 'transformation' with 'change' and simply refuse to entertain the idea of frameworks. It doesn't matter what route you take to create big change and there are various methods and proposed frameworks out there – SAFE, XSCALE, etc. – what's always needed is understanding the pillars of what's different and finding ways to get those comprehensible and intensely emotionally relevant to your own team and the team of teams – AKA your organization. I take that back – it does then matter what route, as if you take any of the prescriptive ones off the shelf, then the thinking and design needed to create a system that truly works for you and is capable of moving mountains are absent, and half the battle lost before it began.

Those pillars have to revolve around big, non-negotiable themes such as these:

Affirming a deep commitment to change – giving your people real permission by sharing your thought process behind wanting change to give validity to how much you do: *'This is what we've read and where we want this company to go and we know we must change our work culture and behaviours to make it happen so this is not empty rhetoric but our plan on how to become part of the digital elite – come with?'*

Decentralized and purpose-driven autonomy in lieu of command and control. Some say this is the hardest of them all – servant leadership comes so unnaturally to every consummate exec that they have trouble even envisioning how a climate of lack of control would even accomplish the enterprise goals they have.

An environment where flexibility and adaptability are aggressively praised – in actionable terms, not on paper only. Shifting from sequential thinking to a continuous loop with things done as needed, not as road-mapped a year in advance is not easy but essential.

Obsession with the customer. Finding ways to prioritize customer feedback above all else and therefore learn to be MVP-driven to gather it. Above all others, this is intensely personal to your particular business and attempting any of the off-the-shelf strategies won't work.

Obsession with the team. Focusing on the idea of the family-like units that do the Agile work is fundamental. As we said before, too much of the rhetoric today revolves around 'the organization' – a nebulous concept if you stop to think about it, which brings the discourse into the realm of the theoretic and unactionable in the same way that the term 'transformation' does. Once the lens changes, the natural need will be glaringly obvious: obsess with the team's Psychological Safety so they succeed.

Obsession with the people and eradicating your Human Debt. Much of this is hygiene in this new world where automation can and will eliminate anything that isn't intensely human and therefore competitive eventually. Giving our people respect and admiration isn't the norm and the implications of that alone have contributed to the Human Debt which needs cleaning up.

Redefining 'results' to what matters. Instead of KPIs and performance indicators lifted off someone else's business manual from the 1990s, sit down and understand what's important and what would be a good measure of success: the company level 'why'. Ideally, the exploration finds that it's cold hard cash in the coffers as that's a perfectly valid reason for living business-wise and it's translatable into objectives and key results (OKRs) to drive it comprised of these pillars here, once it's crystal-clear. These new measurements must reward failure, heart, courage and curiosity instead of compliance and submissiveness.

Culture of experimentation. Once the above is in place and rewards become connected to being adaptable and brave, all that's left to see courage propagate in an environment where mini-results are praised is to consistently underline how making open and honest mistakes is more valuable than being spot-on.

Deconstructing collaboration. Moving the topic from an empty word to meaningful and practical, intense common purpose, mutual help and its immediate and tangible benefits. Instead of talking about breaking silos, unify them by reaffirming the vision and allow them to see the connection threads that will benefit their customer obsession to let them think of ways to grow together, not apart.

Becoming addicted to critical thinking and cultivating passion. No stone should be left unturned and no question unasked by any of your people, your teams or your leaders. If they stop examining everything and attacking the status-quo, they stop being able to always strive for the loop and they stop being in flux. Ironically, a willingness to always exhibit critical thinking is the clearest sign of the presence or absence of passion. When it's there in sufficient quantities, expressed and vociferous critical thinking will be too.

Continuous learning and curiosity – a thirst for innovation and growth are fundamental to each of the above elements, but it often comes as the least natural step considering the state of our knowledge organizations today.

The above list is neither exhaustive, nor mutually exclusive, and it surely isn't 'best practice'. It's hard practice, it's new and uncomfortable practice, but part of the recipe for insidious, seamless and non-labelled change. This isn't to say change shouldn't be openly desirable, defined and declared from the top, far from it, as per the first item there, enough exec-level goodwill and a personal #Agile mindset based on pure business greed and sustainability needs is fundamental, but it is to split it into manageable, realistic and supremely effective 'epics', each with immediate tangible results and to stop only paying lip service.

'Organization', 'Culture change' and 'Transformation' in anyone's vocabulary today should ring alarm bells as even if not intended in the empty demagogic way in which they end up being delivered, they are far from being true levers for change. Ninety-four per cent of 'Agile

Transformations' may fail, I'd bet the proverbial farm 94 per cent of 'Agile Incremental Changes of the Heart and Mind' do not.

You Can't Have the WoW (Way of Working) Without the WoT (Way of Thinking)

Professional Thinking Patterns and Change

In my view, one of the chief reasons why Agile transformations 'fail' or are slow to show expected and revered results is because Agile is, at its core, a radically different mentality and a completely new way of organizing our thoughts than the ones we have been used to as professionals and that complete change is hard – if not impossible – for some to muster.

As we go through our formative years, which in the case of our professional entities extend far beyond formal education and into the beginnings of our careers, we develop an understanding of what the world looks like. This set of 'professional values' inform an internal code of conduct and belief system we are mostly unaware of that remains in the subconscious but influences how we conduct ourselves in the workplace.

Everything from our work ethics to our comprehension of basal topics such as collaboration to our attitude to tasks is based on a combination between what we have learned and what we have observed and becomes what guides us forward. This is mainly because it offers us perceived protection from risk.

Furthermore, because we have had an expectation for education to only be part of our lives for a finite amount of time – i.e. there has been no sustained expectation of continuous learning and improvement over our professional lives beyond completing formal education and some training – we rarely seek to challenge the frameworks we created and re-examine the nature of the way we think in a professional capacity.

As we saw before, the difference between Waterfall and Agile is not minute. Having Waterfall as part of how we see the world means having a very sequential, rigid and linear way of relating. It implies a 1-2-3 pattern where one thing comes after the other in a certain order logically and it also contains the expectation of lengthy amounts of time spent on these steps, which gives the practitioner a feeling of caution and therefore appeals to the risk-averse. Phases are expected to be completed meticulously, judiciously and completely according to a detailed plan and they will, therefore, allow the professional to feel in control of the process.

By contrast, Agile implies a 1-2-1-3-2-1 (and any other combination) pattern with a cyclical, feedback-based view, things happening without the structure or the plan and where they can be possibly completely changed on short notice. There are no phases, no detailed plans and no exact specifications. Furthermore, each iteration feels incomplete and 'undone' as compared to the bigger goal, which of course requires far greater flexibility, mental acuity and risk appetite. The two are nearly opposite ways of relating to the world and the real 'transformation' has to happen in the minds and hearts of each individual before they can make the leap from one way of thinking to the other. In particular when the first is perceived as 'tried and tested' and therefore secure and safe.

Sadly, for organizations to be successful with Agile, they need to have arrived at the need for this radical change without reservations on their own and fully, with nary a soul left in the company who is not Agile at DNA level and has relinquished the need for control and sequential thinking. Everyone from testers to the executive team has to have individually arrived at the need for this change and have taken steps towards challenging and thinking their ingrained linear and rigid thinking patterns. Obviously, they each have to have comprehended the 'Why' behind Agile and wholeheartedly believe it is necessary before that can start occurring.

I have been in rooms with many leadership teams where the need for the change in mentality is painfully clear. Some even understood the need but found it hard to arrive there, whereas most simply paid lip service to the necessity and kept hoping it will 'go away'. At times, there is no shortcut and all you can do to help is introduce them to enough examples of success to inspire them, but there are actionable wins to be tried, starting with asking them all to read Project Phoenix and now Project Unicorn.

The age-old question about organizational change is 'Where do we start?' – 'Bottom up or top down?' and when it comes to taking Agile to heart, we have to find the most effective ways to permeate every level of the organization so I am a big believer in 'the sandwich' method, where both are true and they meet in the middle.

The lower layers of the organization, the developer teams, the product, design and ops teams in the trenches, will take less work to understand and embrace Agile perhaps but they still undoubtedly can use focused work to ensure it becomes DNA level.

At the top, it is harder. Over the years I've collected a handful of ideas that have worked for change makers with the courage to put the executive team in a room and attempt to make them understand:

- Take them away – a 'leadership team building' or 'team re-launch' get-away somewhere remote, where you will have their attention for the day and their mood for the evening;
- Do a mini Team Launch at the beginning of the meeting complete with a culture canvas and obtain agreement on interactions from 'We'll be using a Kanban board and have a backlog' or at least 'We'll only use our phones once every couple of hours/at lunch';
- Start with an uncomfortable empathy exercise – prepare and give them each a printed list of 10 questions of a personal nature (research and use '36 questions to make you fall in love' first published in *The New York Times* a few years ago for inspiration) and ask them to pair up and choose two of those they feel comfortable asking each other. This will let them know the other

person sees what they avoided while they can't escape giving some answers. Ask everyone to return to the group when done and share one question and why they haven't asked it;

- Explain the concept of impression management (see Chapter 4 around this for more reference) and ask them to keep an eye out for it;
- Constantly reference data from DevOps reports that show the value of speed in no uncertain terms;
- Discuss the actual Agile Manifesto and then show them https://www.halfarsedagilemanifesto.org/ – watch for reactions; if they aren't laughing, you haven't reached them;
- If your budget allows, bring in one of the initial signatories of the manifesto to do a talk on the ethos behind it and the journey since – ask them to please keep it own-framework devoid and as close to the core concepts as possible;
- Use the Silicon Valley myth by outlining the speed of innovation and execution in these 'elite performers';
- First, get them to think of their own teams and how they can start and grow a 'People Practice' – explain the concept of Psychological Safety and show its correlation to productivity then show them how to measure it and what to look out for in their own teams. Offer the CEO or top leader in the room some means of measuring it at the leadership team as well and then explain they can round-robin that responsibility in top management meetings to get everyone involved;
- Get them involved in co-creating 'Agile for Us' by acknowledging methods of rolling it out at scale such as Scaled Agile Framework (SAFe) and others are not valuable across the board and therefore explain them all and their pitfalls to the execs;
- Ask them to create a Trello board for something personal – from a summer project to organizing a family trip to renovating their home – then to invite their significant other to it.

Ironically, this last suggestion seems to make a huge difference for some leaders where we've observed massive attitude and behavioural changes once it becomes intensely relevant and personal.

Any true Agile practitioner will confirm it has completely transformed them both as a professional and as a person and that once you 'see the light', there is no turning back. It's a light they come to recognize in others, helping them appreciate the huge investment that comes with the work done to arrive at it.

Agile and Humans

As the concept evolves past project management into leadership and any other function of the organization that can also use fast, demonstrable results, it finds itself compared with other management frameworks such as Six Sigma or Lean and sceptics point out that, apart from a few exceptions, despite their evident advantages they are nowhere as widely spread as they had been heralded in their time. This leads them to believe Agile will meet the same fate of oblivion.

The main difference could lay in the fact that, as compared to the two methodologies cited above, Agile starts at a very practical, results-driven place with undeniable desirable outcomes. Boards everywhere find themselves having to get over the initial eye-rolls and turned noses when approving large Agile transformation processes – at times for the entire organization in every department, not because they have personally seen the light (and this may come back to bite in time) but because they see clear numbers and want to have the same speed and accuracy of delivering new technology and results as the fully Agile organizations they see consistently keeping customers happy.

What some people – boards included – fail to realize about Agile is that doing it 'by numbers' is doomed to eventually fail as it requires a lot more depth of emotional investment than any other method or way of work. This is because Agile is a state of mind and a philosophy above a mere set of practices and processes and as such, it forces practitioners to look inside themselves, both at the organization and individual level. This, on the macro level, explains the push-back some segments of some industries give it. The 'Agile isn't for *everything*'-type objections are typically flippant and unfounded and meant to avoid closer examination. They mean that as it isn't the cure-all that applies to every part of the business in grave need of radical transformation. But is that assumption correct?

What do we *need* Agile for?

Not For Speed, But For True Collaboration

Speed of delivery is an undeniable result of applying Agile to software development (and any other function of an organization really) but to obtain that, this way of work requires real collaboration in a throwback to the team values of yesteryear, in which truly working together towards a common goal was key to making anything happen. Whichever virtual or real-life board or tool one uses in Agile and irrespective of which variation they have signed up to implement, the scope is constantly reinforced; the end goal constantly stated and – hopefully – examined; the reason for making whatever it is that is being created always reframed and declared. This helps deeply align the team. Once that team is 'sold' in their heart of hearts towards why they are building something and why they are building it in this way, they are infinitely more likely to care enough to truly help each other to do so.

In a time when in their work lives everything looks open, from office spaces to tech tools, workers often find themselves feeling insular and isolated and to counteract that, company posters simply mandating collaboration don't work, whereas Agile lets everyone's true collaboration instinct come out.

For Finding Family

Psychological Safety is the core concept and main success lever for any productive team. Feeling supported and safe in one's team is undeniably the single most basal need of workers everywhere. While this is true for all ways of work, Agile in particular demands a team that feels safe. In Maslow's pyramid of needs examining what it is that humans require, safety is at the very basic levels of that pyramid. Beyond physiological needs such as shelter, nourishment, etc., feeling secure is the basal need to be fulfilled and without it, humans can't function and that is true irrespective of the environment that human is in, so no less applicable to work.

Right above safety as we go up the pyramid we find the need for 'love and belonging' and while in our numbers-and-bytes-obsessed society this topic is often regarded as a weakness and consigned to an emotional discourse that has no place in the office, it is an intensely important human need that in large organizations is becoming increasingly difficult to satisfy outside of the four cubicles radius and the common interests groups. Agile requires so much of people as a team that the feeling of belonging follows undeniably strong and paradoxically, it makes many practitioners push back even further at first, as they have no frame of reference for feeling like they are part of a real family (or tribe) at work.

Being part of a family feels warm, safe and comfortable, whereas outside of start-ups or family businesses, in large organizations, in particular, work seems to be meant to feel hard, unpleasant or even painful in most workers' experience so finding Agile is a moment of intense reckoning.

For the Value

Going up that same pyramid, next we see humans need esteem – they need to be respected and feel like they are valuable. Agile gives those who understand and use it a sense of self-worth that's documentable to the business by how its KPIs are so unequivocally speeding it up.

In a sense, the staples of Agile – the velocity and the accuracy of the results – are a metaphorical 'I told you so' from the part of the long-overlooked and undervalued hard-working teams in the field, who are now allowed to use new methods and operate in an intelligent fashion, thanks to a fast process, so can show the business how valuable they really are. Not only that, but being open, honest and vulnerable as a practice in this safe new family they built, they get to shine and show their worth in front of the people that matter the most – their teammates.

For the Sake of the Challenge

Last, on the very top of the pyramid and a luxury most people don't associate with their professional lives, with surveys showing they attach little or no value to their sense of self through their work accomplishments – self-actualization.

In Agile, change is welcomed, the honest and constant dialogue is necessary, vulnerability is celebrated, nothing is ever 'done', things are eternally in flux and often difficult and all this means that it can be intense and demanding. The mechanism through which humans constantly test their own abilities is by accepting challenges and in Agile, holding yourself and others to the highest of standards while questioning next steps and greater purpose at every corner is fundamental. Some claim Agile only suits overachievers as it's demanding that the worker be the best version of themselves they can be, but that presumes only the triathlon athlete types like challenges and have a need of self-actualization, and that is simply untrue as the need to be better is there for each and every one of us, even if the work culture we are in hasn't been able to cultivate that.

For the Licence to be Human

There is no way to really become Agile without exercising some of the best human qualities, starting with empathy and passion. Contrary to the popularized belief that nerds or geeks – or whatever other terms we associate with tech teams – are all but incapable of having emotions, the success of Agile shows, without a shadow of a doubt, that is utterly false. Developers, product owners and project managers everywhere have been able to tap into deep reserves of understanding and kindness to make Agile work.

Oftentimes, being vulnerable, open, creative, innovative and fully emotionally invested is an eerie and difficult exercise for teams of consummate professionals but in achieving Agile organizations, the willingness to push themselves emotionally is evident and consistently pays off. Technology changed everything and Agile is arguably one of the fastest ways to access technology so it is placed right in the middle of that change, which is why it elicits strong responses from both converts and persistent laggards holding onto a hope that it will 'go away'.

Being introspective and willing to be emotionally intelligent in particular in a work environment where there's institutionalized paralysis of thought is hard. Holding a mirror to search for intensely human qualities like courage and passion is extremely uncomfortable. Being vulnerable enough to admit all these needs at work is painfully counterintuitive but all of the above is necessary to redesign the future of work around new, healthy, collaborative, empathic and purposeful habits, not convention and acronyms.

Agile is not business, it's personal, but so should everything else be in our work lives.

It's OK to be personal.

To feel, to think, to be human.

Why Agile is Hard

One of the major complaints practitioners of Agile have is that nothing is 'ever DONE' and that developers and managers alike yearn for their post-waterfall project completion downtime. This is true and very interesting.

It's interesting because in just one symptom it exposes a systemic issue we have in our workplaces today: an ingrained expectation of things working a certain kind of way. That way sadly revolves around organizational ills and ailments as much as it does around structures and processes we no longer need.

Concepts such as 9–5 workdays, hierarchies and the resulting 'monkey management' it brings, in eschewing responsibility and attempting to take on as little as possible, as well as the detailed and extreme planning before any execution, are deeply seated in the mentality of just about any professional in the workforce today. We are now asking them to do things differently. If we want them (and ourselves) to succeed, we have to be honest and explore how extremely different this is from their habits and expectations.

In a corporate environment and part of the Human Debt, most people are stripped of individuality. This is true across the board. Even at the executive level, personal responsibility, ownership and courage are far from being a given. Once you step inside the organization, you feel like you are a cog in a big mechanical organism and therefore you find ways to be human in between mandated processes and directives.

When a long, oftentimes harrowing, incomprehensible and frustratingly slow project is done in a big organization, that is the time for employees to breathe a huge sigh of relief and wait for the next un-relatable task to be bestowed on them. Usually, they failed to understand why they were doing this in the first place, why they were doing it in what seemed to be the most painful way imaginable, and certainly, why it had to take twice as long and have everyone fear for their lives.

The end of a classic waterfall project is like the end of a scene in a horror movie where the characters have sprinted away from the imminent threat and the movie-makers still want us to believe that they stand a chance. Everyone is on the ground, panting, filled with loathing and dread, but pleased they survived. For now. It's done. It's trauma over, they can begin to heal.

In Agile practices that moment never comes, but neither did the trauma. This isn't the ordeal a waterfall project is, this is another way of seeing what all needs doing the fastest to keep making cool things for the end consumer. Developers and managers alike can't rely on the downtime coming from the delivery sign-off anymore, they need to instead learn to be adults and get their own ways to decompress when they know they need them, to keep going and be sustainable in lieu of waiting for the flaws of the system and process to offer them.

In corporations, we not only fall down flat at the end of a project race but take any process or tool flaw or misgiving as an opportunity to take a breather. The missing licence, the machine that broke, the colleague who 'has the ball', the impediment that hasn't cleared, the approval not having come through, the other guys not answering, etc. All of them breathers. Times to dissociate and wait while someone else has the monkey. Of course, humans have to rest. In the old way of work, this rest comes when the system lets them down.

Sometimes the system fallacies even give way to another intensely human behaviour: moaning about things not working. It has become the only humanity moment in a work-life where we repeat acronyms and platitudes ad nauseam. We need the stuff that goes wrong because then we can do the complaining that unites us.

This is the most vicious of circles we will have to break to truly become Agile in big organizations: in the waterfall old ways of work, the system relentlessly reinforces processes and ideas that are fundamentally broken and to survive it, employees reinforce the usage of the broken bits themselves. That's why we need to hit the big 'reset' button; that's why we can't 'introduce Agile in parallel' as a hobby or a side project.

That said, one fallacy I see a lot of these days is the presumption that the tension between waterfall versus Agile is perfectly resolved in start-ups. Much as they would like to have you believe they are intensely nimble, new outfits sometimes struggle too.

Let's be honest: Agile doesn't come easily and naturally – in particular to consummate professionals who have spent many years in corporate environments before starting on their own and have to show investors they have all the answers. At the same time, it's not for 'the new kids' – it's too presently and urgently needed and useful to wait for a change of guard so anyone with as much as five years left before retirement had better learn how to become a practitioner or prepare to fail.

Truth be told, we like Agile on paper but in practice, it's hard and seemingly counterintuitive for anyone who has worked in the old style of work across the board, not only in corporations but in start-ups too.

Agile is asking people to:

Be ballsy. This can go wrong in so many ways, there are so many unknowns and scary 'what-ifs' we have little to no experience in dealing with and absolutely no practice feeling safe to fail.

Be 'always-on' and always speak up. No backlog item can be left un-debated, nothing can be done on automatic pilot, with no thought invested and no-conflict guarantees.

Be creative. Things they've known and tried may not work again. Everything is changing and that's disconcerting and scary but once they see the value of spotting the new way, having a crazy thought or trying out a new path, everything is easier.

Be 'owner'. Once they move that ticket on the board (or get their name against it in Jira or Trello), they must feel as if that were the most crucial task of an imaginary start-up they are the CEO of and they are to make it happen and then seek feedback too, so accountability goes hand in hand with autonomy and it is a new feeling for most.

Be open and curious. Don't take it personally, be prepared to be challenged, questioned and second-guessed, whether you're a product owner or one of the team. By others and yourself. Feel safe enough with your team and trust your magic enough to be comfortable with it.

Stay authentic and human and therefore uncomfortable to keep flexible. Don't try to minimize risk and fall back into old patterns of thinking, stick with the 'uncomfortability' of the unknown, added to the 'uncomfortability' of having to remain intensely human and ever grow your EQ.

None of those asks has ever been asked of our workers before and none of them come naturally. No one can blend in as a cog in a big organization and wait for the blessed relief of the end of the horror movie chase. It's not easy, it's not comfortable. Here are some things to try in order to manage the discomfort:

Celebrate small victories. From doing an internal happy dance when something is moved to the 'Done' column to having team beers after a velocity win, every time we achieve something we should take stock and take pride. It's a hard lesson to learn as compared to the annual stakeholder meeting or the yearly performance review but Agile gives us a reason for often incremental joy and we should use it.

Take breaks, work at your own pace. Teaching people to respect themselves enough to learn and stand up for their own rhythm is paramount. Don't let them yearn for the waterfall delivery point. Is it a sprint? Yes, but sometimes picking up just the one ticket is judicious and wise and the team needs to see it that way and support it. There's no risk of that opening the door for anyone taking advantage because the size of the team would quickly expose that. Can we afford to let people have their own pace when the very reason we do Agile is to be fast to market? Absolutely – you can only win the collective race if every player is irreplaceable so they each took their own marathon seriously.

Keep the heart. Always go back to 'religion'. Why are we doing this? What are we making here? How will the end user feel when they get their hands on this? True customer-centricity is building something you intensely believe will make your end users happy and then reminding your team and, more importantly, reminding yourself of that on a sprint basis.

Remember the alternative. Keep comparing. If you were to waterfall this, when would you be done and where would that put you, as compared to Agile competition?

Praise as a practice. Teams who learn the value of praise end up turning the criticism in retrospectives and evaluations into positives. They seek out failure as a learning and growth opportunity and realize that openly dissecting it is what demonstrates vulnerability and openness to help them make magic.

Don't punish, but shoot straight. Organizations that change the culture of blame and sanction and instead create 'people practices' and reduce their Human Debt through Psychological Safety win. When something goes wrong, it just ticks a bad-turn off the list. This is a tricky one though because in this day and age of political correctness, many outfits confuse Psychological Safety with non-straightforward communication and being 'nice'. Agile is nothing if not honest, open-hearted dialogue. Hiding behind being PC language is fear, speaking from the heart but knowing it lands well and it's well-received and constructive to the team is the courage we need in Agile.

Then this last one is not an immediate fix but one that I believe we need either way. It won't help replace old ways of work with the WoW du jour, but it's the only succession planning we should spend time thinking of – mentality and how our next generations, unblemished by 'corporatitis' and competing with automation, can make themselves indispensable.

Fast forward 30–40 years and hopefully the educational system would have caught up and the few humans still employed would have had their formal thinking processes structured around these new values from their early formative years but for now, we should all roll our sleeves, interact openly and teach each other.

Agile Superheroes

It is undeniably easy to fall in love with the minds of those who truly get #Agile. They may not flaunt it, but they invariably have superior intellect and amazing mental flexibility. They need to be able to:

- **Show self-control as they feast on micro portions.** As speed is all about learning and delivering slices, these need to be savoured and celebrated;
- **Thrive on change.** It goes against our need for safety and security but we can reprogram our brains to embrace it once we comprehend why we need to accept it as the only constant;
- **Be truly open-minded.** It's possible none of the initial assumptions holds water – it's why they shouldn't even be made;
- **Be ready to admit they may have been wrong.** How else would they learn? It's 'for now' or 'this time' and it's to their team, not the world stage – so they trust them and lean on them;
- **Have faith** – in their vision, their purpose and the fact that they have family around;
- **Play well with personal responsibility.** Autonomy and growth depend on a collection of internal moral compasses all pointing to the same North;

- **'Get' the end consumer of whatever is being made, intimately.** At this speed and with this level of expectation, every success is transient;
- **Become immune to the whiners, the nay-sayers and the framework fanatics** who want to see their own version of events happen more than they want to see results;
- **Be an unapologetic perfectionist and obsess over doing better;**
- **Be an athlete – a sprinter and a marathon runner in one.** Have disgustingly superhuman amounts of resilience and stamina;
- **Have huge courage and therefore be able to be authentically and inspiringly vulnerable;**
- **Be intensely human and an extraordinary empath with an obsession for their team.**

Nothing in business is more counterintuitive or goes more against the grain of everything we learned and did so far than #Agile, but at the same time, nothing else comes even close to guaranteeing success in the same fashion so there's little wonder there's so much pushback.

If you 'do Agile right', these are truths:

When you do a 180 and throw away good work because feedback told you to, you won.
When you admit you made a mistake, you won.
When you deliver slower than you liked but you know it, you won.
When you change or pivot, you won.
When you fail and learn from it, you won.
When you're back at square one, you won.

Unsurprisingly, getting to grips with these is extremely hard for all of us. The only advice I have for those who recognize themselves in the lists above is 'hang in there and try not to lose heart while the rest of the world works it out and joins in'. For everyone else: 'Wake up!' If I could shake every executive of every enterprise into getting it, I would. And for their own good too. There isn't any industry, any business and any individual who could happily carry on in the arrogant belief that they can carry on with their sequential doing and their sequential thinking when the world is running past them.

If you're reading this, you're one of the ones above and you're friends, family or beer buddies with a chief experience officer (CxO) who doesn't but may do, here's a karma shortcut: save them from becoming an #AgileFaker, look them in the eye and level:

- Don't hope for any predetermined formula, forge your own!
- Don't copy & paste anyone else's version; you're not them.
- Don't hope it will pass and we'll all go back to a PRINCE (PRojects in Controlled Environments) world.
- Agile isn't 'out'; *you* will be if you don't get it.
- Don't think you can delegate it. Be the superhero – check your back pocket – you have the cape!

Agile, DevOps, WoWs And Reducing Human Debt

So how can the new WoWs (Ways of Work) contribute to reducing the Human Debt and treating these Agile Superhumans better so they become part of Psychologically Safe teams that can make magic? Is it HR or DevOps we should look towards?

To see the connection, we first have to look at the similarities and differences between these two terms even if we are to use loose definitions of what are essentially ever-evolving definitions of philosophies. Agile can be seen as either a description of a set of practices and processes or a set of values and a new type of thinking that guide the way we run a project (primarily in software development for the time being) whereas DevOps refers to an umbrella vision of what used to be disparate functions of the organization from development and testing to other operational functions and the way the magic of automation can redefine the organization. As such, it would seem at first glance as if it's a tactic versus strategy: one execution, the other vision. The reality is that terminology is trivial and both Agile and DevOps are descriptors of a mindset that needs to power a very different work culture than anything organizations have experienced until 30–40 years ago and as such, they are indeed descriptors of the new ways of work.

In my view, the best example of the intersection comes from an unlikely source – a report published in 2019 called 'Accelerate: The State of DevOps' by an organization you should look up called DORA – DevOps Research and Analysis headed by three rockstars of the industry – Gene Kim, Jez Humble and Dr Nicole Forsgren. The report surveys and analyses some of the darlings of Silicon Valley, from Google to New Relic, and in this particular instalment, it retests the findings of Project Aristotle when it comes to the relationship between the existence or absence of Psychological Safety and its relationship with high performance by checking if the findings are 'Google-specific' or they apply to a wider segment of companies. The report shows that they consistently correlate in the case of all other 'elite performers', which are companies showing high achievement across a multitude of technical indicators. (In the 2018 edition, these were 7 per cent of those surveyed, whereas in 2019, the number of companies who were hitting all the markers of success around speed and delivery had risen to 20 per cent, showing that having solid DevOps people-based principles works!)

The report – which remains to this day one of my favourite publications of all times! – not only states its importance under no uncertain terms but ensures that in every visual representation of excellence in software delivery and achieving the same results as the coveted 'digital elite', having a 'culture of Psychological Safety' is in

a box of its own as the starting point of each and every diagram. It doesn't get clearer and more spelt-out than that when it comes to this audience.

In my view, if Professor Dr Amy Edmondson's work has put the concept of Psychological Safety on the map for the medical field as well as offered studies and results in a number of other industries such as aviation or pharma when it comes to the software industry, the DevOps community did the same by outlining Google's Aristotle project finding and then by adding publications such as this pivotal DORA report.

If you look for mentions of Psychological Safety in the report you can find them in every diagram. Right there at the top, everything stems from it. What it says to the industry really is 'You don't have that box on top, you don't have a hope in hell to have "productivity"'.

To me, discovering the report had been heartwarming in a number of ways. Not only as an 'I told you so' link between Agile/DevOps and Psychological Safety but as diffuse confirmation that amazing people are out there. It's like finding unicorn tracks in the forest. People who 'get it' – who think and learn and collaborate in new ways that make them super-human-like are out there and they are answering this survey and working to make themselves and their organization even better. Not news to us as we meet some every day, but the numbers seem refreshingly higher than ever and that means critical mass.

The report is not meant for Agilists or Superheroes or those who already live and breathe the new ways of work but for everyone else who needs more data points and more evidence of how this is the way. The beauty of the State of DevOps Report is that you either believe it or you don't. You either aspire to be one of the elite digital performers or you don't. And if you do, then you can't ignore the big elephant-sized box in the middle that says it all starts with a family-like-team-bubble who makes magic fast, because it is Psychologically Safe.

Beautiful as it may be to me, the DORA paper is a report and as such, not the most exciting of mediums.

Humans learn best through storytelling. That is not news to anyone. Which is one of the reasons why I keep insisting in my keynotes that – aside from reading everything Professor Dr Amy Edmondson has ever written about Teaming and Psychological Safety, all Brené Brown ever put out and other must-reads such as *The DevOps Handbook* or *The Culture Code* by Daniel Cole – one should absolutely consume *The Phoenix Project*, which I jokingly refer to as 'chick-lit for DevOps' because it's the only one of these necessary reads that translate dry, big lessons into an amazingly relatable story.

In 2019, *The Phoenix Project* ceased to be 'the only one' though and I could barely contain my excitement when I realized there's a sequel of sorts created by the same amazing Gene Kim entitled *The Unicorn Project*.

The book follows an alternative story to the first one and this time its protagonist is a female lead developer Maxine exiled from the Phoenix Project. In an interview about the book, the author describes what he entitled the Five Ideals: 1. Locality and Simplicity; 2. Focus, Flow and Joy; 3. Improvement of Daily Work; 4. Customer Focus and 5. Psychological Safety. This is not the order he presents them in and the delimitation is interesting and arguably debatable but needless to say, having one of the biggest voices in DevOps who has authored all the most important books and has contributed to all the most transformational reports underline Psychological Safety so clearly is nothing short of monumental. Gene Kim undoubtedly knows the importance of the topic – he's one of those rare keepers of this truth I refer to at the beginning of this chapter and he also knows that storytelling sometimes gets people listening more than they would to cold hard facts or even the results of a Google study.

While there is growing awareness about the topic, and we meet more and more enterprises by the day who get how Psychological Safety is as equally fundamental to the potential success of the digital elite as the technology chosen, and the way of work it is employed in, having it spelt out in a story form can only help and further that as we need not only leaders to work out – without it, they shouldn't even pretend they are trying to succeed – but everyone to get it bottom-up as well.

Interestingly, Gene Kim confirms that the Phoenix Project was aimed at leadership whereas the Unicorn Project is aimed at developers and I think that's tremendously astute and necessary and they deserve it. The honesty. The dialogue. The promise.

The Human Debt I aim to get everyone to reduce means essentially, we have collectively severely mistreated our people – developers in particular! – by inflicting mindless and soul-killing processes and performance management systems and the occasional wooden-language survey on them, yet not 'hearing them', not focusing on team bubbles that make them productive and happy and generally, not caring about their well-being. As a result, they utterly mistrust the organization when it says it now cares and wants what's best so will herald in a new era of autonomy, respect, better morale, learning and growth, and everything nice. They simply don't buy it in the least at first. Which is why stories like this one, and results such as the reports mentioned above, are crucial because they bring home the point that the enterprise now has to make these substantial cultural changes as a life-or-death business imperative, not a lip-service moral one. So, to use Agile to reduce this Human Debt, we will need all of us who have it at heart to help shine the light on teams that make magic by having enough courageous superheroes that they have Psychological Safety and high Emotional Intelligence.

CHAPTER THREE

Teams and the Search for High Performance

- What is a Team?
- Modern Teams and the New Ways of Work
- Leadership 2.0
- Forming – Team Launches, Culture Canvases, Contracting and Swarming
- Storming – Healthy Conflict, True Dialogue and Dysfunctions
- Norming, Performing and High-Performing: Teaming and Re-Teaming – Team Composition vs Team Dynamic
- Project Aristotle

What is a Team?

Before we can discuss what makes people and organizations better we must first and foremost look at the concept of 'team' as the group is the level where we can affect change the fastest if we understand the dynamic and foster the right behaviours.

The funny bit about 'team' is that one feels it more than one understands it. Any of us comprehends intensely what it means and instantly casts our mind to the time when we were in the most tight-knit group that was 'making magic' together as one.

The most common definition of 'team' which can be found in courses around the world today (including the one from the University of Washington on Effective Teamwork) is 'A group of people with different skills and different tasks, who work together on a common project, service, or goal, with a meshing of functions and mutual support'. By that definition, many groups of people of many sizes can be considered to be a team. When it comes to education, sports, defence or social activities, the concept is clear and its use is widely spread.

The 'Work Groups And Teams' study from Cornell University recognizes the difficulty of producing an exact definition and of realizing who holds responsibility for the concept, saying:

This ongoing transformation in the basic organization of work has captured the attention of researchers and is reflected by new theories of team functioning, a rapidly growing number of empirical studies, and numerous literature reviews written on the burgeoning research on teams. It is also reflected in a shift in the locus of team research. For most of its history, small group research has been centred in social psychology (McGrath, 1997). Over the last 15 years, however, group and team research have become increasingly centred in the fields of organizational psychology and organizational behaviour. Indeed, Levine and Moreland (1990) in their extensive review of small group research concluded that 'Groups are alive and well, but living elsewhere.... The torch has been passed to (or, more accurately, picked up by) colleagues in other disciplines, particularly organizational psychology (p. 620).

So, in the work context, the concept has seen ebbs and flows in terms of both adoption, usage and importance since its first mentions in management practice dating from the twentieth century.

The evolution of the concept in the workplace is best described by Frederic Laloux, author of *Reinventing Organizations: A Guide to Creating Organizations Inspired by the Next Stage of Human Consciousness*, in his interview in the documentary, *Squads by Invision*, where he explains that the first types of modern teams after the tribal society came with the agrarian revolution. They had a wolf-pack character, where it was all about following a leader, after which there were army-like structures brought about with the Industrial Revolution. He then proposes that the model of leadership that suggests we blindly execute orders and follow the one at the top of the hierarchical pyramid is the only model the business world has known until the past 30–40 years, at which point the Agile and Lean ways of work have challenged the perception of those structures and the respective leadership applied to them.

Nowadays, in truly agile organizations the structure is much flatter and is made up of pods, squads, tribes or just groups of people in teams that are self-organizing and coming together with other teams if and when they need to so that they facilitate work. To those of us invested in the concept of people, the periodic loss of emotional investment and sheer intellectual interest in the idea of the team is puzzling, if not utterly incomprehensible. When we examine the Human Debt we spoke about, a large part of it can be traced to this attitude towards the 'team' concept.

Over the years, as I've spoken about people and teams around the world, I've seen the disconnect first-hand. Whether in the faces of the thousands in the audiences of one of my keynotes or in the eyes of a new dialogue partner, a certain sense of blasé lack of interest happens when I mention the word. It's as if it's not heavy enough of an idea, or even not landing in its entirety. I can only imagine this is a reaction to it having been so heavily overused in business jargon for so long alongside how a lot of our culture rewards heroes and individual performers – both financially and with recognition – to the detriment of the team.

To counteract the apathy and lack of connection, I flash a slide which says nothing more than: 'Team = Family'. The reaction is unmistakable – utter recognition. There's a word that hasn't lost its meaning – on the contrary, one of the most intrinsically important words humans even have – and now there's a presumed association, which brings about an instant connection. The very next reaction oftentimes is an incredulous smile or an eye-roll and many immediately quip, 'Ha! Well, you don't know *my* family!', which gives me the opportunity to reiterate the connection, 'No, believe me, I do. We all have one of those. And we don't always love each other, it's not always fun and fuzzy but we all always have each other's backs and always selflessly work towards a common goal which is the well-being of the other one. That's what your work family should feel like too.'

In his book *The Culture Code*, Daniel Coyle describes having asked multiple teams what is the first word they would use to describe their group and the word they came back with over and over again was indeed 'family'. They chose the word consistently over others that would have made much more sense, such as 'friends' or 'tribe' or even 'team'. When asked to motivate it and expound, they all seem to describe this feeling of 'magic' they have together in their team: 'I can't explain it, but things just seem right. I've tried to quit a couple of times but I keep coming back to it. There's no feeling like it, these guys are my brothers,' says Christopher Baldwin, US Navy Seals Team Six to Daniel Coyle in the book.

This feeling of 'magic' is, in fact, the concept of 'Psychological Safety'.

Some oppose the idea of the team altogether. Despite how, in researching this book, I have challenged myself to be empathic towards what look like outrageous points of view around individualism and the ability to assemble pieces of work in an abstract layer where introverts and those who loathe social interaction aren't forced to collaborate, I've listened to those saying we've been forced into the team structure artificially and read all types of definitions and theories regarding everything from how teams are formed to how they perform (or not, as the case may be), I still believe a team is the most amazing collective manifestation of being human.

However we choose to define a team, they all have a few fundamentals in common such as 'trust', 'collaboration', 'goodwill' and 'common purpose'. The trick with the definition of a team is perhaps to attempt to not really have a definition but to make it super personal instead. You need everyone *in* a team to have a very clear idea of what a team is *to them* even if those ideas are vastly different, as long as they have these fundamentals in common. Once you see the essence of a team not as another name for an artificial structure but as a pattern that includes the above, you start seeing it in other groups as well. A family is the best example of a team, but so too is a couple or a marriage. Well, the good ones are. As is the group organized around the executive committee for the school fayre or the local book group or cricket club.

An instant team is everyone who stops by the side of the road when someone falls ill in the street, from do-gooders to the paramedics and the doctors. They instantly slip into collaboration mode, pass and accept tasks as necessary, trusting each other's goodwill and knowing the common purpose is that of potentially saving a life.

Some people thrive in the presence of others and are naturally built for collaboration, investing more trust and goodwill upfront and being able to retain a firm vision of the purpose – the mythical 'team players'. Others think that's just not them and they find it much harder. Both need to iron out those differences and get to where they are 'family' and this takes longer for some than others.

Here's something that is little talked about when it comes to teams: stability, longevity. Often confused with job security and a mad focus on retention at all costs, it is still an extremely important factor in the ability of a team to build and grow together because before teams have been firmly in 'performing' mode for long enough – and this 'long enough' is different for different industries wherein some instant teaming is possible – they aren't at their best.

There are many reasons why the stability of teams is a difficult desideratum to accomplish in most business situations but evidence abounds that in the case of teams, stable and solid social structures are desirable, ranging from long-term performance data to a NASA study quoted by the Harvard Business Review in 2009 which found that fatigued crews who had a history of working together made about half as many errors as crews composed of rested pilots who had not flown together before.

Modern Teams and the New Ways of Work

There are several ways in which we can analyse the concept of modern teams – by the way they were formed, their size and type, by their purpose or industry and by the way they are organized and function together.

When it comes to terminology, the new ways of work – in particular, Agile – have come with a bevy of new names for the concept of team, in particular in the software development industry, which is the field that has the widest spread of the new mindsets and methodologies. We have 'squads', 'tribes', 'chapters', 'huddles' and more. Generally, they all refer to small, nimble, flat structured teams, where the team members pick and choose from a common backlog of tasks together and work in bursts of expanded work energy according to an Agile framework or philosophy, such as Scrum, etc. 'Squads' in particular is said to have originated from world-acclaimed Agile coach Henrik Kniberg, when he popularized his idea of an efficient team in an engineering environment and his concept at Spotify and became part of its gargantuan success, thus coining the term of the 'Spotify model' which is nowadays practically synonymous with distributed, cross-functional and highly efficient autonomous teams. The concept is widely applied and it showed it can just as well work for huge corporations when the Dutch bank ING, which has tens of thousands of employees, decided to apply it to their own team structures and is today organized around 350 squads and 13 tribes.

Size-wise, any group that interacts with a common goal is a team irrespective of size but there is a growing body of research to indicate there is a natural cut-off point for efficient teams – the famous 'two pizza teams' term coined by Jeff Bezos of Amazon was based on his gut feeling and his disdain for groupthink (the theory according to which people start behaving a certain way and adopt the dominant thought pattern in the group to the detriment of their individual opinions, thus resulting in poor decision making) but it is on par with many studies and experiments that seem to place the magic number of employees on efficient teams somewhere in between five and eight.

The larger the team, the more pronounced a number of dysfunctions are.

Put bluntly by J. Richard Hackman, the Edgar Pierce Professor of Social and Organizational Psychology at Harvard University and a leading expert on teams who has spent a career exploring the wisdom of teams, 'Big teams usually wind up just wasting everybody's time.' Simply because the amount of connections that need maintaining is growing exponentially in any teams above five to eight teammates and therefore it becomes unsustainable, a drain on productivity and renders the size of the team a liability.

In an interview for the same *Squads* documentary (*see also* p. 70), CEO of Scrum Inc. J.J. Sutherland emphasizes that in the current structures of work, it's evident that teams of 10 'simply don't work' and there are substantial differences in the performance of those having seven or eight and then nine members, with productivity dropping significantly as that number goes up.

In terms of specific industries, the concept of teams in particular in the modern digital world where the manner of work has to be Agile transcends the exact field where the respective team is active and the only considerations may well be around the amount of time they have to become a team (some teams need to perform instant teaming, such as in emergency services or the medical arena) and the overall longevity of the structure.

When it comes to systems, processes and tools the panoply is ever-growing, with Silicon Valley giants famously reporting they hold licences to thousands of enabling software packages to help these teams best perform their tasks.

In the arsenal of a modern team leader many trendy concepts can prove valuable tools in their People Practice as ideas such as 'Amazon Memos', 'Culture Hackathons', 'Lean Coffees'; 'Private Brainstorming'; 'Google's Conversational Turn-Taking'; 'Permission to Fail Values', 'No Blame Culture', 'Conflict Training' and more are all doing their bit to avoid deeply unhealthy anti-patterns such as the ones cited by Atlassian to be found in interactions that are 'Unstructured', 'Complaining', 'Negative', 'Micro-managing' or 'Bored/Unengaged'.

Above all, modern teams of all denominations are teams that obsess about humans with a diminishing focus on hard numbers and an ever-growing concern for health, family and magic.

Leadership 2.0

If we have spent time examining all the ways in which work is bound to change and agreeing that teams are the structures where this change can be most effective, we can't leave out the concept of leadership.

Leadership is a vast topic and this book is not having its dissection as a goal, but it is unavoidable if we spend time thinking of teams and the ways in which we can have them at their best. To start with, we must assess the idea of fully autonomous teams. Is this truly desirable or even a real-life possibility when the team needs to communicate with the rest of the organization? Is it wise to have no 'throat to choke' and at the same time no one to clear the ice in front of the puck? Is it a good idea to have no one specific in the team in charge of keeping things on track and of supporting the work of those who are creating those things?

The closer we inspect the theories that claim we ought not to have any type of 'head' in a team, the more they become impossible to translate into practice, seductive in theory as they may be. We like the idea of full independence with no reporting lines and complete autonomy but we need the support and help that structure and organizational charts give us so what is the answer?

The answer is a new type of leadership in which those in charge of various support functions do their job exclusively to help and never hinder. They empathize, not chastise; they encourage, not control and they inspire, not dictate. The big themes of modern leadership, or 'Leadership 2.0' as I call it, have to do with the very nature of leading from a gleeful, voluntary and growing perspective, not a constrictive one.

Command and Control vs Servant Leadership

Robert Greenleaf coined the term of 'servant leadership' over 50 years ago and the first body of work into this new managerial mindset originates from the Greenleaf Center for Servant Leadership he founded in 1964, helping to raise awareness of what he viewed as a more efficient business practice as it focused on the employee's needs and enables them to be engaged and innovative.

A lot is said about the selfless nature of servant leadership and this throws the term into the vocational realm and away from business realities. While there is no contesting that any servant leader has to be fully invested emotionally in their team and their purpose, that doesn't mean constant self-sacrifice for the sake of it but a deep understanding of how serving is the more efficient way of doing things.

We all instinctively know that to be successful, we have to rely on others and we will be more successful when we are able to harness the best they can bring. It stands to rational reason that simply demanding someone's best self is a lot less efficient than setting up the environment where it can be brought about. To the servant leaders, the needs of their team members come first because if they have satisfied them, then the employees can achieve high performance and therefore the business wins. It's not a nice-to-have or a moral add-on, it's a clear business imperative.

Johnson & Johnson is one of the most prominent examples of companies who place servant leadership as a central value and their resulting business wins are undeniable, thanks to this mindset. From an individual perspective, irrespective of what level of the organization we are at today, we have all had bosses for the majority of our adult lives. Our relationship with authority at work is as interesting and complex as any other area of our panoply of human interactions but oftentimes, if we examine it, it's fraught with frustration and laced with fear and often we subconsciously model the same behaviours that have caused that down the line.

By and large, we collectively believe management is paid in nebulous P&L connected bonuses. In a sense, judging by how we've been treated and how we feel, we wouldn't be surprised if they are paid by how mean they manage to be – a reign of terror KPI. Is it any wonder we freeze at any mention of 'What can I help you with?' and assume it to be the beginning of a negative review?

Do we ever really believe that a leader asks 'What can I do for you?' in an open-ended way in which they are truly and honestly trying to remove the blockers that stop us from doing the job we want to do? Unlikely. To a degree, it's why so many people are quick to fall in love with Scrum despite its critics as a scrum master is such an immediate evident example of a person who is meant not to manage but to keep the team on track and help. In fact, Jeff Sutherland, one of the first signatories of the Agile manifesto and the founder of Scrum.org, is openly advocating against command and control by saying that he believes the IQ of team members faced with micro-management drops by 10 points.

That same concept, of course, is behind the idea of 'servant leadership'. Leaders are meant to be there not to manage and chastise but to facilitate and ease. A turn of focus from control to enablement. Leaders should have always been around to help, not to oversee and hinder. Somewhere in the life of organizations though, a dramatic shift has happened, where leaders have become the villain in lieu of the hero of the story and more dramatically still, they have bought into that stance themselves. It's now an expected demeanour of 'management' to be unattainable, busy, frosty and mostly exasperated.

External Impetus

In a world where tasks had to be imagined far into the future and assigned by a select few to be executed in a sequential fashion by the many, there was no space for dissent or even basic dialogue. Orders and demands were dispensed and heads had to roll, should they not be executed, so leaders are to be feared to be efficient.

But what if we reimagined how leaders earn? What if it became the case that they couldn't retire before everyone reporting to them is happy? What if they couldn't make the bonus if anyone was left with a problem they would have had an answer for? What if they were rewarded for every time they truly helped? Would we believe them then? Would we be able to shake the eternal 'us vs them' and 'buy it' that they are really invested in serving us?

Internal Impetus

Definitions of 'servant leadership' say it 'inverts the norm in management'. How is this even the case? Why is being controlling and un-serving 'the norm'?

To some of us leadership comes as second nature. Others – likely 'most' – have to work at it. Those who are just born to be leaders are intrinsically also born to be helpful servants. They know that being truly of service is valuable and do so without prompt or because they apply a certain methodology or other. Everyone else went to 'management schools' and is leading 'by numbers' so none of the compassion, empathy and emotional investment of a real leader comes easily or naturally.

Irrespective if we are a natural leader or not, we know beyond a shadow of a doubt that being a servant leader is the decent thing to do. We know it to be the moral, right way to be with others – aiding, assisting, being human – so if we can now be assured that the business is not better off by us going against our decency and instincts, but will indeed instead benefit from us being servants to our teams, that should justify our humanity when it comes to leadership at long last. This to me is yet another way in which Agile brings us closer to our humanity – by demanding that we are leaders who serve, not leaders who crack whips.

In research from the University at Buffalo School of Management published in January 2020, it becomes clear that not only is servant leadership demonstrating undeniable business benefits but that it may usher in an unexpected but welcomed by-effect – diversity, as women proved to be consistently more performant in the role perhaps as a result of the feminine role stereotype. The role of gender in management is well documented and the expectation is that the male stereotype is synonymous with great leadership in popular culture. Yet this is only the case for old-style Command and Control, as the study outlines how women are consistently performing better in terms of Servant Leadership. This may well suggest that the time of iron-fist-masculine energy management styles is on the way out and that we ought to popularize the value of Leadership 2.0 with its focus on deeply human values, nurturing energy and genuine assistance.

For those willing to learn and develop and become Leaders 2.0 there is much to take in and a handful of topics to think of. One of the best voices you'll find on this topic is Karen Ferris and her amazing body of work in effecting practical change by transforming how we think when we are a leader. Find her and others who do the good work of preaching this and have them help 'change the norm' as the so-called norm will hurt you in the long run if left unexamined.

Most importantly, make it a practice to routinely look around you and question: are we, as leaders, truly serving our people? Are we positive, open, fostering, empathic? Are we jumping at the chance to remove any impediments? Are we risking our own comfort to focus on the team's well-being? Are we forever working hard to clear the ice in front of the puck? If not, how do we expect them to win? And if they won't, how would we?

If 'managers' can't be leaders, let go of frameworks and put their hands up willing to admit they are human and none the wiser than any in their teams, while staying obsessed with building connection, compassion and listening, then we will have lost the opportunity to have created stronger teams. It will be little wonder that we feel more Psychologically Safe and connected to all kinds of instant teams, from community volunteer efforts to parents' WhatsApp groups or old schoolmates' Slack or Microsoft Teams channels, than we do with our work team, in particular in times of crisis. This would be a great loss for both the company and ourselves and a loss preventable with the right servant leader with a strong EQ and a worthwhile People Practice.

Forming – Team Launches, Culture Canvases, Contracting and Swarming

When it comes to the way a team comes together or really, whether that is a once-and-done linear process, or, as suggested by some authors such as the brilliant Professor Dr Amy Edmondson in *Teaming* and the wonderful Heidi Helfand in *Dynamic Reteaming*, a live, cyclical and highly susceptible to change process that resides more in the mindset than the structure, it is still likely that the initial mechanism of formation holds clues regarding how they become 'family' and how it is that they can 'make magic' with each other.

While there are numerous theories around what the mechanisms and behaviours of a team are, one of the most reliable of the ones explaining their evolution as a group remains the forming–storming–norming–performing model of group development first defined by Bruce Tuckman in 1965, who said that these phases are all necessary and inevitable for the team to grow, face up to challenges, tackle any problems, find solutions, plan work and deliver results. In short, it refers to the way that groups of people come together and what their behaviours and their need for help or guidance are at these times.

The 'forming' phase is often characterized by confusion, lack of agreement or deep enthusiasm, mistrust and cautiousness as teams first come together and individuals size each other up. This phase is the one that requires most prescription, direction and guidance.

In the second phase, 'storming', the team has been working together for some time, some convention is in place and the common presumptions begin to be put to the test. In this phase, there will be conflict whether it is overt or not, with individuals trying to assess their dominance, 'turf wars', battles over perceived resources, etc. This phase too will need leadership and guidance if in a more conciliatory and advisory manner. Teams in the storming moment can learn valuable lessons about productive conflict, if coached and supported accordingly.

Next up and when a team starts to truly come into their own and starts to become performant is 'norming'. At this stage, the team has been together for a while, has resolved areas of conflict and is now starting to find emerging ways in which they are efficient and performant while developing a close bond and trust. From a managerial (or People Practice) point of view, this phase requires facilitation – in particular around maintaining a feedback channel and ensuring good habits of opening up and expressing everything from agreement to dissent.

Lastly (if we don't count a final phase added by some, which implies the dissolution of the said team called 'Adjourning' for teams that disband after a set amount of time) is 'performing'. While its meaning is clear, during this phase the team 'hits its stride' and they start becoming comfortable with successful routines that closely mirror the contracts they initially made. Therefore, they have solid communication, are clear on purpose, efficient and productive. This is the 'team magic' and it requires very little if any managerial intervention, being the most autonomous of all states.

In terms of autonomy, it can be argued that keeping teams in the Performing phase simply reduces if not eliminates the need for management as they can use a type of swarm intelligence to do the best job possible. 'Swarming', named as such in *The Wisdom of Many – How to Create Self-Organisation and How to Use Collective Intelligence in Companies and in Society From Management to ManagemANT* (Kurzmann/Fladerer) as part of their concept of 'ManagemANT', implies that functional teams can and do learn from the wisdom of ants, who always find ways to collaborate in efficient patterns when it comes to high performing groups. It names the following as prerequisites to self-organizing structures: motivation, independence, diversity, decentralized knowledge, communication, no central control.

Obviously, those are such huge topics that it explains why we rarely find companies who have found models of autonomous teams across the board. If we return to the first phase, what happens at the inception of a team is indeed crucial.

Harvard's Richard Hackman states that he found that 'the things that happen the first time a group meets strongly affect how the group operates throughout its entire life. Indeed, the first few minutes of the start of any social system are the most important because they establish not only where the group is going but also what the relationship will be between the team leader and the group, and what basic norms of conduct will be expected and enforced'.

Here too, there are many theories on what is necessary in terms of team formation and various authors offer various accounts of best practices but in our opinion, the most efficient theory can be found in Scrum's concept of 'team launch'. This is not a descriptor of a phase but a hands-on exercise – a plan of action on how to design the interaction of the respective teams moving forward. Many times it amounts to a full day's exercise that in some ways mirrors the team-building retreats of the 1980s – it gathers all the team in one room (or one virtual space, but this can often be harder) and asks them to go through a set of exercises together to co-create what will be a team they can become invested in.

Often organized as a blue-sky Human Centred Design exercise, it allows new team members to jointly describe and agree on a set of norms and practices they find desirable and that would ensure they are successful as well as allow them to spend time agreeing on purpose and vision.

For the latter, using a Culture Canvas is always a helpful exercise as it helps frame everyone's ideas of where the commonality of vision is, what words are best descriptors, where the common ideas and beliefs lie and what the common goodwill denominators are. A new modern way of uncovering, painting and then articulating a joint 'mission statement' of old.

Often it is the conversations that the Canvas provokes that are the most valuable part of the exercise as they quickly expose deep aspects of the team members' view of the world and of the joint work they are called to do. This quickly allows team members to adjust their expectations of one another, getting a de-facto crash course in the way of thinking exhibited by their teammates, which is especially valuable in the case of teams made up of individuals who have never worked together before.

Once the values and vision are laid out and articulated, the team members can move to the more practical matters of finding the best ways to work with each other. This can be called 'Contracting' and involves discussing every operational aspect, from the methodology employed to manage the project, the processes in place, the way they communicate among themselves and with other parts of the organization and what actual tools and systems will be used. Teams are encouraged to emerge out of this exercise with an actual 'Team Contract' document they can use not only as a good reference point internally – in particular as the Storming phase hits – but also as an external artefact when they interact with other teams.

These Team Launches are typically being led by an external facilitator such as a coach alongside the team leaders but an experienced team leader who has been through a few other 'Forming' phases before and who is high on EQ and has a strong People Practice from working with other teams can easily ensure they 'hold the space' for the team to come together and do this thinking.

Storming – Healthy Conflict, True Dialogue and Dysfunctions

The second phase of a team's life – 'storming' – is often seen as the most dangerous one. This is because it involves one of the hardest parts of human interaction – conflict – and because the determination to avoid it at all costs, in particular in a professional environment, makes many engage in destructive behaviours such as covering-up, cowering, being dishonest and hidden, being catty and bullying, being avoidant and inauthentic and generally being unwilling to speak up for fear of furthering the conflictual stage which gives rise to systemic issues reflecting in bad norming, which unchallenged disallows teams from being productive.

In the organizational development cult classic, *The Five Dysfunctions of a Team: A Leadership Fable*, Patrick Lencioni outlines that the biggest challenges a team may face are: a lack of trust, fear of conflict, lack of commitment, the avoidance of accountability and a missing focus for results.

Even if a team went through a healthy amount of co-creation through the work they invested in their team launch to rally around a common vision, chances are that the respective vision is theoretical and that to achieve honest commitment towards what they outlined they will need to traverse a deep dive into their innermost attitudes to work that will often include conflicting ideas. If they are unable to manage conflict and transform it into a positive and constructive exercise, they will lack the ability to debate openly and therefore may never achieve commitment and accountability and these dysfunctions will circle viciously towards a lack of trust and then a lack of common high performance.

The way a team can remain grounded in the task of being 100 per cent open and honest, speak up, be vulnerable and welcome productive conflict is the cornerstone to their ability to advance to the further stages of norming and performing. If they miss out on this crucial step, they will start creating a set of bad behaviours that will undoubtedly play against them and see their productivity never materialize as compared to teams who have found ways to navigate conflict in a healthy way.

Learning how to hold an open debate and not take things overly personally, learning how to remain respectful during heated opinion exchanges, not engaging in one-upmanship behaviour and remaining empathic while employing the famous concept of 'radical candour' (AKA extreme honesty) are all incredibly valuable skills which are formed during the storming phase and can avoid Lencioni's dysfunctions moving forward. Some teams such as those at Atlassian and Airbnb openly admit they revel in this phase as it brings about more learning and creativity through open dialogue and debate than most other ones.

Storming is, above all, the phase where the team learns from valuable experience that speaking up is indeed not only permissible but desirable and a true value, that there is a safe haven for honest dialogue in their social group and that they should not see their willingness to be open and state their point of view as risky, thereby laying the foundation for the work on Psychological Safety.

Norming, Performing and High-Performing: Teaming and Re-Teaming – Team Composition vs Team Dynamic

It is in the last two phases of Tuckman's group development model that 'the magic happens'. Obviously, the first two are sine qua non and no team can jump over any of the steps in either forming or effectively avoid the storming phase but both are of little value productivity-wise. While the team may well have been asked to do work day one and few have the luxury to be given dedicated time, even for team launches, the reality is that their output is simply not very good before they reach at least the norming phase and it doesn't get to its full potential before the performing phase.

In norming, much becomes easier and there's a collective sigh of relief at the level of each team member as they realize they have now achieved commitment, they are clear on the purpose and they have good working methods to work and communicate effectively while allowing them to do good work fast. The speed and sense of common good can well be intoxicating. Teammates realize they can absolutely trust each other, that they are a functional and productive cohesive group and they are starting to get comfortable in their new shared reality.

During norming, it is especially important for the team leader to plug in the healthy People Practice they may have referred to in the team contract before because it is now that people need sustainable support they can count on and they need to feel like their well-being is being taken seriously. That's not to say that the mental and emotional well-being of the team is a job for the team leader only or that they are to go around fixing these nebulous potential issues and encourage a set of mysterious behaviours, far from it. Everything a team leader does in their People Practice ought to be utterly transparent and they should enlist the help of the team to outline issues or praise beneficial behaviours while thinking of ways to improve.

Consistent work on the human aspect in the norming phase only strengthens the bond the team has and allows them to feel even safer with each other and convince them taking risks is safe, speaking up is desirable and they can – and should – be vulnerable and utterly open with one another.

If any phase underlines a sense of familiarity coupled with a sense of achievement it would be norming in particular by contrast with the uncomfortable sense of upheaval that the team may have felt in the first two stages. This is the right time to underline that the consistent work and high degrees of attention are not any less important in any of the other phases and that the phases themselves are not strictly linear but may indeed be interwoven with teams slipping into storming from either norming or performing in times of crisis or uncertainty and with forming being necessary either when there is a significant amount of new additions to the team or when the team seems to have lost its way and strayed from the vision and the purpose. A good team leader can sense this by a dip in the general sense of shared goodwill or through sudden dips in courage or engagement. Nonetheless, norming is typically an intermediary phase as well and not a goal as the phase we all want our teams in is 'performing' and with that in mind, any team leader should want to get there the fastest way possible and stay in the respective phase for as long as possible. This is because in performing, this is when the team's true potential is realized and when results and outcomes clearly reflect this.

The team is relatively free from the dysfunctions, it jives, it feeds off each other and it functions like a well-oiled machine, giving everyone extreme satisfaction. Teams in this state will be achieving their full potential and they are typically behind some of the greatest achievements mankind can boast, from scientific breakthroughs to productivity records being smashed. They are high-performing 'dream teams'.

We often hear talk about 'dream teams' and our reaction is to presume it has to do with their composition. That the members of the team have a special bond because they are each, individually, a certain type of personality and their respective personalities happen to perfectly mesh together.

This isn't a surprising assumption and the business world is awash with attempts to exemplify the power of composition and 360-degrees assessment tools and personality tests. One of the big four consultancies is anecdotally so in love with the concept of the perfect team composition that they have hired the team behind Match. com's algorithm to build them one like it, but for work, supposedly putting people together in the best possible way – Business Chemistry. Unsurprisingly, the reports are not stellar.

At PeopleNotTech we have had our own path of having courted the topic of 'dream teams' so much so that we have created a prototype software solution to ensure that the best possible match happened when teams would dynamically come together. It all started with our extreme indignation at the simple fact that in some corporations, whether they liked to admit it or not, new teams for new projects were put together through a method as much fine art as an exact science: Excel-picking based on availability.

Many enterprises, in particular in the banking sector – which was where we had seen many a case where they were using this hypothesis – openly not even used any of their data or knowledge about their employees before sticking them in an aleatory fashion into teams with no regard to anything more than a broad brushstroke of their skills. This struck us as shocking and even irresponsible, not to mention absolutely unnecessary in this day and age when we can so easily get live and deep feedback from our employees to learn where their interests and passions lay, to understand what they would want to be involved in and even to measure the degree of trust that their teammates may have in their abilities to be part of a certain team at a certain moment in time. We developed a mechanism that, based on the data the enterprise already had about its people and, more importantly, based on the new data acquired from asking the right questions at the right time, used machine learning to suggest possible team members for a specific project and then subjected the team proposal to a voting process to see what the other employees thought of the suggested team composition. At the end of this exercise, teams of highly invested and skilled individuals which already had the trust of their peers could be assembled. A whole new way of putting people together.

In the process, we also spent a lot of time examining the work of matchmaking software out there in an effort to find one reliable enough to overlay it to the mechanism described above, adding theoretical matching to purpose and trust. We couldn't find any which we would have bet the farm on, and while we were investigating why that was, we came across Google's Project Aristotle and realized composition and even our bet on initial purpose and trust were sorely insignificant as compared to their findings, which stated without a shadow of a doubt that the main predictor of team success and high performance has nothing to do with who it is that makes up the team, but whether or not they had Psychological Safety.

Project Aristotle

Following a 2008 project focused on understanding the role of management and the attributes of a good manager at Google entitled 'Project Oxygen' which outlined a number of the qualities and behaviours of a good leader and demonstrated their importance to their vast engineering workforce, Google took a step further in deeply understanding their workforce and uncovering what makes them a high performer and launched another project entitled Aristotle.

Spanning a few years of intensive research and looking at 180 teams and 37,000 employees, Google asked a pivotal question – 'What makes teams effective at Google?'

A tribute to Aristotle's quote, 'The whole is greater than the sum of its parts', they focused on the team for all the reasons outlined above as they call it 'the molecular unit where real production happens, where innovative ideas are conceived and tested and where employees experience most of their work' and did a deep dive comparable to the one done for Project Oxygen. Famously, they expected the results to focus chiefly on how the Google team magic was a result of a combination between the famous Google gruelling hiring practices giving them the best-skilled individuals and the fact that they treat their employees equally famously well. In other words, they expected the results to reveal how they have hired engineers with the highest IQs and the most experience and then given them resting pods, Google bikes and ping-pong tables so it's little wonder they make up efficient teams.

'We were pretty confident that we'd find the perfect mix of individual traits and skills necessary for a stellar team – take one Rhodes Scholar, two extroverts, one engineer who rocks at AngularJS and a PhD. Voila. Dream team assembled, right?

'We were dead wrong. **Who is on a team matters less than how the team members interact, structure their work, and view their contributions.** So much for that magical algorithm.' Google re:Work

As you can see, the results surprised them. The factors above – IQ, experience, satisfaction with present work conditions – they were never the top most important conditions to the success of a team. Instead, they found five common characteristics of high-performing teams. They have Dependability, they have Clarity and Structure, they are clear on Impact and Meaning (AKA purpose) and most importantly, consistently coming on top above all, they all exhibit high degrees of Psychological Safety.

This is when they found the concept. Around since the 1960s when it was coined by MIT's Edgar Shein and Warren Bennis, and then reinvigorated in the 90s by research by William Kahn it had been as we now know, heavily studied and well established by Professor Dr Amy Edmondson's research but never had it truly permeated the vocabulary of business before the results of Project Aristotle.

We need to learn from Google's research as it was built upon a great mountain of evidence about the power of Psychologically Safe teams and it immediately follows from that research that the 'team' matters the most because any other structure is either inefficient (the individual) or imaginary (the organization). If we want success, we must become invested in the ways to empower it through Psychological Safety, so that it stays anchored in the performing state and creates magic in this invaluable, family-like structure.

CHAPTER FOUR

Psychological Safety – The Only Lever for High Performance

- Psychological Safety at the Top
- What Psychological Safety is *Not*
- Trust
- Flexibility and Resilience
- Speaking Up, AKA Courage and Openness
- Learning, Experimenting and Failing
- Morale and Engagement
- Avoiding impression management
- The Dialogue of the Bubble
- Team Happiness and the Human Debt

Psychological Safety – The Only Lever of High Performance

As we learned in the previous chapter, what Google found was that the way a team was created, or indeed who it was that made up the team, was largely irrelevant and not nearly as important as other coordinates that make or break the company's success, key among them the team's healthy dynamic of Psychological Safety.

This is a better-researched and infinitely better-articulated finding, but it's not personal or exclusive to Google in the least and many other Silicon Valley darlings have been proudly focusing on their people for many years and have done so by encouraging some of those same values and creating similar visions.

'We are a people company' is an adage often heard out of Netflix, Apple, Zappos and Amazon these days as they are not only examples of enterprises who have done very well for themselves from a business perspective but also share a conviction that to win, they must keep humans – be they their own employees or customers, or at times, the communities they are part of – at the centre of their every action.

Zappos is a shining example of such a people company. A lot of amazing employee and customer practices come from them. Most of their time and effort is spent on the happiness and engagement of the employees and examples of their outcomes are scattered throughout this book, but they also spend time investing heavily in the value of the shared vision. For example, they're famous for paying new employees to quit. After new employee training ends, each employee is offered the opportunity to quit their job and walk away with $1,000. They do this because one of the Zappos core values is 'be passionate and determined', and paying people to quit ensures that those who remain are incredibly enthusiastic about their work and in it for the long haul – an early litmus test of the effectiveness of their culture canvas.

It's easy to believe this fierce stance on caring about humans is only corporate rhetoric, but if we examine some of their actions, the way they treat people is consistently reducing any Human Debt and protecting safe, happy environments where their preoccupation with an employee's well-being spans every topic from how they remunerate them to how they engage them so chances are, they have understood that their people are their true competitive advantage.

A recent example of a company who live and breathe this respect and focus on people is the way that Airbnb has responded to the financial crisis and its devastating effects on their workforce. When CEO and Co-Founder Brian Chesky was faced with having to let people go due to how heavily they were hit by the lack of travel brought about by the pandemic in 2020, he not only wrote the right letter with a humane, kind, empathic and connected tone, but demonstrated he had put genuine and honest thought into how he can help those he was parting ways with. After announcing a package of very generous measures to help out those leaving, from monetary compensation to allowing them to keep the company laptop as he recognized how crucial it would be to have the right kit when searching for a new job, he closed by saying:

[...] As I have learned these past eight weeks, a crisis brings you clarity about what is truly important. Though we have been through a whirlwind, some things are more clear to me than ever before.

First, I am thankful for everyone here at Airbnb. Throughout this harrowing experience, I have been inspired by all of you. Even in the worst of circumstances, I've seen the very best of us. The world needs human connection now more than ever, and I know that Airbnb will rise to the occasion. I believe this because I believe in you.

Second, I have a deep feeling of love for all of you. Our mission is not merely about travel. When we started Airbnb, our original tagline was, 'Travel like a human'. The human part was always more important than the travel part. What we are about is belonging, and at the centre of belonging is love.

To those of you staying,

One of the most important ways we can honour those who are leaving is for them to know that their contributions mattered, and that they will always be part of Airbnb's story. I am confident their work will live on, just like this mission will live on.

To those leaving Airbnb,

I am truly sorry. Please know this is not your fault. The world will never stop seeking the qualities and talents that you brought to Airbnb, that helped make Airbnb. I want to thank you, from the bottom of my heart, for sharing them with us.
    Brian

You can always tell a true people company by the way they apply humanity, like the Airbnb message above, and by how willing they are to invest time and effort in Psychological Safety. Alex Kroman from NewRelic says, 'Treat Psychological Safety as a key business metric, as important as revenue, cost of sales, or uptime. It will support your team's effectiveness, productivity, and staff retention, along with other key business metrics.'

And to do so, to treat it as being as important as it is, we must learn what it truly is about and spend time dissecting it into its various components.

Psychological Safety at the Top

I believe the lack of Psychological Safety at the top, in the management teams comprising all other lower-level managers as well as those that are at CEO and CxO level, is the root of all organizational evil we see in the vast majority of organizations. I believe that impostor syndrome, risk aversion, fear, dread and stagnation are running rampant among C-suites and until we resolve this at that particular level and until such time as we restore the team at the very top it's not going to be sufficient that we work on Psychological Safety for every other team or that we try to make real mentality and cultural changes in organizations.

The higher up you go in an organization, the more leaders think of teams as structures that are executional and exist in the layers beneath them. This is part of the reason why, at the very top levels, there is no talk or expectation of Psychological Safety because even if they should admit its importance at the team level, they don't actually feel they are part of one themselves so they aren't expecting it in their particular group.

In many ways, this is not surprising as focusing on the team requires so much in the way of establishing an empathic and EQed People Practice based on courage and demonstrated vulnerability, trust in yourself and others, perceived reputational and financial risk, a thirst for learning and growth.

One telling fact is that if you Google 'Psychological Safety for Leaders', nothing comes up that is in fact aimed at helping leaders with the Psychological Safety of their own leadership team. A shocking discovery as the term in itself is widely acknowledged in any other type of team that wants to be fast and productive.

I think a chief executive should be little else than a team leader or product owner or even project manager or scrum master of their own leadership team. If he chose them correctly and can ensure they are truly valuable and their hearts are in the right place (which admittedly are big ifs worth extreme measures to attain), little else is more important than ensuring they really are a team and they are a secure, thriving one and just as no other team leader can avoid it, the CEO themselves will not be able to shun the work of investing thoughtful interventions and strong emotions into their well-being.

A good litmus test is to look around the room in a management/leadership or board meeting and see if you can even think of them as a team working together to accomplish something in place of a collection of disparate individuals there to impression manage, posture and read press releases out loud.

Here's some practical advice for the Emotionally Intelligent, Servant Leader 2.0 CEO clued in enough to have tested and found their management team is far from psychologically safe …

Do a Leadership Team Re-Launch

- **Spend disgusting amounts of time discussing mission again and painting a picture of the future that has them excited and reinvested** – whip out the Values and Vision Canvas mentioned above and re-launch the team as often as needed;
- **Focus on re-contracting and critically examining every interaction to prevent the unengaged power parade happening today** – How do you work best together? Should meetings happen with a certain frequency? Should they perhaps all have Amazon-style memos that are being read out by every leader that leaves space for open and honest dialogue after? Is there a Kanban or Trello board for what you are accomplishing together? Where are your sprints/epics/hopes defined other than in the shareholder reports?
- **Use the power of 'Pay it forward'** – Set up a culture of mentorship. Instead of the handful of favourites each CxO has, have leadership offer mentoring to several employees – say one new hire, one problematic leader and a randomly chosen other one – and show what they've changed by that direct contact and advice;

Change the Narrative

- **Less BAU (Business as Usual), more New** – Change the focus by ensuring what is rewarded is directly relating to new and innovative not accomplishing P&L connected results – point out (not sanction) when what is accomplished is trivial and/or hygienic only and contributing little to the goal of moving ahead and encourage extreme experimentation;
- **Demonstrate Permission** – and ask them to communicate it to their teams. It is now OK to be human, have emotions, focus on your People Practice and empowering teams; it is now desirable that you fail, it is now needed to be open and honest;

- **Leaders' Book Club** – If you're meeting your leadership team once a month or once a trimester (hopefully for sprint kick-offs), have them mention a book to read that they found inspiring each time and update on the blogs they follow. Learning together increases closeness – the beautiful minds of your executives are a terrible thing to waste and as a top mind told me the other day, it's astonishing to see that at the top no one reads anymore.

Better Them

- **Encourage them to grow their own brand** and build their own hero stories – you want your leaders so valuable they absolutely do not fear mobility but choose to stay with you and recommit to the purpose every morning. Make sure they build a voice in your industry, encourage them to write and speak and become influencers – it always pays off. Even leaders on their last career leg will find value in building a publicly visible hero narrative so ensure they do that;
- **Agile management sprints** – If you're not doing this already in your leadership team this is the number-one change lever you can introduce today. Break down the yearly objectives into a backlog and set up epics and sprints, then get your team to grab from the pile irrespective of their department. Why shouldn't your chief risk officer (CRO) help with the digital transformation, or your chief technology officer (CTO) sort an HR restructure if they have the willingness and resources? If nothing else, by doing some form of Agile in your leadership team, you quickly show them that rapid experimentation and collaboration is possible and with no disastrous consequences is possible and that failure is intrinsically connected to progress.

Make Them Feel Safe

- Use some team solution like ours to focus on the same elements any other team has to mind – your leadership team, maybe more than other teams, needs to be flexible and resilient, they must always have the courage and they need to be open, they have to find ways to keep learning and there should be a focus on how to keep them engaged and connected to the idea of the strong management team you have built;

- Help them avoid impression management (not speaking up for fear of looking incompetent, negative, disruptive, intrusive or ignorant). Start with ignorance and incompetence, eliminate them as fears. Tell them the story of former CEO of Xerox Anne Mulcahy, who was so comfortable with saying she didn't know the answers that people nicknamed her the 'Master of I Don't Know'. This gave Xerox employees the confidence to engage fully in tackling the company's challenges, and under Mulcahy's leadership, Xerox came back from the brink of bankruptcy;

- Obsess about new ways of setting a physical or mental Team Action, complete with various interventions to build more closeness, from humour hackathons to sharing in 'Leadership Truth or Dare' – maybe over monthly dinners (if you don't have those with your core team, get them, even if online!) and not around the boardroom. Encourage your team to constantly open up with new and personal titbits or to act as silly as they would if they were out socially at a pub with their best mates – in the olden days – or on a Friday Zoom with a pint in hand and a willingness to share during quiz night with the family.

Lastly, does your management team, however you define it, have a regular engagement method? Perhaps a WhatsApp group? Or Slack channel, daily bloated email list, Intranet group, Workplace space, or Twitter DM? The incarnation is irrelevant. Is there a space where dialogue between all of you is meant to be open and continuous? If not, how do you expect that you are a team without it? Get one today. And if yes, keep an eye out for who stops ever coming back to kids and sporting results and take it as a sign that they may have stopped feeling psychologically secure enough to be open.

Your managers, your leaders, your CxOs – the top structures of your company are made up of people with immense talent, great IQ and who were once in love with the purpose of what they were building. You're getting none of that today but instead a half-hostile, fearful, under-utilized, overly-consumed-with-politics-and-numbers set of checked-out disparate entities – the opposite of a real team.

If you can reignite their initial spark, if you can get them to renew their vows with you, if you can reassure them that they are safe to experiment and grow together as a team, if you can help them move fast, use their EQ and be brave, knowledgeable and passionate once more, then you have a Psychologically Safe management team and should be in with a good chance of making great things move from 'Doing' to 'DONE!'

What Psychological Safety is *Not*

As with every other 'human topic' Psychological Safety, Google and academia, endorsed as it may be, has had its fair share of eye-rollers and detractors. Typically, those who know instinctively that this is incredibly important, but sense a lot of work is necessary to affect it for the better and are unwilling to put that work in. Over the years we've met hundreds of executives who were at first willing to discredit it and throw every objection they could think of at it to get out of having to do any of the heavy-lifting their People Practice needed – to avoid starting to pay off their Human Debt.

We must clarify what Psychological Safety is not – Professor Dr Amy Edmondson, Shane Snow and yours truly are only a few examples of authors who have had to take on the task of dismantling half-baked myths and objections around the topic but anyone invested in the concept has probably had to do so at one point or another.

Psychological Safety is not …

… a fluffy concept fit for charity shops

This is perhaps the most infuriating misconception regarding the applicability of the concept. Anyone who has looked into the subject knows that to coin the term, Professor Dr Amy Edmondson started her research in the medical community. Much of the subsequent foray in the data comes from that same healthcare industry and aviation and it wasn't until Google's project Aristotle that the concept has even been applied to teams that work in less critical environments. It is anything but a side note to do with smiley faces and offering free hipster beard-oiling classes. If in business it gives us blessed productivity through high-performing teams, in the fields where Professor Dr Edmondson studied, it can easily be a life-or-death matter.

… a ticket to Lazy-town and complacency

Psychological Safety is in no way a licence to take the work or the team for granted and slack. In fact, in teams that are secure and invested, it is far less likely members will be tempted to resort to subterfuge and eschew the actual work. Moreover, this is particularly applicable to working in Agile teams and while a little-discussed benefit, Agile is an absolute antidote to laziness in any form due to the visible nature of the process.

... guaranteed employment

We've all heard horror stories of how in some Nordic countries it is notoriously impossible to discard useless employees and private companies find themselves trapped in endless loops of politically correct retraining cycles. Psychological Safety is not advocating instilling a sense of guaranteed employment in teams. While the above stories may be gravely exaggerated, there is a grain of truth in the social safety valves in place in some Scandinavian countries, where it is indeed much harder to demonstrate the need to let someone go and despite this, there is no evidence that their teams are more daring, open to risk and criticism, willing to learn and be vulnerable together. In fact, according to critics, the opposite seems to at times be true, which would make for an interesting research position I wish some organizational design scholars would undertake in the region.

... the death of performance reviews and any other measurements

Turning a blind eye to how the team is performing is never a good idea and it is certainly not what advocates of Psychological Safety preach in particular, seeing as how our main driver is better productivity, which of course cannot be tested in the absence of measurement.

Of the few places innovative enough to actively concern themselves with this topic, some have adopted a concept called The Just Culture Model, which was introduced in 2001 by David Marx and advocates searching for the root cause of the various possible types of mistakes and mishaps, which of course in itself involves an openness to admit to them and discuss them, but also encompasses an implicit review of performance even if it isn't formally recognized as such and is a lot more stomachable.

Additionally, Agile has intensely clear and blissfully easy-to-measure outputs so judging performance is nearly impossible to avoid and furthermore, paradoxically the more psychologically secure a team, the more likely it is that they are comfortable with personal (team) responsibility so reviews and measurements are actually welcomed and often initiated by the teams themselves.

... a mandatory pair of proverbial gloves

There is a fair amount of confusion between individual psychological safety and team psychological safety. While both desirable, and evidently to a degree interconnected, they are two different concepts with different sets of drivers.

An individual's sense of emotional safety hinges on many things and the way they get on with their team at work is but one. It has to do with a series of factors, most of which are personal and out of which work, and its nature is an arguably small proportion depending on where it sits in the individual's self-definition and actualization mechanisms.

The intersection lies in the team's spirit of interpersonal trust and respective ability to exercise empathy but the team's overall Psychological Safety is not a collection of the individual senses of security of the team members, but an independent construct so while human decency and deep knowledge of one's colleagues can only make for better interactions it doesn't follow that they translate exclusively into teams willing to take risks and debate.

... a licence to forgo all morality filters

This one is hard. To have any hope of instilling Psychological Safety in teams we must first and foremost ensure they feel they have freedom of speech. Dialogue is paramount and being able to speak up without fear of judgement or repercussion is the key. This, of course, invites the age-old questions around morality constraints on said freedom.

When this dialogue is at a certain-sized team level, it is visible and submits itself to the same moral accountability norms individuals employ in their day-to-day lives. In other words, a team is as biased or bigoted as its weakest member and when everyone is permitted and encouraged to speak up that is evident and regulated through normal group dynamics.

Nonetheless, critics rightfully point out that, in some enterprises – Google is no exception if you look at some of the recent scandals of employees' extreme behaviour and intensely politically incorrect opinions or even prejudice – the eagerness to create forums for utterly free dialogue has led to insufficient consideration being given to the modality of doing so, and anonymous extreme feedback has been encouraged in lieu of human decency and personal accountability.

The intention is not to build an internal 4Chan, where each team member takes turns showing their worst sides and tries to outdo the other in adolescent *enfant terrible* mode for mere shock value, but to open the floor for dialogue within the expected moral boundaries of grown-ups, so they learn and grow together. So, in essence, it is not about making people feel no matter what they do, or worse, do *not* do, they are meant to remain employed. It is not about having to mollycoddle teams ad infinitum. It is not about a set of individual definitions of well-being. It is not a cute little side employee engagement and well-being lever with no direct correlation to the enterprise's success. It is not about dissolving common sense and decency to create a safety net.

None of those.

It is about telling teams it's OK to make mistakes, it's fine not to know everything, it's good to open up and be vulnerable, it's right to have a passionate common purpose and desirable to be human, to be family, to make magic. Most of all, Psychological Safety is not a feel-good, nebulous, unaffectable concept that is out of our hands but a set of behaviours and a handful of components we can focus on to effect change and we owe it to ourselves, our teams and our organizations that we do so.

We must be willing to pry and probe and uncover and research to do so. Some of us will have access to team solutions like ours and others will have to do this 'by hand' but the need for the work remains. Above all, we must measure. We must ask. We must care enough to measure and ask. We must apply our collective mind to deconstructing this major, nebulous concept into actionable bits and then look at each of them with open-hearted curiosity.

Trust

The first thing that comes to mind when it comes to Psychological Safety instinctively is that it is all about trust. And in a way it is. Some refer to it as trust, but at a team level, as compared to trust between two individuals, for instance. While I don't disagree with the evident connection, we at PeopleNotTech are betting the farm on it being deeper than that. And on how trust too is a nebulous term that can and should be dissected further to allow us to better our team dynamic.

In some of our research, we have looked at the various frameworks that do deconstruct trust and we have used some of their findings to ensure those elements are accounted for in the Psychological Safety components we have eventually settled for measuring.

Zenger/Folkman's review of 87,000 leaders' 360 assessments published in the *Harvard Business Review* in 2019 generated three areas they ought to focus on to build and maintain trust: Positive Relationships (i.e. staying closely in touch, demonstrating empathy and concern, resolving conflict, generating cooperation, giving feedback in a helpful way); Good Judgement/Expertise (i.e. demonstrating good judgement and knowledge in decision making, having well-respected opinions, contributing to team achievements) and Consistency (i.e. being a role model and a good example, honouring promises, keeping commitments, follow-through, etc.). While all these elements were important, they found that there was more emphasis put by the team on the first one when scoring their level of trusting their leaders.

Entrusted by Shane Snow, author of *Dream Teams: Working Together Without Falling Apart*, a study from 1995 entitled 'An Integrative Model Of Organisational Trust' cites three major characteristics of trust: 'Ability', 'Benevolence' and 'Integrity', and in *The Trust Factor: The Missing Key to Unlocking Business and Personal Success*, 2020, Russell von Frank does a critical and extremely detailed exploration of the concept as it spans work and personal realms around language, core values and the different ways in which we can 'matrix' our way to trust.

But the model that spoke to me most was Brené Brown's definition of trust in *Dare to Lead: Brave Work. Tough Conversations. Whole Hearts*, where she proposes the BRAVING framework for trust. In essence, she proposes that for trust to exist in any meaningful fashion, one has to have Boundaries, Reliability, Accountability, a Vault, Integrity, Nonjudgement and Generosity, and while this is a case in finding synonyms to go with Brené's trademark topic of courage, the list is all-encompassing and includes practically all the models cited above and more. What is remarkable with Brené's framework is that, as compared to other trust dissections, it isn't meant as a sterile theoretical exercise but as a method for increasing trust in a team. She accompanies the book with a workbook and speaks about 'operationalizing trust' – a lovely actionable departure from the academic side of things, offering leaders and teams straightforward exercises and advice to include in their People Practice and better their trust.

Despite how valid all of these are, I didn't think that trust in itself was a valid and sufficient measurement of Psychological Safety in particular since many of the concepts proposed above remained staunchly unmeasurable so at PeopleNotTech, after our brush with *Dream Teams* and when we realized we had to find ways to become forensic about Psychological Safety, we interviewed a few hundred professionals with a mix between developers, leaders, technical architects, strategists, project managers, scientists, operations, designers, support personnel and others. We have settled on six other components to measure Psychological Safety through and then overlaid them on Professor Dr Amy Edmondson's questionnaire and included Google's Aristotle findings, such as 'Dependability', 'Structure and Clarity', 'Meaning' and 'Impact', therefore arriving at a much-enhanced version measuring Flexibility, Resilience, Courage, Openness, Learning and Engagement.

These are measured by a proprietary algorithm that takes into account whether a question is based on feeling, intuition or knowledge, on whether the question has a behavioural component (we measure how people interact with the team solution as well), whether the question is self-reporting or referring to others, whether light, neutral or heavy in tone and importance, whether it refers to one of the fears exhibited with impression management or demonstrates the existence of trust or not.

Flexibility and Resilience

First, the difference – a lot of people confuse the two or find them to be sufficiently close in terminology to lump them together but the reality is that teams may well exhibit an extreme appetite for change and flexibility for a period, but that may well not last them over time and then their Psychological Safety as a team would directly be under attack in the absence of resilience. In other words, they'll bend a lot but then they'll break. If we were only to measure their appetite for change, goodwill and emotional availability to attempt it at a certain point, that wouldn't also measure their overall ability to adapt and their lasting power.

In *Workplace Wellness That Works*, Laura Putnam says, 'Then there is emotional well-being, also called resilience. This is your ability to bounce back from changes and it can be fostered by practising mindfulness.' The latter is true, the former disputable to my mind. Wellness is a bigger encompassing term of which resilience is only part but even so, the topic of being resilient is the cornerstone to the stability of a team and with it, their emotional well-being as a team and therefore their Psychological Safety.

When we designed our team solution, we spent quite some time defining resilience in a team context versus an individual context and thinking of ways to measure and improve it. Far from a straightforward topic with ways to check or affect it out there, resilience is a new one on everybody in a work context.

While as humans our ability to sustain perceived hardship and remain stable and strong is the cornerstone to our ability to thrive, this hasn't been expected of us in the workplace. In fact, on the contrary, over the last tens of years, the overall expectation is that the better we understand and acquire a set of skills and the better we employ them in processes, the more we are expected to eliminate the risk brought about by sudden change, so we are to expect great stability and predictability and these are to be celebrated and hailed as supreme markers of success.

And having predictability and feeling stable is indeed a good foundation to thrive and progress. It gives us collectively a sense of safety that only the known and familiar can bring, and a sense of security that we are prepared and on track.

Except none of that is still true in our VUCA world. And there is no way to gain stability and predictability with the tools and means we have employed so far. Not only that, there is no reason to believe that whatever we learned in business school, whatever course we took, whatever process we successfully employed before will ever work again and help us compete with the lightning speed some go at.

So, we collectively, at a macro level, have lost the certainty and comfort of a known, understood world, where we can search 'best practices' or be 'smart followers'. We're now all up the same proverbial creek with the same flimsy paddle in this strong current of these rapid falls.

At an individual level, this chiefly reflects an acute need to become flexible and develop a set of practices that allow us to remain calm and engaged despite the great discomfort instability brings.

At a team level, resilience can only be discussed in the context of those teams who already have Psychological Safety. In its absence, there is no hope of resilience as everyone is too paralyzed by lack of safety to exhibit any adaptive and courageous behaviour as a response to fast change.

In teams who have it, preserving it in a VUCA context is essentially the greatest challenge and simultaneously the greatest predictor of success. Finding ways to stay connected, flex together, grow together and not let any of the outside changes shake the feeling of family that achieves magic in teams is being resilient. And being resilient as a team is conserving that state of bliss that allows us to create and achieve.

Families as social units have a degree of resilience that is inbuilt. Despite any of the challenges of life, by and large there is no real fear of failure as a unit. Even in fractured families riddled by conflict, there is an expectation of the structure being perennial enough at the end that said conflict could be resolved at one point. That there is a future and there is enough goodwill and alignment through affinity and affection to attempt resolution and gain support and rebuild a nurturing environment. That is what makes families as strong as they are. That expectation of the structure lasting and enduring is not in-built in the workplace by default. Instead, teams must work to develop it and then preserve it at all cost.

Things that teams can and must do (and this often starts with team leaders so hopefully whoever that is has a relentless eye on it; there's your servant leadership homework #1 'build resilience') is to celebrate failure, reinforce the value of learning and vulnerability, restate and question purpose and vision until it's etched in everyone's heart, relentlessly foster transparency, show the value of collective risk ownership, obsessively nurture a sense of family and reshape the discourse to view each sharp turn and each change as a winning opportunity.

The beauty of training resilience is that every knock, every setback, every hardship is an occasion to grow and reaffirm safety. We get to fall and break and utterly fail, and to see how that is not terminal but a reason to celebrate. Much like weight training, where new muscle fibre builds only once we've broken the existent one, when we reinforce that it's safe to fail together, we learn, we improve and we grow, and ultimately we survive in this new world of change and speed because make no mistake, it's only the resilient that will make it.

In the next 20–30 years, a lot of businesses will grow or die in this VUCA world. The winning ones will have found ways to be resilient. And winning organizations are not so as a whole but as a collection of resilient team units. Resilient teams are Psychologically Safe and consciously working hard to preserve it, hence the need to measure flexibility as a precursor to resilience and resilience as an absolute fundamental of Psychologically Safe teams.

Ensure both flexibility and resilience are measured when you ask your people the questions that will determine if they are

Psychologically Safe – make sure you test whether they are simply exhibiting appetite for risk or indeed excited about change. Patty McCord of Netflix fame says in a famous Ted video, '8 Lessons in Building a Company People Enjoy Working For', 'We need to have teams running as fast as they can to the left and we come in some morning and say they need to start running to the right and why, and they will enthusiastically start doing so fast.' Measure if they will, and repeatedly.

Speaking Up, AKA Courage and Openness

No one needs much convincing around why expressing one's opinion honestly in a team without fear of negative consequence is beneficial. It is, after all, the key to communication, innovation, growth and all the other sugar and spice of the business world, but historically, doing so, being able to speak up, has become near-impossible for so many for a multitude of reasons that it is now a firm part of the Human Debt and until such a time as we reinstate a habit of completely and gleefully opening up for every member of the team, we will never have high performance.

To speak up, one has to be brave and then add a willingness to take the risk of opening up on top of it. This is why we would recommend that anyone measuring whether or not their team is regularly speaking up relentlessly measures both courage and openness separately from what they answer on the topics, and from how they behave around moments that require them to take a risk and avoid impression management to express their opinions.

Even seemingly confident people experience moments when they find speaking up difficult and engage in impression management instead. Note the example from Amy Edmondson's *Fearless*, where she mentions business innovator Nilofer Merchant, labelled a visionary by CNBC, and in 2013, awarded the Future Thinker Award by Thinkers50. But in a 2011 *Harvard Business Review* article, Nilofer shared while working at Apple, she would keep quiet about problems she noticed because she didn't want to be wrong. She's quoted as saying, 'I would rather keep my job by staying within the lines than say something and risk looking stupid.' This is, of course, a classic example of impression management, where she was avoiding looking ignorant but that doesn't make her not a courageous person in general, it simply shows she wouldn't score high on openness.

There are numerous examples of companies that didn't have the luxury of Psychologically Safe teams that would speak up against behaviours that later proved disastrous for their business in the past few years. One example is Wells Fargo, where many people were appalled by the practices they were employing, which were unfair to both employees and clients if not actually morally reprehensible, yet no one spoke up against them.

Another example comes from Nokia, which during the 1990s was the top mobile-phone manufacturer globally, but by 2012 had lost this spot, along with over $2 billion and 75 per cent of its market value.

In 2015, in a graduate business school INSEAD study of the company's fall, we see clearly that Nokia's executives didn't communicate openly about the threat from emerging competitors Apple and Google. At the same time, managers and engineers were afraid to tell their bosses that the company's technology couldn't compete in an evolving market. As a result, Nokia missed the opportunity to innovate and soon became irrelevant.

Both classical examples where people didn't have the courage and the openness to speak up and likely didn't have the Psychological Safety foundation that would have enabled them to express themselves in their teams.

For Psychological Safety to happen within a team, all of these have to be true. There is no chance they could be missing and the team would still be winning:

'We have to be passionate and deeply care'

'We have to be ourselves'

'We have to feel immensely connected to each other and like we have a safe bubble'

'We have to cultivate and practise empathy'

'We have to be flexible and we have to be resilient'

'We have to learn to experiment relentlessly and fail "growingly"'

'We have to never be afraid of appearing negative, incompetent, ignorant or disruptive/intrusive/unprofessional'

'We have to speak up'

And all of these, every single one of them, has an underlying theme: they require us to be brave.

'We have to be courageous'

And isn't that the hardest one? How do we allow and model it because let's face it, motivation alone will fail to transform kittens into lions. We can dream ourselves valiant and daring and consistently not act that way.

And why should the awareness and energizing vernacular be enough when historically, it was never really demanded of us? We showed up and did some things and that was all that was required of us to be a functional human being, even a model employee. Being brave was for movies and legends, every day did not require superheroes and the most we'd exercise putting ourselves out there would be on karaoke nights out after a few pints.

In general, as human beings, we need to strive to minimize risk. However, experimentation and progress imply it. This is a conflict less apparent in our personal lives, where we strive to have all of Maslow's needs covered at all times, and it is only on the brink of major life decisions that the value of our character as a valiant human being is tested, but one that is impossible to avoid in our VUCA world at work.

Things change ultra-fast – stability and lack of risk are no longer possible. What is required of us is a collection of acts of courage, from the small ones of raising an unconformable point to the major ones of attempting things that are new and unheard of. Constant challenge. Constant push.

A new paradigm where showing up and applying what we know is no longer sufficient, but where we are expected to show up and be wide open and ready to fail, learn and adapt every day.

With courage comes the dreaded vulnerability, which we have been predetermined to avoid in every management course. A true leader was measured by the size of their Achilles heel apparently and therefore had to have a tough, impenetrable armour on at all times. No one rewarded them for chinks and many had even forgotten how to take it off, even for the annual dip in the sea with the kids, whereas now we tell everyone, leaders included, to rip it off and have their entire skin made of vulnerable material to allow their teams to do the same. This is because you ought to have nothing to protect against in a team that has the magic bubble. When there's no fear and when there's protection what you have instead is openness and the ability to experiment, learn and create together.

So, vulnerability is not only allowed and desirable but deeply needed.

Practical suggestions? Here's some we use: plaster the walls with Dr. Seuss and *Wizard of Oz* posters – corny, but shockingly effective at being motivational when it comes to courage; model questioning – wonder why anything is the way it is and discuss it openly, from operations times to process and vocabulary used; share an intimate thing in every meeting; put yourself out there and ask for anonymous feedback about something; speak up when it's not in your best interest and make it a point you did; try something absolutely new or opposite your usual modus operandi every week; come up with a measurement of courage that makes most sense to your own work and team … the list goes on.

Most of all, celebrate each of these. Laugh and learn, commiserate and communicate, share and grow. Every instance of daring. Every time that 'courage' translated into an actionable and measurable win and was no longer just fodder for demagoguery.

Learning, Experimenting and Failing

Teams who learn together, perform well together and the fact that they can and do learn as one in the team context enhances their Psychological Safety and makes them entirely more productive than those who won't engage in this growth behaviour, that's plain to see for anyone who has studied highly performant teams, but with the concept of continuous learning being relatively new and contrasting our previous attitude towards the conclusion of education at the end of our school years, how we are curious and collectively acquiring new insight and skill in the workplace is a complex topic.

In some organizations the permission to learn and its most raw manifestation – 'curiosity' – is highly praised. Those are the organizations best positioned to win. An example of one is how the giant pharma company Novartis' CEO Vas Narasimhan is a staunch supporter of the concept and has expended vast amounts of effort democratizing it, while demonstrating his belief in the essence of being curious.

Vas remarked, 'Curiosity is critical for success in our increasingly complex world.' This is far from empty rhetoric but sustained in practice by a serious internal preoccupation with demonstrating acquired learning that each Novartis employee is encouraged to do and measured on and supported by numerous #WeAreCurious internal campaigns. This simply says that Vas and the Novartis leadership team have a clear understanding of the size of the Human Debt when it comes to employees truly believing they have permission and encouragement to keep learning while at work and coupled with their understanding of the value of Psychological Safety makes Novartis one to watch.

The role of having a solid appetite for learning in our new VUCA reality in the context of Psychologically Safe (and therefore highly performant) teams should be clear to anyone with an interest in competing in the digital age but surprisingly, isn't as evident as it should be.

'Is it safe to fail?'

'Is it safe/encouraged to learn?'

'Can you have Psychologically Safe teams in the absence of failure and learning?'

And if we can all agree it's desirable, 'How do we ensure inbuilt curiosity in the DNA of a company's culture?'

'How can we ensure the top keeps learning as well?'

'Does impression management not directly disallow us from effective learning?'

'What is the relationship between curiosity and courage? What about learning and vulnerability?'

'Are teams who learn together exhibiting higher degrees of engagement and are they more resilient?'

'Do all types of learning count equally towards building Psychological Safety?'

'If the emphasis on curiosity outweighed the fear of failure, wouldn't that breed a much-needed culture of experimentation and innovation?'

Those are just some of the questions we asked ourselves when we decided to measure learning appetite or curiosity in our software solutions as one of the components that indicate the level of Psychological Safety a team has. We highly advise anyone wanting to better their team should ask them too.

What can you observe around you and within yourself? Are you more or less thirsty for knowledge than you were in other jobs and with other teams? Do you feel like your team learns together and shares efficiently? Do you gain from interacting with them around new information, shared experiences and acquired knowledge?

Depending on the type of industry and job you are in, the necessary pace of learning can vary (and aside from information, there is also the more pressing matter of the steep learning curve we are all faced with in increasing our EQ fast enough to remain competitive in our new workplace realities), but there is no argument for believing it will slow down in our VUCA world so let's get curious about learning or learn more about curiosity and watch the exploration make our teams feel more Psychologically Safe.

But learning takes time and it takes feeling like you at least have permission, if not encouragement, and both are luxuries most of us can ill afford.

Not enough has been written about the paradoxical effect of taking actions to improve oneself, enhancing one's impostor syndrome in a world obsessed with speed and efficiency, but I think it ought to be worth a lot more exploration.

There is an honest dialogue on learning led by some amazing visionaries out there but the mere fact that they have to fight a battle speaks volumes. Over the years, there have been some rumblings around the topic, such as when Google publicized their 20–80 per cent rule allowing employees to spend time on what they deem necessary to satisfy their curiosity and passion for 20 per cent of their paid time, as well as whenever we read reports on how leadership spends their time but overall, there seems to be this perception that at work, they pay us to do work, not 'other things'.

Tragically, this 'other things' umbrella lumps together a variety of things to do with learning, passion, interpersonal relationships, emotions and all varieties of improvement. My theory is that this occurs because we have grown to believe work has to be a stiff, unpleasant if not painful exercise, or else we wouldn't get paid to do it. As a result, we associate all unpleasant tasks and unwanted activities with our work life and anything that is even remotely pleasurable with our leisure time and if anything happens to feel good at work it must be cheating the company out of an honest dollar if we don't do it 'on our own time'.

This has far-reaching and stupendously negative implications in how leaders treat people-issues because to effectively lead, they need to strive to spend masses of time on thinking of the humanity of it all – the emotions and interactions of their teams, their peers and their own, and let's face it, who feels like they get paid to think?

Another big theme few of us feel they are being paid to do is learn in general. There's no DevOps nature to our perception of life. No CI/CD pipeline of thoughts and actions. Because of the sequential, waterfall-like way in which we have been taught to view the phases of our existence we expect to first accumulate knowledge in our formative years, then download that accumulation by utilizing it in our work life. Step 1 – learn. Step 2 – use the knowledge. Step 3 – if you survive it – relax and then you can do anything pleasurable, such as learn or take care of yourself.

It is because of this rigid subconscious mental demarcation that we have phrases like 'going back to school' or 'affording to do a PhD', etc. Once you're in the work field, you feel the sum total of your knowledge and skills have already been acquired in your hiring phase and you are now expected to demonstrate just those. Nothing less, but nothing more either.

Why would employees ever think they are expected or at least entitled to keep learning? Nothing in the hiring interaction led them to believe that is valuable, no one asked them how, when and what they read, or where they want to improve themselves and once in, every time they wanted to go to a conference, buy a book or listen to a podcast on the company money, they've been made to feel like it's a perk they hardly deserve. The entire system is geared to reinforce these sequential steps that leave no room for learning in our adult work lives.

Of course, humans can't stop being curious and if they have the least amount of passion for their work, they will keep learning but reading has become something they do 'on the side' or 'on their own free time' irrespective of how what they acquire is given back to the company.

How unfair an exchange and how short we sell ourselves when we allow that!

How many of us reading this have negotiated at least the Google 20 per cent in our work practice? To read, do some Yoga or code on the side. To daydream about how the world will be once machines take over, or consider why Jane in accounting has been quiet lately. To open a book or listen to a podcast. At our desk. In plain view. During working hours. And get paid for it.

Few is the answer. We need to stop thinking work is doing us a favour by empowering us to be better versions of ourselves. Why would they be paying for less?

Nonetheless, once we have 'learning' inbuilt in the team's core culture we need to let them know they are truly encouraged to use it so they experiment heavily and by extension and necessarily, at times fail. You can't innovate without failing. It's – sadly – just not possible. And if you fear failure, you refrain from all the behaviours that you need to create and innovate.

One of Professor Dr Amy Edmondson's favourite examples of the importance of failing is Pixar. Animation studio Pixar is behind 15 of the 50 highest-grossing animated films of all time, and co-founder Ed Catmull makes a point of telling staff that every movie is bad in the early stages. This minimizes their fear of failure and makes them more open to feedback.

Catmull's book *Fearless* is brimming with examples as to why failure is desirable and necessary. A 2012 study by Taiwanese researchers Chi-Cheng Huang and Pin-Chen Jiang on 60 research and development teams whose work demands innovative, outside-the-box thinking showed that teams with Psychological Safety performed better, while members of the other teams were too scared of rejection to share their ideas. And at the pharmaceutical company Eli Lilly, they go so far as throwing parties to celebrate and share failed experiments. This may seem extreme, but cementing the idea that failure is a positive thing ensures that people don't continue to waste time and resources on experiments that aren't going anywhere.

The book also outlines how some higher education schools in the United States now offer courses to help students understand failure not as a setback but as a step towards learning, thus increasing their resilience and ability to function in this VUCA world that demands us to be ever-learning, open to failure, thirsty for innovation and ready for change.

Morale and Engagement

First of all, the terms as components of the team dynamic – we spent quite some time working out if the two can be considered truly interchangeable and concluded that in as far as we can see, yes, they ought to be. We then spent time trying to work out how and why has the term 'engagement' eroded; but quite frankly had to leave that exploration (fun as it is) to consider recent-years-HR-failure-folklore (which also comprises other mysterious cases of erosion and disappearances, such as those of 'employee satisfaction', 'employer branding', 'purpose', 'motivation', 'well-being' and even of the term 'team' in itself). Understanding why it has come in and out of focus in the consciousness of organizations is not going to help the status quo.

And the status quo is that the current situation of 'engagement' is rather dire indeed. As mentioned before, its dog day never really came, despite being part of the rhetoric of many an HR initiative over the last 20–30 years.

According to Gallup, 70 per cent of the US workforce is disengaged at work. This is toxic for any work environment and costs around $450 billion per year. Further *Harvard Business Review* articles and many pieces of research of late suggest two in three employees feel utterly disconnected and 72 per cent report 'never having felt truly engaged in my work' and even if we simply look around with honesty, we'll see that the overall levels of engagement of our employees are at an all-time low and that we've also abandoned most of the concerted efforts of yesteryear to do anything about it.

Fanciful places here and there have given the topic some life by replacing the terminology with the semi-hipsterish 'employee happiness' instead, and grated as some of us may be by seeing the *Harvard Business Review* rebrand containing variations of the word in Silicon Valley hopefuls' job titles, the move works because it allows us to talk about it once again.

Some will also argue it's not a rebrand at all as 'engagement' veers more towards 'purpose' whereas 'happiness' is all-encompassing and looks at the well-being of employees holistically. That's perhaps true, but in a world where people are as chronically unhappy and disrespected as our employees are today, and where we have created masses of Human Debt by discouraging authenticity and flagrantly disregarding emotions and wellness, we have a lot to do, no matter what we call it.

'Happiness' works too because, at the end of the day, the question we are trying to answer – and, more importantly, the question we are trying to make sure every team leader obsesses with – is: 'Are they happy?' but we settled on 'Morale' because it sits at the heart of it all when it comes to a team.

Contrary to what some may imagine, despite being central, morale is far from the only marker of success and predictor of a psychologically safe – and therefore high-performing – team but it's a very important one.

'Are their hearts really in it?', 'Are they in high spirits?', 'Do they care deeply about each other?', 'Are they emotionally invested in what it is they are doing and who they are doing it for?' – those questions need to be answered at a team level by asking each employee morale-related questions that indicate how good they feel about themselves and about each other.

Establishing how a team is doing on morale as a component of their Psychological Safety means finding out if team members socialize with each other, whether they laugh in their team, if they genuinely enjoy their time together and have fun, if they share secrets, if they open up, and if they truly connect. If they feel that 'magic' together when they feel close and strong enough to be vulnerable and grow.

The stats are staggering. Even in the lowest estimates in the most optimistic of studies, one in three employees reports they feel alone, unauthentic and depressed at work. Every organization knows that's not sustainable and that it kills performance (and sadly, whether we like to admit it or not, eventually kills people as well), but they have trouble isolating levers of change and effective solutions no less because improving morale/engagement/happiness in itself, needed as it is, doesn't immediately reflect in the bottom line. It's a huge part of a puzzle but not big enough to make a difference in isolation. It needs all the other elements to show how it moves the needle results-wise, which is why we measure it in conjunction with the other components and why we think organizations should too.

I believe the topic of 'Engagement' itself will be greatly helped by the ascension of the topic of Psychological Safety and its importance to achieving high performance. If we finally let the success stories and studies speak and concede that the only human measurement that translates into innovation and sustainable performance is Psychological Safety in teams, and that engagement is one integral part of it, then we stand a new chance to see it elevated to the level of importance it rightfully deserves, not in the name of an ill-understood moral imperative, but through the prism of a healthy business one, because we'll find it pays to work on happiness at work.

Avoiding Impression Management

Impression management is the set of behaviours we engage in to manipulate the opinion of ourselves we imprint on others in all walks of life. The energy spent on managing impressions in this day and age extends outside of the work context into our everyday social lives, particularly due to how social media has exacerbated our need to be favourably seen while offering us increasingly more ways to show ourselves. This calls for a larger discussion about the sense of community, whether or not we feel connected to those we broadcast to and whether or not this behaviour will reveal disastrous consequences in time, but that is not the exact same definition of 'impression management' as that which we imply in the context of work and Psychological Safety.

While first coined in a larger sense by Erwin Goffmann in the 50s and further studied by Leary and Kowalski in 1990 and in the context of what makes teams productive and healthy by our hero, Professor Dr Amy Edmondson, in her studies, it is both a surprisingly relatable concept that everyone instantly connects to and a really difficult set of behaviours to avoid even once people are aware of them.

The oversimplified idea is that one of the reasons why we are not more willing to be open and vulnerable with each other, we don't speak up and therefore do not create Psychological Safety in teams is that we are all hardwired to maximize pleasure and avoid pain, and as a result, we are all working hard to mitigate against being seen in a certain fashion which we deem negative and therefore risky to our well-being.

We eternally work hard not to give off the impression that we are either Incompetent, Ignorant, Negative, Disruptive or Intrusive. Every time we stop ourselves from speaking up or contributing it can always be traced back to one of these four fears. To these, I would personally add a fifth: the fear of 'looking unprofessional', which makes employees stop themselves from honest reactions in many instances in particular when it comes to reacting to new and anti-normative circumstances or when employing spontaneous behaviours such as humour.

One evident way to combat the fear is to model the opposite fearless behaviour, so leading by example in daring to flaunt lack of knowledge, lack of experience or lack of extreme political correctness is key to team leaders with solid EQ and a strong People Practice who have created a habit of exhibiting those behaviours to the team, but what about recognizing when impression management happens and coaxing the opposite out of their team? And what about the team becoming savvy enough to notice and change these behaviours themselves?

In other words, spotting and stopping impression management in its tracks is not a job for the team leader only but should be every team member's to-do. One way to accomplish this is to outline it is desirable to police against these fearful behaviours in both ourselves and others by asking hard-hitting questions of yourself and the team. It is important to mention that none of these answers need to be public and simply getting used to using an internal 'mental counter' of these instances – which we call a 'Catch Yourself' counter – will help reframe the behaviour:

'Have you noticed anyone including yourself refrain from giving out critique?'

'Have you seen anyone express it after a retro maybe over a pint?'

'Has anyone in the team felt like they were on the verge of admitting something in the last month? Have you nearly said something about any topic?'

'Are we as a team becoming more open or more reserved?'

'Have you praised any of your colleagues over admitting they never used a tool but been willing to try it?'

'Have you heard any questions among your teammates that you thought were too personal?'

'Can you think of a time when something said made you feel defensive before you remembered you are among "family"?'

Questions like the ones above are not open-ended for survey and diagnostic purposes but suggestive and hopefully guiding towards certain desirable outcomes in behaviour.

Because of the nature of work and because of the climate of political correctness in the workplace, 'incompetent' and 'ignorant' are easier to spot and mitigate against than 'negative', 'disruptive' and 'intrusive'. The latter in particular will be heavily problematic in our new remote-and-office hybrid reality so affecting even minute amounts of these levers is bound to make a substantial difference in increasing Psychological Safety and therefore the team's ability to grow and perform together.

For Psychologically Safe teams we want the team leader to keep the question of 'How many times have my people avoided looking negative/incompetent/intrusive/disruptive/ignorant in the last month?' front of mind because they know that the more they have done so, the less open communication, trust and learning there is, and the less productive and psychologically safe they are.

The answer in our team solution was to help them see it, monitor it, and the cleanest way to achieve that was by exposing the data through a feature on the leader's dashboard called 'Impression Management Alarms' that simply displays the overall number of concerning answers the team provided so that the team leader can do something about them before those behaviours translate into broken bigger components, such as a lack of openness, engagement and resilience.

But in the absence of supporting software asking for them, the team leader simply has to obsess with identifying impression management themselves and notice when it happens in the team's day-to-day interaction, hence mitigate for it. The team leader should think of themselves as a cross between a referee, a doctor and a teacher forever on the lookout for signs that in lieu of being open and behaving like they are comfortable, someone is trying to save face and project a certain image. They should wonder why that is and what they can do to prevent that behaviour from happening.

Being honest and staying with a vulnerable state is difficult, especially if circumstances change and defence mechanisms are triggered where employees revert to tried-and-tested neural pathways that demand we say and do anything to protect against looking like we don't know, can't do or are causing issues for ourselves or others. Thankfully, impression management is one of the topics that are most instinctively comprehensible to anyone when it comes to Psychological Safety and the reason why we can all immediately understand why being closed-off and projecting an image instead of being authentic and honest is bad is because we already have a practice of being on the lookout for that in our personal lives.

Everyone does this impression management constant watch when it comes to our partners, our friends or our kids. We can immediately tell when either of those is obscuring their true feelings from us, or when they are afraid to be open, and we become immediately alerted and try and understand why that is to protect the loving status quo.

Thinking a loved one is 'hiding something' or simply not engaging openly the way we expect them to, but instead attempting to project a certain image, is causing us immediate distress and that is because we instinctively know the importance of having a strong, intimate connection based on full disclosure.

This is no different in a team and the mental barrier between 'personal' and 'work' relationships is the only reason why we don't routinely focus more on it in the office, but once the discourse of the team leader permits us to think of our team as the family that it is then we will quickly transfer that watchful and caring state of mind.

If we can imagine a world where being vulnerable is rewarded because it signals a willingness to learn, where admitting mistakes or unknowns is celebrated and where asking potentially intrusive questions and offering possibly negative comments is not seen as disruptive but on the contrary is desirable and laudable as it signals courage, then we'll start fearing less, creating more Psychologically Safe teams.

The Dialogue of the Bubble

None of our path to Psychologically Safe teams is possible in the absence of a clear, trusted and solid dialogue path. How are we to probe all of these separate components if we aren't told how our people feel? By the same token, coming from organizations where they were asked once a year and where they had to either answer irrelevant questions and see no evidence they had given their opinion or, worst even, expect punitive measures for having done so – why should our employees tell us anything on a regular basis even if we should manage to convince them we cared enough to ask open-heartedly?

Several things need to be reinforced for a true communication channel to open and remain open with our team:

- **The Frequency** – As Patty McCord from Netflix says in the video mentioned earlier in this chapter (*see also* p. 113) – 'We ask our people things once a year and we complain they don't want to tell us more – have we asked them?!?' – as part of any team leader's People Practice declaring the channel open is a priority, and affirming the cyclical nature of the need for feedback is the mandatory next step. Creating a communication habit may take time but is essential. In distributed, remote teams of the post-pandemic world this is slightly easier to attain with rolling team meetings in the calendar and one-on-ones being in place but the tools and expectations should be firmly in the 'team's contract' from the Team Launch all through the 'performing phase' to count on the results;
- **The Clarity** – In *Dare to Lead*, Brené Brown recalls a circumstance where she asked her team for brutal honesty in their feedback and on receipt, she was at first taken aback and hurt, only to then realize that 'being clear is being kind' and ambiguity or sugar-coating would have been insulting and unproductive. It is worth testing the limits of the common degree of acceptance towards what the team regards as welcomed 'radical candour' instead of gratuitous offence in team launches and re-launches though in particular as different team members have different levels of sensitivity;
- **True 'No blame – no punishment'** – Many teams boast having a 'no-blame' policy but simply affirming it won't be sufficient. As part of the Human Debt, team members are often scarred by the times that they have trusted management or the organization, have offered a candid opinion or have experimented and been chastised or even demoted so it's little wonder they find it hard to engage in that positive behaviour again. The only way to

demonstrate 'no blame' is to invite extreme experimentation, praise failure and ask for all opinions incessantly;

- **The Value** – Reinforcing how important and valuable the dialogue is to the team should be a constant preoccupation of the team leader as part of their People Practice;
- **The 'Bubble'** – Demonstrating to the team that the communication channel exists at the team level only is paramount. What is said in the team bubble stays in the team bubble and no team leader should take anything to the enterprise unless agreed with the team and for the good of the team.

Psychologically Safe teams communicate. Openly and abundantly. In 2006, Professor Christina Gibson of the University of Australia and Professor Jennifer Gibbs of Rutgers University studied innovation teams with members scattered across the world and found that Psychological Safety helped teams communicate more openly. When teams can not only share their thoughts openly but work through them together, they're much better prepared to tackle whatever challenges come their way.

But ask, don't spy.

In February 2020, Barclays Bank made the news with one of the biggest HR fiascos of the past 10 years as an investigation showed they had installed software on their employees' machines without their knowledge or permission to check what they were doing with their time. I would have loved to have been a fly on the wall when the company who designed the Barclays 'employee spying software' sold it as a good idea. How did that conversation go?

'Do you even know how much time they spend actually working?'

   'Well, we know how much time they spend in the building'

   'What about at their desk? How about which program or browsers they're using? What about their breaks? How do you even monitor if they aren't spending far too much time on a toilet break?'

'Well …'

'That's how you gain access to unprecedented data and therefore optimize cost and performance – you monitor all these things and change behaviours by advising that they spend more time "in the zone", that they take shorter breaks less often and you categorize their trips to the loo as "unaccounted activity" so they know it's not OK to be messing around on company time! Get our software in and watch your employees triple their productivity!'

What was their tagline? 'Measuring performance by time chained to a desk'. Or maybe it was: 'Trust. Who needs it when you can measure toilet breaks?'

Here's why this is sad: outside of all the common-sense ways that have escaped the execs who got this in, it's a setback for data exploration in general and that's a major pity. It's a pity because the tempting conclusion is that we should enquire less in the lives of our employees when in fact we ought to enquire a great deal more except not in ways that deceive them and ruin any ounce of trust we should be striving to build.

The 'organization' owes its employees a major amount of investigation and probing. They have a lot of Human Debt in enquiring what their employees think and feel but that curiosity has to be caring and open-hearted, not misguided and sneaky. There is no case for observing behind an interrogation mirror but for sitting in the same room and learning.

You have to wonder what possessed the executives who deemed the foolish spyware a good idea and what it was they were attempting to accomplish. The only explanation would be that maybe they were trying to baseline lack of engagement when physically present, i.e. that the assumption was 'we need to do something about this: our employees are in the building, but they are not engaged and if you don't believe us, we'll show that to be the case with data'.

Perhaps they had a lofty goal in mind – they were going to show these figures to the bank's board and they would slap their foreheads with a firm revelation in the presence of undeniable data and let everyone work flexibly from home thereafter as a result. Perhaps they were going to kick-off a massive 'employee respect' – wish that was a thing! – project where, in light of showing management that their people are emotionally detached, they would be able to bring their happiness back into serious focus once they had this data of how long they were spending hiding in the toilet and how many times they had accessed the *Daily Mail* from their desktop. Perhaps. Most likely, none of that is true and they had simply committed a colossal error in judgement. One of monumental and potentially irreparable proportions.

The relationship between the employee and the organization is so very fractured already that any sense of 'company level team' is nonexistent as it is. Even before stunts like these, humans everywhere feel spied on and distrusted. What will such episodes do to that trust?

At PeopleNotTech we do think that measuring anything at an enterprise level is almost always futile, ineffective and gives little in the way of practical ideas and that measurements should instead be done at the team level and kept private to the respective team, the only productive bubble unit that matters and the only group where any lasting and important change can be done for the good of the employees by instilling Psychological Safety. But being curious, asking, wanting to decipher what your employees think and feel is never a bad thing so long as you do so overtly and considerately.

Here's some common-sense advice for those organizations who do care and do want to measure from a good place, not a love of *1984*-esque surveillance:

- **Extend a hand.** Spend time showing enough genuine, open-hearted curiosity to get your employees' buy-in. It's not till they trust you to have good intentions in attempting to find out that you should start designing how to enquire;

- **Get a real agreement.** Design this probe together – you have smart people in your enterprise, use them instead of some random consultancy to help you design this exploration and have it be intensely emotionally relevant to your own team;
- **Make it feel truly safe.** Be open, be clear, be forensic in demonstrating safety, lack of repercussions and permission to fail.
- **Be 100 per cent open and honest.** Hide nothing, ignore nothing, spy on no one! (Who would have thought that last one had to be spelt out?!)
- **Measure what matters.** Finding out what to measure so that it truly matters is not easy. We spent the better part of a year thinking of what are the core things that create Psychological Safety and what are solid ways to measure 'courage', for example, but here's a tip: whatever you learn is important. It's almost guaranteed it will never be 'time spent moving the mouse' or 'time spent on a certain browser or app'.
- **Build strong feedback loops.** Show what changed as a result of what you learned, what improved. Keep asking and demonstrate the feedback loop is solid and this is now an ongoing dialogue and they are being 'seen' and truly 'listened to' from hereon.

'Ask, don't spy' ought to be a good first commandment if we are to collectively attempt to grow together by learning about each other. This should not become 'permission *not* to "intrude" or "pry"', this should be a moment to reflect on what it is we could do jointly, curiously and open-heartedly to build a Psychologically Safe 'Big Team' by asking the right caring questions.

Team Happiness and the Human Debt

Companies that are winning these days have – despite what sensationalist reporting may have you believe – immensely more engaged and happier and productive employees and teams that are highly performant. The key ingredient is that their teams have a fair amount of Psychological Safety and while indubitably possible to replicate that blessed state, it requires a serious investment of time and effort.

Creating value takes time. We didn't create the Human Debt overnight – we didn't make our workforce feel unsafe overnight, we won't build them back again mindfully and with respect and admiration fast either. But how can we prepare for a long, arduous road when we're not even positive how important it is to be on this path?

First and foremost, we have to move the topic from a 'nice to have' to a firm and urgent 'must-have'. I don't believe in business concepts done in the name of higher moral ground. Not exclusively. At the very least some part of the motivation needs to be of a commercial nature, where the business can immediately see the connected value.

Before Psychological Safety, despite the efforts of scholars and specialists who could show the negative impact on turnover or the positive impact in hands-on KPIs of employee satisfaction, the topic of keeping your workforce happy was viewed as a 'nice to think of after we do the real stuff if there is any time and budget left'. Psychological Safety changes the game on that – it has such a clear connection to productivity that for the first time, here's this concept that – incidentally – means employees are happier at work, while lo and behold, they are very evidently more productive and useful to the business in being so. Digitally native companies such as the big tech in the Valley know their intrinsic value is not in the technology they create that is entirely replicable, but the fact that they have built safe, happy and invested teams, and now have resilient, strong and healthy organizations. They wouldn't dream of thinking any of this is a side note as they know it's the secret sauce of their success.

Psychological Safety or Employee Happiness?

Much as the Psychological Safety of teams transcends several ideas it is indubitably also contained in the ethereal, fluffy concepts of employee engagement or employee satisfaction, etc., with the pivotal caveat being that Psychological Safety can be diagnosed and affected, hence it is an execution lever for bettering the bottom line, whereas the other ones have remained anchored in un-actionable rhetoric for the enterprise.

For a while, some 10 years ago, those terms were en vogue enough that a few studies to show the direct correlation between satisfaction and productivity had time to emerge, with results ranging from 20–45 per cent across the board. X per cent more profitable, X per cent more valuable in the stock exchange, X per cent more likely to survive the next big shift, etc. Every chief experience officer (CxO) carried one or two numbers like this in their deck and vowed to achieve them, but as time went by and they found nothing in the way of solutions to aid them in making this a priority, those numbers dropped and were replaced by trendier and seemingly more actionable ones on diversity. After all, when the only suggested solutions are around desk placement in open office spaces, little wonder no one feels empowered to tackle the less evident and much bigger topics of whether or not our people feel heard, respected and pleased.

As a sombre side note, 'happiness' is not the first people-related concept to have been all but dropped by management decks. A few years back, the term 'talent', with its reverent notes, was everywhere and it is now all but gone from anyone's job title or recruitment ambitions, which is very telling indeed and in line with how we think of people as 'resources' not 'capital'.

From Ethereal Concepts to Concrete Solutions for Change

Patrick Lencioni of teams and network concepts fame speaks about this in his book, *The Truth About Employee Engagement*, and postulates that to improve it, one needs to make people feel like they matter, like they make an impact and like they are advancing, making progress. Those become a lot more actionable and thankfully, the last two improvements he mentions, the group ones where purpose and relevancy are underpinned by transparency, rapid feedback and visibility of progress, are covered in the concepts of Agile and other new ways of work.

What this means is that for the – mainly – software development teams that are Agile, part of the work of building happiness is realized by the power of the process and ironically, partly by how the process is only secondary to people. In these teams the remaining part to cover by Lencioni's theory is the part where we make people feel like they matter, what we at PeopleNotTech believe is the very crux of the issue: making people feel heard as a first step to tackle the steep Human Debt.

It looks deceptively simple and straightforward. 'Feeling heard' means the team not only hears, but listens. That implies they care. That caring can only happen when the group is cohesive and as a result benefits from how teams who demonstrate they have close relationships with their teammates are 51 per cent more engaged. Also, crucially, it means that the organization 'hears'.

It's an umbrella term for recognition, good morale, understanding, healthy group dynamics, responsiveness and more. Also, it's the cornerstone of any open dialogue and this in turn is the cornerstone of any ability to feel safe enough to be vulnerable and learn.

Improving Employee Happiness is Now the Day-Job

Executives will soon have to face the music and completely reframe their ideas of priorities as it is becoming more and more common sense that to compete with people-savvy enterprises which deliver outstanding technology and service they have to become people-savvy themselves. As disruption rolls over the industry and the wheat is separated from the chaff by sheer consumer demand, many see their survival in question so this time it's urgent and this time they no longer have the excuse of lacking the tools to effect change.

They are no longer asked for a nebulous concept of improving satisfaction but have clear solutions and tools to effect levers that accomplish that. It's as if, after years of whining and diffuse generalized complaining by a spouse that the other one should 'make them happy', leaving them bedazzled as to where to start, they begin to break it down into exact 'do the dishes more often' tasks and even hand them the tabs and help them learn how to program the machine.

There are no more excuses, there's software out there to increase morale, trust and transparency, there's the software to gauge people's emotional state and there are clear proven ways to better EQ by teaching our people and ourselves to listen. So, it's time leaders put all the comfortable to-dos about revamping legacy core systems, moving applications to the cloud and delivering against regulation down, replacing them with the far less comfortable and monumentally bigger tasks of hearing their employees and creating a true People Practice.

High time.

Psychological Safety may not be an easy-to-have but it's an essential, crucial, sine qua non 'to have' – not a 'nice' one for anyone who intends to stay in the game. Psychologically Safe teams are happy – substantially happier, that is. And therefore yes, they stay and they develop, but more importantly, they work harder and smarter, they are open, curious, resilient, flexible and they innovate and grow and perform highly.

At Google, at Amazon and even at smaller but recognizable names such as Spotify and Airbnb, there is a number on Psychological Safety. Not only a number for employee happiness, although that exists too, but a specific measurement and bottom-line correlation to

Psychological Safety. The number is not a public one, in some cases not even one that's known to employees as heaven knows political correctness works in mysterious ways, but it exists and it informs more actions and decisions than surprisingly many of the traditional other business KPIs. This is why they do well. This is why they can employ technology to react fast to what the consumer needs and build addictive experiences, making them win. This is why they have 'culture' that is envied across the board.

This is their secret sauce.

They say money can't buy you happiness but in the case of your employees, their happiness can increase both your money and the time you have left in the game, so only ignore it if you can afford to.

CHAPTER FIVE

Putting a Number on Psychological Safety and Emotional Intelligence

- Making a Dent in the Human Debt
- Behavioural Foundations
- Interventions and Bettering Teams – The 'People Practice'
- Lessons from Different Industries
- Why Business Won't Care About People and Teams Before They See a Number
- The Experiment of Trying to Experiment
- Measure Small, Obsessively and Often to Win Big

Making a Dent in the Human Debt

There are but a precious few truly people-centric big winners. Aside from GAFA (Google, Amazon, Facebook and Apple) and some other Silicon Valley winners, we could maybe also count all the start-ups who are so close to their initial cultural impetus that they put their people at the heart of everything they do, and lastly, add a handful of big incumbent enterprises who understood the need to rebuild around their core value: their people. The total of all of these still constitutes a minute percentage of all companies though.

Obviously, building right is a lot easier than having to rebuild and execute on deep change. The old adage of change only being possible when there's a clear recognition of the need and a willingness to invest stands for big organizations just as it would stand for the individual. The necessity for cultural change only becomes clear to big organizations if they feel their existing ways – which are unbeknownst to them riddled by technical debt and Human Debt – will no longer carry them and they will possibly be threatened and face the fate of some other great mammoths that have been 'victims' of the digital revolution.

No company wants to be the next Blockbuster or Kodak, who have ignored the need for change and innovation and gone from being a success to being nonexistent within a few short years of the digital era and those examples weigh heavily on the minds of many executives who care about the enterprise they are leading.

On the flip side, there are examples of companies who got it right in most industries, so their 'old school' competitors have all had to pay close attention in the past 20 years to see how they have achieved these levels of success so very fast. And what traditional enterprises notice when they look towards Google or Amazon is a completely different way of doing things: Agile mindsets and people at their very heart of anything they do.

Even when these big enterprises look at models of success, they are still oftentimes lost in their own laudatory narrative and unable to see their faults and therefore have trouble understanding the delta between their practices and philosophies and those of the winners. Should they accept that there are obvious differences, they need 'proof points', numbers on slides, studies and research to substantiate risk mitigation and data from best practices – they use these to have enough fodder for cathartic 'we need to transform' revelations and impetus.

One doesn't have to be a numbers' person to understand the intrinsic value of having referenceable data points when it comes to attempting to usher major change into any organization. Historically, human themes in the workplace of the incumbent organizations have either had no numbers to point to – perhaps because we have collectively presumed that common sense should be enough and prevail – or, by the time they were brought in, they were already 'too late'.

This 'too late' of numbers may well refer to how once a notion becomes ingrained in the collective subconscious of the business as a 'fluffy' topic, it never recovers, irrespective of the mounting evidence to show it has practical application and a direct connection to the much-revered P&L. As such, a bevy of topics has eventually brought its data and numbers to the 'too late' bucket.

Many organizations know that the quality and stability of their Human Resources capability is paramount to their ability to succeed. There are numerous studies to show exact figures on the effectiveness of engagement and diversity, there are recognized numbers to underline the importance of having an inclusive work environment and there are others that speak of the importance of various skills.

Survey after survey – such as 'Employee Engagement, Satisfaction, and Business-Unit-Level Outcomes' from Gallup, or Accenture's 2018 'Getting to Equal' study of disability, diversity and inclusion in the workforces of 140 US companies – has found a direct correlation, with those doing better on engagement and inclusion having 28 per cent higher revenue. Many other studies have numbers to show the importance of employee retention or talent acquisition but if we analyse the nature of all these numbers we see that they are mostly operational. They refer to the effect of having or not having a certain amount or type of employee or know-how on the organization's bottom line but they say nothing about the lives of these employees, who they are, what makes them happy and high-performing.

Have we been measuring the wrong things? (If any …) Does it matter if people stay, or if they are happy? Does it matter how many we are, or how efficient and profitable? Does it matter where and how we do things, or what the things are and whether they are getting done or not? Is it an operational or logistical challenge, or should we focus on collaboration and creativity? Do we need presenteeism or creativity and impact?

So much of what the enterprise has been measuring has been turned on its head by the speed of technology and the new paradigm of the digital age. What business school drilled into the heads of multiple generations as to what is important became very suddenly unimportant and yet many executives never 'got that memo'.

Most offices still keep a tab on when people come in or leave despite how they know full well presence is not productivity. Most companies that could have gone to full-remote did not, despite the opportunity the pandemic of 2020 demonstrated. So undoubtedly there is a great big grey area between the need for people topics being brought to the forefront and business leaders' understanding that comes from a business-led, productivity-driven impetus and not solely as a goodwill or moral exercise. This area has to be filled with numbers. Hard data to show that eradicating Human Debt is actually good for business and the only way to remain competitive in our digital economy.

Unfortunately, historically, whenever business measured anything data-wise in people topics and in particular, performance, they tended to do so with a 'command and control' and 'stick and carrot' lens on. People were evaluated in one-sided exercises that felt harsh and disrespectful and often unfair and then the findings often brought about punitive measures so it's little wonder that humans are wary of all types of performance reviews in the workplace. The risk of suffering a loss (be it of financial or status) as a result of one such evaluation is high and people are naturally fearful.

Individual performance reviews in theory designed to identify areas that may need improvement and subsequently work on them for the common good have too often become punitive and are therefore seen as a pit-stop for blame assignment instead of a collaboration moment where the employee and the company are to co-create a better reality for both.

Nowhere is the idea of data more important than in understanding the relationship between an employee's well-being and 'productivity', which could be defined as the relationship between the amount of work invested and amount of desirable output, irrespective of how this is measured. And most importantly, this has to be reframed away from the exploitative connotation it carried and into the collective and invested space where we all want to bring our best selves to our work for the good of the team and the company.

Whether we call it 'experience' as an umbrella term, or 'happiness', or even if we lump all its components under the idea of 'engagement' – inexact as that is as it comprises so many other components than simply having high morale – the topic of well-being is often overlooked and when it is finally reluctantly explored, this happens in the absence of the correlation to productivity, which eventually renders it an unsustainable preoccupation.

When it comes to workplace Psychological Safety, even diagnosing its existence – or lack thereof – is difficult. As a result, identifying new ways to increase it constitutes an even greater challenge when it even occurs in the minds of the execs, in particular, as very few tools and best practices currently exist in the field. This means that those of us working to create them operate at the border of research and business, basically experimenting in continuous integration mode while convincing the business of the value of this and showing them why it so intensely matters.

A 2018 Censuswide survey of 1,000 managers, C-suite executives and employees at global organizations commissioned by City & Guilds Group found that 52 per cent of staff said they felt psychologically unsafe, which City & Guilds Group defined as 'not feeling supported to work to the best of their ability and feeling worried about speaking up about issues'. Although 94 per cent of survey respondents said Psychological Safety at work is important, only 10 per cent of organizations are believed to have it as a priority and of the remaining percentage, most would not even be familiar with the concept. City & Guilds Group said that furthermore, 43 per cent of senior managers expect HR to deal with the

Psychological Safety of the workforce, while 56 per cent of employees believe it is the responsibility of senior managers and leaders.

While the results are evidently dismal, I personally actually found it encouraging that there have been enough respondents to have at least brushed against the topic and formed an opinion because the most terrifying category are those who never have. Why does this matter? It matters because Psychologically Safe employees experiment, innovate, stay, perform, hit their KPIs, etc. Irrespective of the yardstick companies use to measure performance all the way down to the end-of-year results, it can all be mapped back to their people's degree of Psychological Safety when we manage to follow the data.

Even though it is far easier to measure and therefore more evident in Agile project settings, the same concept applies to any type of team doing any type of work. While the occasions to demonstrate courage, initiative, passion and grit may be less easy to spot in an old-school organizational structure that doesn't benefit from the speed and introspection space of the new ways of work, stories of extraordinary employee acts happen all around us and the heroes are always the employees who feel they are safe to be themselves and grow.

While a lot should be said about a company's moral imperative to make the employee's life better, I find it to be as effective an argument as the imperative to go paperless hinging solely on saving the rainforest. No company reduced their printing until they saw clear numbers on what they can save by doing so. Moral imperatives in themselves are nice, moral imperatives when coupled with business cases are better and thankfully, when it comes to Psychological Safety, its correlation to every measurable dimension can actually be quantified in cold hard currency.

Behavioural Foundations

To start showing that correlation, we first have to be sure we can identify and quantify Psychological Safety in itself. In the previous chapter, I detailed some of the elements I believe are a sine qua non when we speak of Psychologically Safe teams (*see also* p. 115). They all exhibit positive behaviours, such as speaking up and always offering their opinion fearlessly, being flexible and resilient, learning and experimenting together, being inquisitive, etc., and are as a result open, positive, engaged, vulnerable, real and trusting with each other, but also display negative behaviours where they avoid speaking up as they fear looking incompetent, ignorant, negative, disruptive, intrusive or, I might add, unprofessional. These are all the case and they all need dissection and focus, but the reality is that the work is greater than we sometimes anticipate and keeping a keen eye on all of these is no easy task.

Empathy is to me the greatest variable here. We can and do measure so many other aspects of our human practice but if a team leader or even a team member will not find ways to avoid impression managing against 'looking un-professional', dig deep and relate, how would they ever begin to work on their EQ in earnest when it all hinges on their ability to recognize and value emotions? In the next chapter, I go more in-depth on the possible avenues of constructing empathy, but at this stage, it is simply worth pointing out that outlining it as the bedrock of any People Practice is paramount.

Even describing empathy and its clear desirability in the workplace will serve as an enabler as it spells out permission to have a healthy preoccupation with our own emotions and those of others. And improving on our ability to understand the world through each other's eyes can only have beneficial results in every realm, powering a true thirst for diversity and inclusion. Nonetheless, because of the Human Debt, people will be naturally hesitant and resistant to believe the change in the organizational rhetoric when it comes to empathy, so one of the easy ways to hand out much-needed permission slips that we advise companies can attempt is to hold 'Empathy Up!' spaces. Whether quick sessions once a week or a focused day's work, asking simple 'How would you feel if ...' questions to accompany various scenarios will allow participants to believe that putting themselves in another's shoes is indeed permitted and valued now.

An effective way to further that work is to grab a hold of Brené Brown's *Dare to Lead* workbook and have coaches or team leaders walk through some of the rest of the exercises she outlines to increase empathy.

Measuring how empathic someone is constitutes a serious challenge. Empathy resides at a largely subconscious level and while we believe it may be trained and bettered, it is never an easy ask as it requires deep and genuine connection, which is not easy to achieve for many people due to individual factors such as childhood trauma, emotional or cognitive underdevelopment or large amounts of unconscious bias. This doesn't make it impossible, just extremely difficult to achieve at times. In other words, the healthier and more stable someone is mentally, the more likely it is that they can be empathic and therefore they stand a better chance of becoming even more emotionally intelligent but at the same time, even those of us who struggle in some departments can achieve the state eventually with enough preoccupation and support.

I find that for some teams, a shortcut to greater empathy that's borrowed from every version of meditation practice out there is underlining the commonality of suffering, or really, just the commonality of experience (although yes, it's human nature that the negative experiences bond us faster at times). When we find ways to outline that we are having a shared reality, relating to each other comes naturally and takes no effort, so at times simply vocalizing and describing situations that are intensely emotional and intensely similar works wonders.

Depending on the context of the work, the field of practice or the industry, the need for 'external' empathy (towards the people we interact with, in our work, AKA the public) can be greater or smaller (those in emergency services, crisis and medical personnel, etc. have an undeniably greater need and different challenges in maintaining it), but the need for developing it as an overall skill and applying it intentionally and intently on a consistent basis to our teammates is constant across the board.

Other sine qua non group behaviours we have to reinforce to get to a position where we can even start laying out the People Practice building work are courage, curiosity, honesty, goodwill and a passion and purposeful underbelly. If these are in place in a team alongside empathy, then they can start admitting the importance of remaining urgently curious and intensely vigilant through a People Practice that focuses on all the other elements of Psychological Safety, such as resilience and flexibility, overall engagement, trust, learning and lack of impression management.

Courage, in particular, comes up over and again in this book because every negative behaviour that saps a team of Psychological Safety and eventually renders them unable of high performance comes from fear. Every time they hold back, every time they cover up mistakes, any avoidance, any doubt, any untruth and any lack of care are all easily traceable back to fear so we must realize bravery is the cornerstone to avoiding any of the dangerous ways of acting with each other.

The very reason why Professor Dr Amy Edmondson entitled one of her books *The Fearless Organization* is because fear really is the root evil of any of the organizational anti-patterns and all the toxicity we see today. Unless we find ways to directly attack and eradicate it, we shall not be able to achieve our full potential, innovate and create the magic that Psychologically Safe teams have.

Another crucially important behaviour any team or organization needs to have to start making a dent in their Human Debt is Curiosity. Being truly and genuinely interested and invested in finding out everything to do with the people in the team.

In a sense, an open and inquisitive stance is implied in one's ability to build empathy based on a deep and common understanding, but a step further from that, always probing and always being thirsty for data points, is the truest manifestation of caring we could offer each other. Hence why we ought to check and ask and measure constantly and obsessively.

In the absence of a culture of a relentless quest for self-discovery, no organization can produce the self-reinforcing data points that show the people work is paramount to getting amazing business results so making an inquisitive nature the norm is a foundational exercise.

Detailing and then encouraging any of these behaviours in an organization or even a team is directly dependent on the ability to change the narrative towards them being necessary and desirable. The concept of 'permission slips' applies both to individuals and to companies who at an organizational level understand the great importance of making these behaviours a priority as a way of fostering every other beneficial result in their business. When companies comprehend this at an honest and deep level, when they feel the need for the people work 'in their bones' and when they can then manage to communicate this revelation believably to the extent where employees feel they have their permission and encouragement to be courageous, to be daring, to be empathic and caring and utterly invested in the people work, that's when great things can happen, 'People Practices' spring up and the Human Debt starts to reduce.

Interventions and Bettering Teams – The 'People Practice'

If we collectively have clarity on the importance of making a dent in the Human Debt in the workplace, we have laid the behavioural foundations down and we have understood the elements that make up Psychological Safety and the importance of EQ – what now? With all the organizational permission in the world, what is the next actionable step and if the step is 'build a People Practice', who should do this and how?

The evident answer is that while a 'People Practice' in its purest definition – which is 'a habit of paying attention and caring about the people around us' – will eventually have to become everyone's business, it has to start with the team leaders. This isn't a certain title and position and it's not necessarily referring to the people leading the smallest and most efficient team units but really, anyone who has any amount of people reporting to them (as an aside, that term is heinous and a vestige of the command and control management culture), whether that's two or 200,000.

When a leader has a realization of this being the most important part of their work moving forward, and once their EQ is at a certain level, and they start paying enough attention and employing the right tools to measure and diagnose, they will quickly start to see patterns of behaviour in their team that they would like to stimulate or discourage. They will then realize doing so will require some type of action at a team level, an intervention in the way they interact.

Many leaders will rely on the help of coaches to organize different interventions and in turn, they will employ a variety of methods depending on the frameworks and schools of thought they adhere to themselves. Typically, an intervention, irrespective of the problem and the agreed actions, will contain:

- **An Awareness Campaign** complete with best-practice recommendations – clarifying the topic to the wider team, popularizing the concepts behind it and showing its importance is critical when introducing any intervention. (Say a team has an issue with being open, a team leader or a coach may first bring it up to the team and then outline the importance of honesty in teamwork complete with data and stats as to where it affects teamwork and productivity and then show what others have done to increase it);

- **A Goal Definition Exercise** – the team leader or coach encourages the team to think of a quantifiable outcome where the encouraged behaviour would be easily observable;
- **Setting an Action Plan** – a phase where there will be a clear formulation of the actions undertaken by the team for a specific period of time to see improvement in the areas they are targeting, ranging from further information campaigns to hackathons, team exercises and innovative practices resulting from the team's own brainstorming process that aims to aid the outcome;
- **The Execution of the respective intervention** – which varies in terms of length of time and contents depending on the behaviour they are encouraging or discouraging and, finally,
- **A solid Review/Retrospective Phase** so that the team can learn from the intervention, irrespective of whether it succeeded or failed. This last step is crucially important and should be governed by extreme honesty for best results.

These components seem borderline unnecessary in terms of spelling them out, as they are so evidently part of any plan of action to effect any change in any circumstance, but ensuring they exist in a clear and well-formulated manner when it comes to people is half the battle, as it reaffirms the need for a structured and diligent approach to the necessary teamwork, where in its absence it would be tempting for some people leaders to simply confine it to an elusive and unmeasurable afterthought.

Any of the components of Psychological Safety can be improved with the right interventions in place. This is why in PeopleNotTech's software we focus less on exposing tips, tricks and best practices and a lot more on developing the leader's habit of bringing what their EQ helped them observe – with the help of our data and training – to the team and asking for their help and assistance in defining what can be done to effect behaviour.

The role of the 'Coach me!' feature in our team software solution is to provide the teams with guidance 'at the point of head-scratching', meaning when they are looking at the data and trying to make sense of what the issue is or what the best next actions are. The coaches we work with tend to have very non-prescriptive approaches and remain staunchly invested in being good 'sherpas' in people practices. In other words, they are typically a lot more interested in helping teams develop self-sustainable and self-governing emotional and group dynamic techniques and behaviours by supporting with advice, guidance and facilitation than they are in dictating what these teams should do step-by-step in each instance.

When choosing coaches or mentors for your teams, always ensure they are of the infamous – and occasionally frustrating – 'And how does that make you feel?' denomination as any other stance such as a collection of prescriptive orders is not adding any value to your team's EQ and ability to progress independently long term even if they seem like quick fixes at the time. Some of the tools that would be part of interventions on specific behaviours and become part of the general arsenal of one's People Practice are:

- **People Hackathons.** Borrowed from IT, a 'people hackathon' is typically an intervention where, for a period of time – ranging from a few hours to a full day – the team gathers to co-create new and innovative ways to deal with a certain topic. From humour to culture and engagement, any behaviour or goal can be translated into a hackathon where mini-prototypes of various interventions would be brought to light by the team;
- **Team Re-Launches.** As mentioned in previous chapters, the act of regrouping around the basal needs and values of a team can be very powerful and should be done regularly, but in particular if there is an element of 'forming' where there are any changes to the team. These times serve as a good reset and a checkpoint for

team contracts and shared purpose and tools such as contracting and culture canvases should prove useful every time. As opposed to hackathons, the structure for team re-launches is tighter with clearer protocols and requires a lot more tight-fisted facilitation, but the time commitment to such an intervention is as big, if not greater;

- **Challenges.** These are more granular examples of exercises and they sometimes derive from the two bigger actions above, where at the end of a hackathon a series of challenges may have been designed by the team as a way for them to improve a certain behaviour, such as communicational ones to encourage speaking up (i.e. an 'Always invite twice' challenge to ask for everyone's opinion multiple times for a team that has trouble with honest participation across the board or the 'Be outrageous week', where people are encouraged to be at their most 'out there' in their examples or opinions to demonstrate vulnerability and therefore model safety, etc.);

- **Design Sprints.** Nearly identical to Hackathons, they may use dedicated Human Centred Design techniques and elements such as personas, stories and research to encourage empathy and then offer more depth to the experiments resulting from the brainstorms, the white-boarding and the blue-skying efforts of the team;

- **Immersive Exercises.** Where applicable, role-playing is an effective way to get team members to understand the core issue when it comes to human values as the simple act of 'putting themselves' in the shoes of another human being forces a higher level of empathy that lasts them past the actual intervention so designing moments like that with techniques borrowed from performance arts – in particular, improv – can be very efficient;

- **Accountability Training.** To encourage a general sense of responsibility towards the People Practice work some form of accountability reinforcement should be inbuilt regularly in the

People Practice of some teams. In particular in teams where their sense of autonomy has been undermined by the organization and where they are less confident in their abilities, taking control and assuming responsibility for their own team well-being can be very empowering. There is an array of actions that pertain to accountability which are worth investigating, from encouraging a higher sense of personal responsibility to remaining aware and invested in the team's overall people goal and reminding the group about it to calling each other out over negative behaviours. Needless to say, the greatest accountability need of them all is that of the team leader towards the team so keeping them honest and focused on the teamwork is crucial and can be accomplished by the team remaining vigilant and willing to observe their progress closely;

- **Re-framing.** Borrowed from Cognitive Behavioural Therapy (CBT), the act of changing the lens and re-positioning a certain problem or issue is spectacularly powerful. If the team can identify negative behaviours and discuss their roots, then follow the thought pattern and change the perspective from a negative to a positive one, they can instantly change that behaviour – i.e. 'I am afraid to speak up for fear someone would think I'm whinging' and then follow them through the individual narrative's path, 'If I'm whinging then I will be seen as a bad team player who is not constructive and people will hate me' and instead reword them and offer alternative explanations such as 'What if whinging would be rewarded as a good idea in our team because it meant people are aware and attentive and willing to call out issues'? and then 'That would mean that any whinger is a great team player who has the courage to express themselves and has the well-being of the team at heart', etc.;

- **Rewards.** Finding the best ways to reward good behaviours is difficult but extremely important as when we get it right, it can be very useful in encouraging behaviours the team can benefit from. In our team solution, we've incorporated the ability to offer rewards for behaviours such as honesty and feedback offering but also for reinforcing the behaviour of speaking up but the nature and value of these rewards are irrelevant. Many of the teams we work with often hold an 'Our Team Rewards' Design Sprint or Hackathon, where they come up with innovative, cost-effective and intensely personal rewards that make the most sense to their team – from days off to badges, takeaway surprises or children's birthday parties (according to Professor of Psychology and Behavioural Economics at Duke University, Dan Ariely's, 'rewards substitution' theory, micro-rewards that are well-timed are as efficient as huge ones).

People Practice interventions and tools and the team coaching that can facilitate them are the new 'team-building' – although we highly recommend teams find ways to construct closeness and engagement in fiercely personal ways as well. If we further spend time wondering about the necessity of the practical experimentation in our People Practice as compared to the idea that we can take any one theory and apply it exactly we need to look at the few models proposed out there. Perhaps rather tellingly, while Professor Dr Amy Edmondson often writes powerful articles to accompany her books which have morsels of practical advice typically centred around strategies to encourage safety in failure and learning to encourage innovation, she rarely offers any prescriptive steps on how to achieve this and always implies a non-linear character to the Psychological Safety work.

One of the other theories out there about Psychological Safety is by Timothy R. Clark and in his book, *The 4 Stages of Psychological Safety: Defining the Path to Inclusion and Innovation*, he names them as being:

Stage 1: Inclusion

Stage 2: Safe to Learn

Stage 3: Safe to Contribute

Stage 4: Safe to Change the Status Quo.

We spent some time analysing this theory and eventually found it lacking. My main objection is that for one thing Psychological Safety isn't a linear progression as suggested by the idea of stages. I believe the elements which are behaviour-specific to the respective team's dynamic will change and produce multiple intermediate and interwoven stages like the ones above. I rather think that Psychological Safety is fluid and always in flux. Also, I can't agree that feeling invited to contribute is different to the feeling of having the ability to change the status quo. It simply doesn't make enough conceptual sense to me that those two are separated – if you speak up, you speak up, and you do so because you believe change is possible.

We also have to discuss how the idea of learning fits in. Being able to learn together implies a sense of hope, a foundation of trust and a sense of purpose all in one so teams that manage to share the experience undoubtedly feel a lot more connected and likely more Psychologically Safe than others. That said, the mechanisms of intellectual and emotional curiosity are complex and deeply rooted in individual belief systems, evolutionary past and personal motivation. When we add cultural components, this is already a complicated canvas and on top of it, layered firmly and dictating group behaviour is the organization's own attitude towards learning. Is it permissible? Is it laudable? Is it seen as connected to innovation and growth? Is it encouraged? Is it deeply rooted in permission to fail?

That is not to say learning shouldn't be measured – we measure it by looking at both intellectual curiosity and sense of team appetite to new information but as one of the elements only and it cannot be seen as 'a phase' as suggested above. In a sense, it can be argued that Clark has seen it as a reflection of an organization's culture, whether or not people feel mandated to learn, and that is indubitably important but I put it to us all that it's secondary to whether that team feels there is firm permission to fail and desire to experiment and innovate within their own team.

That is how we get all the incredible examples of innovative teams existing and thriving in the midst of the most horrendous of organizations. They have an appetite for learning and improvement even when the organization around them doesn't. This is – aside from my objection to the phased approach which suggests linear progression which isn't accurate – the other main reason why I grapple with any framework or theory, which like the one above, relies on any of the reflection of the actions and culture of the mythical organization – because Psychological Safety is an inside-team job.

The idea of the bubble, of finding things out and working on them 'just between us', is incredibly important to us and we expend vast amounts of effort reinforcing the 'private to the team' character of the software solution we made because of this very need to preserve the intimate character of the group. Unless the team feels a firm sense of 'bubble' where their human interactions are to be authentic, irrespective of what surrounds them in the work environment, they won't be able to do better.

One approach I absolutely applaud belongs to Richard Kasperowski, who followed his book *High-Performance Teams* with one called *The Core Protocols: A Guide to Greatness*, which, despite the title is a real purist and non-prescriptive perspective of the value of EQ and the work that needs to go into establishing productive teams that are Psychologically Safe. He is implicitly one of the great advocates of intent human work by how he designs individual training programs for each organization's People Practice to elevate their performance.

While I am firmly of the opinion myself that nothing replaces the in-person, bespoke magic workshops and hands-on human work can accomplish, my bet and the reason why I started PeopleNotTech is that taking that approach would simply be too slow a change curve to make a sufficient dent in the Human Debt and what we need is intelligent software solutions to lead some of the People Practice with minimal coach intervention. This is why we believe that increasing EQ and thus making leaders and teams alike self-sustainable and self-sufficient in their human work is where we should focus our efforts.

A guide for any team leader (be they lead of a team or CEO of an organization) when looking for software solutions to support and empower a People Practice with EQ and Psychological Safety at its core would be:

- Don't listen to anyone with a framework and self-aggrandizing terminology or acronyms. This topic is difficult enough and it requires simple definitions in plain language;
- Don't think it has phases and instil a 'once and done' feeling to Psychological Safety. It's never a question of finding what to tweak to afterwards forever have it, but a constant variable where multiple elements change and the overall state does accordingly so it needs to be seen as taking the pulse, not as a one-time process;
- Don't pay attention to anyone who excludes the connection to EQ and People Practices. While 'radical candour' or 'conversational turn-taking' are wonderful ideas that can be tried, none is the silver bullet. They are but some of the interventions in what should be a constantly evolving list of hundreds on the backlog of any EQed team leader who knows their main job now is helping teams to evolve and have Psychological Safety;
- Don't trust anything with enterprise-level reports and measure-ments – this is not a whole organization HR or Management topic, it has to stay within the team. We have burned far too much trust capital from our employees over the years in the 'human

debt' – we can ill afford to burn any more and failing to protect the team privacy 'bubble' level of Psychological Safety would be disastrous. If the organization wants to know how they do, they can take a look at the overall month-on-month improvement, nothing more granular than that;

- Don't mandate the questions answering – focus instead on building a true dialogue as there will always be a need for more answers;
- Anything that doesn't measure impression management is not taking its importance seriously;
- Don't consider anything that is not a 'live tool' – nothing that is even remotely reminding us of a yearly survey;
- Find solutions that dig very deeply into granular data at a team level and that hold space for the team to define what their next actions are on their own or with the help of a coach;
- Only consider solutions that work hard to reassure employees of absolute privacy but measure their trust in it;
- Find ways to reward desirable behaviours, such as speaking up.

Lessons from Different Industries

The concept of Psychological Safety is a general team dynamic one and as such, its application cuts across industries and applies to any field. Nonetheless, it is a young concept for the workplace and, alongside the numbers the business needs to place it centre stage, there will also be a need for anecdotes, stories and examples where its importance would be undeniable.

Being that the vast amount of the knowledge we have about Psychological Safety is coming from Professor Dr Amy Edmondson's body of research – the industries we know most about from the perspective of teams who have this amazing sense of 'magic' are the medical field, pharma, technology and the airline industry, which sadly offers us the most disturbing and recent example of a lack of Psychological Safety being extremely dangerous.

In Boeing's 737 tragedies (the Lion Air flight 610 crash in October 2018 and Ethiopian Airlines' flight 302 crash in March 2019) later unearthed emails show, without a shadow of a doubt, a climate of fear where employees were acutely aware of horrendous issues and had major doubts yet only spoke up among each other. A glaring example of lack of Psychological Safety. Professor Dr Amy Edmondson describes the organizational culture at Boeing as being 'a textbook case of how the absence of psychological safety can lead to disastrous results'.

The concerns were multiple, from the aggressive production schedule to the fact that management was keeping costs down by avoiding things like additional pilot training, which was much needed considering how the 737 Max had a very different technological presentation to its predecessor. All non-trivial concerns that were never raised for fear of retribution.

In the medical field, there is no shortage of studies regarding the disastrous effects a lack of willingness to speak up or challenge medical decisions can have on patient safety and ultimately, mortality rates, with nurses, residents and doctors alike being now acutely aware of the importance of open communication as an intrinsic safety measure. In the case of healthcare, this is often further complicated by the fact that the context is that of 'teaming', with many teams not having the luxury of stability and a comfortable, tried-and-tested team dynamic when they have to form teams on the fly, as is the case in emergency medicine.

The behaviours Psychological Safety needs to avoid, such as impression management, are common and equally problematic across all types of industries and examples such as the ones above come from other fields as well, like the Wells Fargo scandal, the lack of speaking up in the film industry #MeToo debacle and so on.

In a 2016 study on Turkish immigrants employed in Germany, researchers found that greater Psychological Safety promoted engagement, mental health and lower turnover. This correlation seemed to be greater for the immigrant segment than their German colleagues employed in the same workplace, which suggests that for those who perceive themselves as more disadvantaged or vulnerable, the benefits are even greater. Perhaps the best example of its application in business comes from our friends at Google again, who openly say when they discuss the findings of the Aristotle Project on their incredibly useful re:Work page:

> Googlers love data. But they don't want to sit idle with it. They want to act. So [following Project Aristotle], we created a tool called the gTeams exercise: a 10-minute pulse-check on the five dynamics, a report that summarizes how the team is doing, a live in-person conversation to discuss the results, and tailored developmental resources to help teams improve. Over the past year, more than 3,000 Googlers across 300 teams have used this tool. Of those Google teams, the ones that adopted a new group norm – like kicking off every team meeting by sharing a risk taken in the previous week – improved 6% on psychological safety ratings and 10% on structure and clarity ratings. Teams said that having a framework around team effectiveness and a forcing function to talk about these dynamics was missing previously and by far the most impactful part of the experience.
>
> From sales teams in Dublin to engineering teams in Mountain View, we've seen that focusing on this framework helps all types of teams improve.

Why Business Won't Care About People and Teams Before They See a Number

At PeopleNotTech, we are betting our farms on how Psychological Safety in teams is the most important performance lever we have ever investigated in the workplace. As we said many times before, these big human topics are relatively new in the vernacular of enterprises and institutions, but in the absence of clarity on numbers to tie them to productivity and performance (and for the avoidance of doubt, these numbers do anecdotally exist, thankfully), they too are in danger of being lumped with all the other 'fluffy', 'soft', 'human' topics, where important elements of success are bundled together and collectively disregarded.

Employee 'engagement', 'satisfaction' and 'happiness' have long been heralded as immensely important to every organization but if we're honest, to this day, they are consistently demoted to second-tier priorities and inevitably lose ideological and budget fights in favour of 'real priorities', which are mainly of a legal or operational nature. No board will tell you they don't care about their employee's happiness, but I have yet to see the director pointing out in any strategy meeting that they are not part of any risk strategy and are never considered first priority.

Empirically and from arms' distance from the plight of HR over the years, I would speculate that this lack of importance, this disregard and this demotion that is assigned to these topics in some environments, is the direct result of how the main metric that was used to illustrate them was 'retention'. The organization was told: 'Look, you're haemorrhaging people/talent, this costs money. If you want to reduce turnover by X, make your employees happy'. Aside from how oftentimes, this was never accompanied by a map of steps needed to achieve that, and aside from how practical suggestions and actionable serious plans never existed, this has somehow failed to resonate in the way intended. I postulate that this is because it's appealing to the 'fear' side of motivation whereas where it would have made an impact, it would have had to appeal to 'greed'.

While the retention stats are all correct, would the enterprise be as sluggish to respond had they been told: 'Make your employees happier by 1 per cent and you'll see a 40 per cent increase in business'? Absolutely not. They would have clamoured to figure out ways to do it. Mind, that would have incidentally meant they would have had to start with figuring out what their current level of happiness was – a nebulous area for most, if not all.

Somewhere along the way, the establishment's lack of interest became justifiable to professionals and they stopped being intellectually curious and eager to find the numbers that would have appealed to 'greed' – i.e. the correlations to show how the 'fluffy topics' resulted directly in coins in the pockets of the stakeholders – and everyone just quietly accepted that the bits about their humans are simply not as important as the bits about the printers, the new regulation or the data centres.

Incidentally, I feel like resignation to this bizarre status quo is what has (or will) precipitated the demise of HR as a function because they failed to elevate the importance of the humans they were meant to understand, help and better. Had they done so, including finding some of the numbers I am referring to, then the ladder of the importance of functions and topics would have tipped where the people issues are at the very top and regarded as critical in ways that operations and finance would never be.

Seeing as now the new rhetoric on measurement is being driven by other areas of the business – there are at times many more people-centric chief technology officers (CTOs) and chief information officers (CIOs) and even risk officers interested in repairing and bettering the Human Debt than HR professionals in the enterprises that win – and how the numbers that prove the importance of people in trying to build anything digital, innovative or lasting are coming from DevOps communities, it's clear that they are the new beacons of advocating for better, cohesive, open and happy teams comprised of courageous and happy people because they can show how that correlates to better, faster and lasting business results.

Conversely, other industries such as healthcare have a much firmer imperative – patient safety. There, numbers are crystal-clear, thanks to the work of Amy Edmondson and scholars regarding the direct effect of the lack of Psychological Safety of the medical teams on the safety of the patients. That's an un-ignorable metric that no hospital can choose to ever de-prioritize. Ironically, not even this measurement is about 'morality' or 'decency' but has a very well-defined number in healthcare, which puts our reticence to define it in business to shame.

Some voices deplore numbers when it comes to human topics. Some claim it's dehumanizing to dissect and focus on productivity. Some find it in poor taste to show the dollar sign at the end of humanity. I put it to us that a lack of numbers will continue to keep our employees in a vicious circle of being treated appallingly by the enterprise – the lack of feedback, lack of listening and lack of respect will continue. We won't have Psychologically Safe teams and we won't have happy, fully human, EQed employees and team leaders if we don't have and then incessantly declare the numbers.

In the places where they started from a culture where the humans matter most, where teams have to have Psychological Safety and individuals feel heard, they measured what that means to their bottom line – the Google, the Spotify, some of the other Silicon Valley darlings and as of 2020, hopefully, some incumbents too! – and the percentage they found is unbelievably high. Ask anyone who knows their internal research and prepare to have your mouth drop.

Turns out treating your people right, making them happy and safe, and improving their lives at work pays – who knew? Not the vast majority of incumbents, they didn't, and we believe that to make them stand up and pay attention to the amount of work necessary to reduce the Human Debt, we need to first make the numbers connecting Psychological Safety and productivity to become one of the strongest measurements in business and a recognizable, undeniable figure.

The Experiment of Trying to Experiment

Seeing as how my thesis is that, in the absence of a firm number, directly correlating productivity to Psychological Safety, the business world will never make it a priority, I decided to find a way to obtain this number.

Considering my Agile fetish and my conviction that its true calling is to underline the importance of happy humans, I firmly believed there is scope to create the number we need for Psychological Safety by looking through Agile KPIs lenses, so I've kicked off that endeavour by loosely defining a possible piece of research and immediately reached out to the community to find the best teams.

In my call to arms, I said, 'The idea is simple: we agree on some universal Agile KPIs to start with, then measure the Psychological Safety of both teams and then we support only one of the two team leaders in increasing their EQ. We ensure they are mindful of it in every kick-off and retro and generally do some pointy interventions to better their People Practice in general and the components of Psychological Safety in particular for two sprints and then we see what happens. If my hypothesis is correct, then we should see a direct correlation between increased Psychological Safety and the Agile KPIs (I know, I hate that term too!) in even that short a time frame.'

When I sent the call to arms, I was only left with a short time frame (three months) to collect the data in, so I asked specifically for companies nimble enough and devoid of red tape enough to participate.

What happened next surprised me. While I didn't anticipate a deluge of companies eager to be part of this who believed they satisfied the requirements: Agile and measuring and nimble enough to get organized around starting to use PeopleNotTech's Psychological Safety Team Solution fast enough for us to have a workspace to improve one of the teams, I certainly didn't presume I would encounter some of the challenges I did.

To spare you the suspense, this book doesn't contain this magical number I was hoping for and the resulting two case studies. One day I will have that number for us all – I'm nothing if not stubborn when it comes to eradicating Human Debt and this would go such a long way – but there were several reasons why it hasn't happened now and we've agreed that lifting the curtain and letting you see some of the anatomy of the experiment is useful. All of us reading these pages are a team after all, and as a team, we should always openly share what we find.

Of the many teams I spoke to, some proved to have weak leaders who provided so little true inspirational leadership they were breeding a sick environment – despite how they were convinced they were valiant 'woke leaders' with 'no bad ideas/no blame' policies – some had strange and incomparable set-ups and most simply couldn't get their ducks in a row fast enough and they knew they couldn't be responsive in the time frame that was needed.

Perhaps the most surprising part has been realizing how few of the Agile companies I was evaluating for this actually even measured anything. Often they would be convinced they did, and it wasn't until I got down to the nitty-gritty and asked them for some historical data on their Agile KPIs that the absence was clear. The measurements I was hoping I would uncover would have been software development specific, say around the velocity with which they get through tasks together or the way their coding output tested and how 'clean' it was, etc. I was even willing to extrapolate that to simply include Scrum KPIs in terms of the speed, accuracy or the type and quality of their body of work in the backlog which would have potentially transcended software-making teams and applied to most other industries where they have implemented Scrum.

As I said above, the number one empirical observation in all of the enterprises I have evaluated to be part of this, was how they all thought they had these measurements in place. Whether my internal champion was an Agile coach or the chief technology officer (CTO) or even an individual team leader, they all, without fail, dismissed my concerns regarding whether their measurements were present and reliable and assured me they were.

Witnessing their surprise when they realized that either the measurements existed on paper only, had become individual to the respective team or product or hadn't been used at all in ages was very interesting indeed. It's only five of the eight that had any measurements in place, and two of them did not have them correlate to any Agile KPI at all despite their impression of it, but instead to old organizational P&L goals and measurements. The remaining three did indeed have ways to measure both velocity and accuracy, even if they were using different terms internally. They formed the bulk of my preoccupation and I have then focused on getting two of their teams on board.

In each case, a pair of teams had been earmarked, we had explained cursorily the concept of Psychological Safety to them, we had given them a small amount of training to show them the ropes on how to answer questions (the only prerequisite to team A, who were then not to do anything or even use the software's Dashboard until they were asked to measure again in a couple of months; whereas team B was given more in-depth training to prepare for the hands-on interventions to come, designed to improve their People Practice depending on what the data on Psychological Safety showed us) and we had theoretically shaken hands on the idea of trying to do this together.

Company X is a software maker – they had the makings of becoming dream study participants. Smart, clued in, knowledgeable and Agile 'in the heart', they had a relatively healthy distributed teams make-up that hadn't been forced by the 2020 pandemic but had been their modus operandi for years and they were making cutting-edge products and running as fast as they could. We had started getting organized when they realized that they had run our endeavour past no one internally and they became fearful as to whether they should, despite how they knew there was an opportunity for me to include the results in this book, even if they remained anonymous.

Once the thought occurred to them, their ability to fully engage seemed to drop sharply and they asked for several documents to send to HR for a miraculous stamp of approval. We halted everything while they attempted to get clarity. I spoke to HR myself. At first openly hostile, in fairness they eventually opened up, seen the value and then even became excited about the project themselves. A few weeks delayed already, we could now continue. Except a day later, we heard differently. We couldn't. HR had decided they didn't want to make the decision and re-sent it to Legal for 'a formal permission document' after the former department had already examined the book agreement and then given their green light. Seeing as I knew the backlog of the legal team at a time when Covid-connected liabilities were rampant, I had to concede with regret that the fear-based-approvals-carousel may well have never stopped or never stopped in time. Psychological Safety and Agile: 0, Bureaucracy and Fear: 1.

Company Y – I was about to dismiss as the deeper we were getting into their internal history, the clearer it was that they had deep organizational challenges with immense amounts of destructive behaviour, politics, subconscious bullying, lack of merit and a generalized fear of speaking up. I was worried their results were going to be so disastrously skewed by these deep challenges that they wouldn't bring about any good news, but before I had communicated my concerns, the decision was taken out of my hands when the innovation champion spearheading our access was brought into a meeting, interrogated and accused of thinking about silly things by management – they weren't productive if they were dealing with these topics, you see – and the respective leader of team leads was told he 'lost the reign of his people to allow them to waste time on this'. Psychological Safety and Agile: 0, Ignorant Command & Control: 1.

Finally, Company Z – had an amazing 'Agile Superhero', exceptional two teams reporting high levels of Psychological Safety anecdotally and pre-measurement was all on board but their organizational hell made it impossible to communicate effectively and exposed masses of red tape they were utterly unaware of. They had some of the same challenges Company X and Y had had, but they overcame those. What they didn't realize was how overworked they were, how ineffective in communication, how unable to organize in the new remote world and how shaky from the point of view of the team's overall well-being. All those factors meant that they thought they were in when in fact they were out because they were unresponsive and unengaged. This wasn't out of malice, but a degree of dysfunction already existent in their teams and it just meant a case study in a time frame I was envisioning was impossible.

These are the stories of the companies that aren't in these pages today, giving a definitive number you can use to better the lives of your employees, but I remain resolute to keep researching this and find a way to prove the correlation – hopefully through Agile – beyond a shadow of a doubt and have already taken up the companies who needed more time. I am currently evaluating their suitability with a view to publishing some results in the future.

Measure Small, Obsessively and Often to Win Big

If we can't measure Psychological Safety in itself at an organizational level – and if we're honest, what good would that be? – let's keep measuring it at the team level. Let's become obsessed with being guided within our own individual bubbles by indicators such as the ones outlined in the previous chapters.

How open and honest are our people? How flexible and resilient? Do they learn together? Do they do courageous things together? Do they feel safe to fail? Are they having fun? Do they impression manage? Do they speak up? If we break it down into these themes, we can start both quantifying micro-interactions and hopefully, affecting them positively through the above-mentioned interventions in the People Practice.

We can not only collect these data points, correlate them to internal performance measurements and bring them back to the organization in support of the importance of Psychological Safety, but more importantly, we can learn enough to inform our own team actions and People Practice goals meanwhile so that in the absence of the business' awakening we can still be doing enough winning at the team's bubble level.

Some traditional measurement and polling devices employed by big enterprises which tend to be clunky, weighed down by wooden language and at times utterly disconnected from the day-to-day reality and language of the employees, such as their 360 performance reviews or their Annual or Pulse surveys will at times attempt to expand to include some of the elements of Psychological Safety. But the reality is that a complete change in lens needs to happen before there can be effective measurement where we start with fundamentals around feedback frequency, complete honesty, demonstrable care, lack of punitive measures, etc. There is a real question in my mind as to whether these structures even ought to survive long term as they no longer serve our honest purpose of growing the People Practice.

Alternative methods of polling can and should remain and some may offer glimpses into the necessary people work. For instance, originating at Spotify, many teams of software developers who use their same team structures and work in an Agile method such as Scrum employ a 'team health check' model where participants are asked to score a series of topics such as 'Support', 'Teamwork', 'Pawns or Players (AKA Autonomy)', 'Mission', 'Health of Codebase', 'Suitable Process', 'Delivering Value', 'Learning', 'Speed', 'Easy of Release' and 'Fun' at the end of a sprint, with a stoplight system ranging from green when things went well to red when they didn't. It's beautifully simple and in conjunction with the elements of relative stability, the nature of the work and the beauty of the Agile ceremonies it's incredibly efficient at providing a snapshot of the team.

If we exclude the technical opinion from the list of elements, they verify there is a great overlap with the components our team solution measures, so what a Spotify team health check shows is whether or not the team feels they have Psychological Safety. It's rudimental in some ways but cornerstone to awareness in their People Practice.

Above all, measuring and diagnosing cannot, and should not, be a sterile exercise. The correlation to action has to be immediate and transparent to the team and it must be carried through in either one of the interventions described above or as a series of micro-changes at an individual behaviour level. As an example of the latter, one of the companies we are working with is experimenting with implementing cues inspired by 'nudge theories' and how they can encourage desirable behaviours to the detriment of unhealthy ones. In PeopleNotTech's team solution we already use rewards and the incognito mode to outline a specific behaviour and inspire a better one.

In a sense, the mere decision to start paying attention as a cornerstone to a specific team's People Practice will bring about a need for tools, ideas and interventions and the very act of creating that space of introspection and analysis of the team's emotions and behaviours will translate into higher Psychological Safety and higher performance and will prove its value in practice to the business. So while we should all work towards clearer 'THIS!' type numbers to make the business wake up and then enjoy the easier life coming from their attempts to lower the Human Debt with cultural change and clear permission to be human, we needn't stop our obsession with keeping a finger on our team's pulse or postpone the people work we can do ourselves at the bubble level until they see this magical number materialize and understand its value.

CHAPTER SIX

Soft Skills are Hard

- Hard Skills and the Future
- Feelings at Work
- IQ vs EQ
- Courage and Vulnerability
- Passion and Purpose
- Can We Do 'Empathy By Numbers'?
- Permission to be Human
- The 'People Practice'
- Beyond the Team

Hard Skills and the Future

Recent research from the Carnegie Institute of Technology suggests that only 15 per cent of one's financial success is linked to one's technical knowledge or IQ and if we are to presume that to be a fair monetary representation of one's work contribution then it's fair to assume what we know is much less important than other factors at work. Presumably, the remaining percentage is linked to our ability to relate to others, team up, engage and most of all, read and interpret our emotions and the emotions of others with empathy. And yet it is these very attributes that are neither measured nor compensated in most workplaces.

One of the keys to this lies in the definition of 'knowledge' – confining it to formal education, industry-specific skillsets and conventional IQ can make it become a hindrance in today's work environment, where with the democratization of access and the consumer demands ever-growing, we see rapidly increasing necessary volumes of formal knowledge being necessary to perform our jobs. If we add the speed with which technology changes and grows, having formal knowledge in the sense we have referred to it throughout the centuries is no longer even truly possible. In addition, the complexity of navigating ever more complicated hierarchical structures while having to relate and perform 'teaming', involuntary as it may be, means that humans have to display different abilities than those of a theoretical nature only.

In some industries companies have seen this shift from 'hard skills' and traditional definitions of 'knowledge' and have veered towards hiring people from unexpected backgrounds or with formal education and experience in diverse and seemingly unconnected fields. Companies such as J.P. Morgan, Unilever and others have announced they are after graduates from other disciplines than the ones they would have traditionally recruited from. Other enterprises have gone a step further and have extracted formal education completely from their list of criteria, with Apple, Starbucks and DBS famously not requiring it. In many places, this has started with an experimental diversity goal in mind but it has proven to have multiple benefits and is a sign of an overall departure from conventional hiring practices.

As we said before, the World Economic Forum predicts that in the Age of AI, while 75 million jobs are to be axed, 113 million are to appear instead and one has to wonder, of these new jobs, how many will be based on the old definitions of skills and knowledge versus the ones that will require our humanity and the bevvy of 'soft skills' this entails.

If a few years ago it was the staple of a hippie leadership retreat, the discourse around the importance of emotional intelligence, growth mindset, empathy and purpose is finally becoming mainstream and there are more and more studies cropping up to support it. This is, nonetheless, only the beginning of a long arduous road for even the best-intentioned of companies as our work culture is not best equipped to search for, grow or even accommodate 'soft' skills.

Technical knowledge can be acquired easily and is ultimately a cheap commodity to those who have the curiosity, the drive and the motivation to pursue it. And arguably those who possess the wisdom and focus to weed through the information inflation this era of data inflicted upon us all. Nonetheless, training to the detriment of uniquely human attributes in an era where the most basic of chatbots can replicate it is a highly dangerous strategy. Showing empathy and compassion, striving for growth, having a purpose, true flexibility, the agility of the mind and of the process, believing in the shared vision, having the flexibility to apply new lenses and change courses, always striving for better, a relentless quest to attain higher peaks, missions focus, kindness, intuition, EQ scores ... that's what we need to search for when we search for the best.

Feelings at Work

To get to all the magic we require out of our humans at work, we need to give our workers many things, from genuinely flexible working environments to new ways of work to natural light, childcare, small surprising perks, psychologically safe teams, leadership that is inspiring and helpful, etc., but most importantly, we have to give them permission to feel and be human in the organization.

This lack of permission is an integral part of my concept of Human Debt. Being intensely human at work was never even acceptable or tolerated, leave alone encouraged. For the most part in the workplace, we are faced with the eerie and unexamined convention that being professional equates to being unemotional. That emotions have no place in a serious workplace and they ought to be checked out at the door by any employee. This is, of course, ridiculous and impossible. Humans can no sooner turn feelings off than they can stop breathing and all this nonsense accomplished was to train us all to feign a lack of feelings, fake insensitivity and see us 'do the robot', where we pretend we are devoid of feelings and natural human reactions. A charade that became the norm in nary all incumbent enterprises and has only been challenged in the past 10–15 years when cultures were built from the ground up and devoid of Human Debt in the digital elite.

IQ vs EQ

Despite being first mentioned in the 1960s, the term EQ was popularized by Daniel Goleman in his book *Emotional Intelligence* in the mid-1990s and it has then faced arguably modest amounts of research. Consider the fact that despite having been established as a term 40 years ago, emotional intelligence benefits from only one main test (MSCEIT – The Mayer-Salovey-Caruso Emotional Intelligence Test, which is a test measuring an individual's abilities to perceive, comprehend, act on, and manage emotional information) and even this one is highly disputed and criticized. Meanwhile its counterpart, IQ, sports hundreds of standardized terms.

Interestingly, the reason for this lies both in the insufficient body of study and in the fact that any testing to check the ability of a subject to recognize and name emotions or behaviours relies on conventional agreements of a complex nature, from language and terminology to social contracts.

While many flavours exist, the definitions of EQ revolve around the ability one has to know themselves and others enough to recognize emotions in both and use that knowledge to inform their thinking and behaviour. Therefore it stands to reason that having this ability is paramount not only to be a leader but to remain a competitively employed human in the near future. Then the question has to become: 'Can we train or better EQ?'

Over my career, I've never wanted to 'end up being about the fluffy stuff'. I gravitated towards technology, I built products, I ran teams and developed a fetish for Agile methods, all to avoid having to focus too deeply and delve too seriously into 'the feels'. Being on the autistic spectrum myself, I always thought that if only all the answers lay in the technology we employ, it would be *so* much easier!

I struggled with how mainstream media portrays EQ as being conventionally inaccessible to the autistic mind and knowing I am on the spectrum myself, I simply presumed I would score low on empathy and ability to intuitively recognize emotions and presumed that that's the sum total of my capabilities on the matter. Like many techies, I was even a little bit proud of being emotionally tone deaf at times.

I admit, former Mrs 'Emotional Banking' wanted as little to do with emotions and as much to do with technology as the world of FinTech (Financial Technology) allowed. Which is painfully plenty. So believe me, I get it. Examining the intangible – and what less tangible is there than human feelings? – is unsettling and the road to making the conclusions useful is treacherous. Not for the faint of heart, that's for sure. Not for the security seekers either. Unless you're willing to take risks, you can't do an honest open exploration of anything.

My eyes were opened to the possibility of training EQ in recent years when I noticed how, highly improbable as it would be, my little boy was a mini emotional Einstein and an extreme empath despite being autistic.

My kid is 10. Everyone's brood is their dynamo for accomplishing anything and mine is no exception – gaining his approval gets me out of bed at 4.45 a.m. most mornings and sadly, he has a raised bar in terms of what it takes to be impressed with his mum – gone are the days when he would have been tickled pink by a webinar or a radio interview. Since the *Emotional Banking* book was published, he expects uber-excellence, which is equal parts exhausting and insanely motivating.

Partly because of the book and his interest in my work and partly because, having recognized early that he is also on the spectrum, I have focused on giving him clarity on emotions in their definitions and usage. This education landed on what should have been barren terrain in terms of EQ and empathy, as it would have done for anyone on the spectrum, but in his case, it hasn't been like that. A sponge for every morsel of information he spent time observing and distilling and even though he is considerably more inclined to analyse feelings in others rather than himself, he is now somewhat of a little Rain Man of emotions. He recognizes them with uncanny clarity for an autistic kid, he enquires about them all the time and they are now clearly his 'special interest', which can be a powerful and lasting driving force in non-neurotypical individuals.

Like him, many autistic individuals, in fact, have plenty of affective empathy (being able to instinctively have an appropriate emotional response to someone else's thinking or feeling) and they may indeed struggle with cognitive empathy (being able to recognize that someone is indeed having a feeling) but only if they are not curriculum accessing and able to take in learnings or become interested, which seems to have been his case.

I believe that as we learn more about the levels of the spread of autism in our society, where there is currently a vast amount of underreporting and lack of diagnosis for high-functioning, well-adjusted, high-achieving people on the spectrum, we will start unlocking more of the mechanisms we can use to help everyone train themselves to recognize emotions, even if this initially comes with a degree of difficulty to them.

As for my kid – here's the kicker – I wish I could tell him to 'get into something else' like any good parent who hears their progeny express interest in their firmly vocational career. The artist guiding their kids towards medical school, the footballer nudging their kids towards law, the singer hoping theirs will go into accounting. The reason being that in wanting what's best for one's child, one hopes they will choose easier paths and guaranteed payoffs from sure, stable lines of work, of course.

In my case, more than the examples above, there's a world of exact science to be the opposite of what uncomfortable sea of unknowns about individuals, teams and organizational feelings and dynamics that we examine every day at PeopleNotTech so surely, every time he mentions my passing of the baton (and unsettlingly, he does that a lot), I should immediately redirect – but is that still the wise and caring thing to do? What should he do that, when he grows up, would give him guaranteed shelter from:

Empathy
Intuition
Common sense

and

Emotions?

If the advent of AI is as fast and dangerous as the tin-foiled heads of billionaires sometimes herald it, shouldn't we immediately safeguard by teaching our kids and ourselves how to do more of our only competitive advantage? Feel?

While the time frame is disputable and we're still smarting from how slow flying-cars are to arrive, it's also likely that at least half our young kids' professional lives will take place in a world where the jobs we see today will not exist. Asking them to train to be an accountant is conceivably no more useful to them than having them learn how to drive horse-drawn trams.

His father wants him to follow in his footsteps and become a programmer. Really? Are humans the ones best poised in cornering that trade as compared to their counterparts in the next 30 years? – save of course for the jobs where they guard the red button that will keep them from overpowering humanity, etc. Once we shortlist what the robots can and will have a monopoly on, we should next wonder, what are the jobs that will remain irreplaceably human?

None exclusively so, of course. All professions rely on hard data and science and those bits will indisputably be replaced by AI faster than we can say 'episode of Netflix's *Black Mirror*' but most – or arguably all – lines of work have an element of being human baked in. It can be found in our passion for the job, in having and using our sixth-sense based hypothesis to innovate, in how we see the bigger purpose and tap on a myriad of motivators to achieve it, and in how we care deeply about other people around us. That is the real competitive advantage and the hopefully irreplaceable secret sauce that we need to hold onto for as long as we can and push our little Sarahs and Jimmys towards.

Not what profession to choose, but how to invest themselves in it once they do. How to apply themselves fully, how to learn to understand emotions in themselves and others, how to go with their gut and have the courage and flexibility to do so, how to be open-minded and even more open-hearted and understanding, and ultimately, how to feel.

I put it to us all that letting our kids spend 20+ years in school learning all of the hard facts and none of the tools to deal with the soft, fluffy bits is at best, irresponsible. This ailment of not encouraging 'the feels' is unsustainable for any industry and should our education not understand that and reform to focus around 'soft skills' and EQ then our kids won't be competitive.

And if it is possible to educate EQ in our kids, is it possible to instil it in our employees as well?

It is.

Understanding our emotions and those of others – which is the basis of EQ – is highly trainable and it starts with education. Sheer awareness is spectacularly effective in particular as once people start learning, they immediately connect the dots to their own feelings. In other words, putting names on emotions and comprehending their mechanisms, in general, is the first and most efficient step in recognizing them in our own selves. Between the external awareness and then the self-awareness, a practice of focusing on them encompasses higher EQ.

Furthermore, if we are to start working on it intently and early enough, will we then have young employees entering the workforce with a completely different view of what is 'soft' and what is important, who will be so much better equipped to interrelate with their colleagues and understand healthy dynamics and ways to stimulate them?

The leaders of teams in most industries are often professionals who are subject matter experts and have risen through the managerial ranks to now be in charge of people. It's rare that anyone is in a role that was exclusively managerial to begin with, and if they are, they are likely poorly equipped to empathize due to the lack of practical experience. By the same token they are highly intelligent and motivated individuals who genuinely want the best for their teams and want to do their best work so chances are, once we start exposing them to the right permission and the right information, they will take to it fast and start developing their people practice.

Our mission in making the PS Works Team Solution at PeopleNotTech is easy – increase the Psychological Safety of teams so they can become highly performant. As explained in previous chapters, we measure their current state, we diagnose their current situation and arrive at a snapshot showing where they are at any particular time in their team's life. Now to steer behaviours, and apply any helpful interventions to move the team towards acquiring more Psychological Safety, the data needs to be read and understood so it informs next best actions.

The software will then take this data and based on it, automatically suggest some courses of action, tips and best practices, but they can't even begin to emulate the creative solutions a well-intentioned leader would be able to offer to see their team's well-being increase. Nothing, not even an external coach or advisor, can replace it. No one knows them better; no one is more invested. The only sine qua non condition for that leader is to have a high degree of EQ to 'see' their people.

An EQed leader could in fact 'read' the data as well as the software could and add their creativity and innovative spirit to the different ideas of betterment or even take the problems to the team so they solve them together. The only trouble? Most of the people using our software were in no way high on the EQ side so reading the data was not an easy task. We substituted that by us telling them what to do next for a long while until a time that it occurred to us it was a classic fish vs fishing rod case. That indeed, if we believed EQ could be improved and understanding emotions was trainable, then we should instead guide them to learn to interpret the data they see, so we constructed a feature called 'EQ Trainer' that helps them better focus on the topics that matter and over time gives them the neural pathways to become their own coaches. As with everything else in our software, it's early days, but we would love to one day contribute our findings to proving substantial improvement in EQ for team leaders.

Courage and Vulnerability

One of the most powerful and beautiful ideas of the last few years is that of the importance of courage and of its manifestation – 'vulnerability' – and we owe the democratization of the topic to the inimitable Brené Brown. Her deeply relatable, clear and searing work is so efficient that at the end of a handful of methods of dissemination – a few books, chief among which *Dare to Lead* and *Daring Greatly*, and a very successful few TED Talks, execs everywhere are now at least somewhat familiar with the idea that leadership requires true courage and that, as opposed to what they had been conditioned to believe, demonstrating it requires no posturing, macho-displays or demonstrations of force but instead requires them to demonstrate something entirely different: vulnerability.

They now know that to lead and inspire in lieu of command and control they have to find within themselves the resources to bare it all and be unprecedentedly open, dropping all their defence in front of their teams, however public and however frightening that would be.

Brené's message resonates so powerfully that her talk about vulnerability and bravery, entitled 'The Call to Courage', has even been picked up by Netflix as the only semi-business talk they show on their channel. The reason why Professor Brown was so successful in the messaging has to do with how she has managed to remove the stigma commonly associated with 'vulnerability' that equated it to 'weakness'. She has been able to deconstruct the misconception and show that it is, in fact, the very opposite – the more able you are to be vulnerable, the stronger you are in actuality as it often requires going against the need to impression manage and all types of other self-protectionist measures.

Raising our EQ, learning about our emotions and the emotions of others as well as practising to increase our ability to be compassionate will, in fact, render most people to report feeling a lot more vulnerable and exposed. Learning how to deal with the discomfort of that is a courageous act that's deeply inspiring to their people though and transforms them from managers to true leaders by demonstrating extreme amounts of courage that people want to follow and model themselves against.

Doing something despite a perceived risk is the definition of what courage means. The greater the risk, the greater the needed amount of courage and the more emotional energy we need to dispense to act. Some of the determination on the nature and size of the risk happens at a subconscious level, where we decide on the next course of action without perceiving it as rational thought. Most of all acts we do every day have at one time required a dose of courage to go through and have since become automated as the risk was reassessed and the reward was clarified together with the method of acquiring it. These formed paths for our trivial daily tasks as well as informed our general appetite for risk and associated ability to be brave.

If we consider courage in general and the things we commonly associate with it, we never refer to these semi-automated moments but instead to invariably majestic, heroic examples of monumental acts big enough to write a movie script around. The savings, the self-sacrifices, the leaps of faith. No songs exist about the micro-acts that make day-to-day life. The times when we draw breath and still do the things we have to despite every instinct screaming against it – when we cross the street in a hurry, when we enter a conversation while waiting in a queue, when we go for the colourful shirt or make eye-contact on a tube train. So many things we need to be ballsy for. When we ask for that raise, tell the truth when it doesn't suit us, admit a mistake, ask for help, learn something new, change course or keep the course.

Modelling plays a big part in diminishing the perception of the risk and when it comes to bravery in our personal lives we have a lot of examples to draw on, ranging from common sense and folklore to Hollywood movies and all the Russian literature we can handle, but when it comes to professional examples there's precious little to cast our minds to.

So yes, courage ranges from minuscule everyday acts to – in the context of Psychological Safety and the reason we obsessively measure it – the conscious choice to always be honest, engaged in the dialogue and not holding back, and it culminates with modelling vulnerability. Nonetheless, irrespective of its incarnation and its dose, it is a sine qua non condition to being intensely human at work. Oh, and here's the thing: courage is not only necessary, beautiful to witness and inspiring, but it's awfully addictive. We all have that superhero under-armour that makes it feel darn good to let out, so loosen that tie and let it out, then reach over and tend to the tie of others in your own team-family so they too can breathe in and you can make heroic, ballsy and yet safe awesome things together.

Passion and Purpose

When it comes to discussing the topics of 'purpose' and 'passion', no one is more clear than motivational speaker and author Simon Sinek and his ability to focus on the 'why'. He talks about finding the reasoning behind the actions we do both as individuals and as teams or organizations to provide enough motivation and driving force to achieve our goals.

'Average companies give their people something to work on, innovative organizations give their people something to work towards,' he says, emphasizing the tremendous role having a shared vision plays. He goes on to advocate doing an honest and open personal exploration to find the deeply individual drivers we each have regarding the work that we do and suggests we keep those top of mind even if we don't share them in detail with the team. As such, any winning company would in effect be made up of a collection of individual 'whys' whether they are public or not, a strong team-level goal and an even clearer and more noble and exciting company-level purpose.

Changing the narrative to focus on intangible topics in lieu of numbers hasn't started with Sinek, but it has always been challenging even going as far back as to the originators of the concepts in the 70s, Richard Pascale and Tom Peters. The topics of 'purpose', 'vision' and 'mission' remained etched in the vocabulary of most companies but their relatability, their degree of truthfulness and ultimately the weight they carry is never easily quantifiable and many employees struggle to relate deeply and consistently to these 'company values' as they are meant to act as a motivational dynamo.

In 2016 the Global LinkedIn Report 'Purpose at Work' found people would pay money to gain purpose; that they would literally trade a portion of their salary to add more purpose to their work. That's the measure of how thirsty we are for a higher goal in our work life and yet companies we work for think the yearly shareholder press release should motivate us enough. Multiple other studies before it including HBR's 'The Attack on Pay', or Barnard's 1998 'What works in rewarding problem-solving teams?' showed that there is only a certain amount of motivation that can be affected monetarily. After a certain cut-off point, the only differentiator in adding and retaining talent is how good companies are at establishing and reinforcing a higher sense of purpose.

Even for the best-intentioned organizations, attaining company-level purpose is not easy. Often it requires a deep cultural change for the term to be taken seriously before it can become a serious objective and for the 'woke CxOs' – a 'Management Epic' if you wish.

Harder still, just as is the case with the permission, this is not a 'once and done' task as once defined, it has to be reinforced and the spark has to be reignited and that's no easy card to have – 'Jointly define the purpose, and ensure every employee has it ingrained, that they are truly, in their heart of hearts, and at all times, emotionally invested' – but it's important to say that the flames of the fire should be fanned not only by leadership but personal responsibility too and that is why smart companies invest in employees' own voices.

To gain or reinforce purpose employees have to have a firm eye on the goal for the end consumer. This is so often sorely missing from our work. How will what we make better anyone's life? How will it play into the end client's day-to-day?

With the advent of human-centred design, customers are regaining their central role in the proposition creation beyond the empty rhetorics of 'customer-centricity' of yesteryear, but if we want to let them take their rightful place as purpose drivers we must find ways to democratize the impetus behind human-centred design (HCD) and ensure it trickles through the entire organization.

This is where it all falls into place in the concept of Psychological Safety – once the team believes the collection of individual purposes rhymes and that they share the ultimate vision, mission or goal, they truly work 'from the same backlog' in the emotional sense and that's when team magic happens. As we all know, it's team magic that makes money for the company, so Psychological Safety is ultimately the ingredient we need to demonstrate the value of purpose to the bottom line.

Can We Do 'Empathy By Numbers?'

'When we are engaged in shared mind awareness, the possibilities for mutual aid and collaborative problem solving abound,' says Helen Reiss, MD, in her book, *The Empathy Effect*. Having and bettering empathy will become the number one skill that will keep people employable in the near future. That leaders ought to have it in spades, as it is the cornerstone to anything they do, and it's their gateway to creating happy, productive and psychologically safe teams, should go without saying.

But it doesn't.

No less because among all other wrongly labelled 'soft' skills, empathy is the most complex to define and construct. Depending on who you ask, there's even a degree of polemics when discerning between the concepts of 'empathy', 'sympathy' and 'compassion' and many argue the latter is the most involved of them all as compassion includes both 'awareness of suffering' and a sense of 'sharing' said suffering. We choose to ignore that debate and use them interchangeably. There is very little in the way of practical advice on how to create empathy but the little there is seems to require in-person interaction.

There are a few different ways of breaking down the types of empathy but one of the most intriguing models postulates that the following exist: Cognitive Empathy (the ability to intellectually comprehend the emotions of others, which incidentally includes self-knowledge as a prerequisite), Affective Empathy (the ability to emotionally relate to others) and Conative Empathy (the actions stemming from the mimicking type of deep relating that happens when we feel so connected to others we emulate their behaviour subconsciously, i.e. yawning).

The latter is the hardest of all three and whenever you hear of a team's magic serendipity with stories to suggest they share a mind or even a heart, such as what they exhibit in the army in heroic combat situations, they are displaying this type of deep empathy, which typically takes years to build and requires deep knowledge of each other.

To try and short-circuit that, the most efficient of exercises are based on some empathy-inducing exercises from the US Army and mostly revolve around improv and intelligent human closeness. When PeopleNotTech does workshops, it's a lot easier to employ those and almost force empathy, but seeing how the PS Works solution we make is a digital vehicle, and how many teams today work in a distributed, remote fashion, the challenge is tougher.

What we decided to focus on at first is how to improve Cognitive Empathy by teaching people how to recognize emotions and Affective Empathy by setting up monthly team challenges. We focus on gathering data regarding what each team needs and how each team leader acts, we analyse this behaviour data and we may suggest exercises to develop active listening, monitor sharing of emotional data (such as doing '1-high and 1-low' exercises periodically – say, incorporated in retros) or encourage emotions pattern recognition in our solution. We don't yet know which one of these interventions will have the best success rates but since we score leaders on empathy month on month, we'll likely start seeing patterns as to which is more efficient in making people more empathic.

In a former design sprint we even tested a children's emotions recognition app aimed to help kids – in particular those on the spectrum, who as established above traditionally struggle with this more than neurotypical children (much like software developers, some might argue!) – understand social cues, including facial expressions, body language, etc. We tested this with four different groups – two of which were children and two were adults, with different professional affinities – and we found that all groups scored better once they had had initial exposure to concepts and an educational injection.

Who reading this can't do better at putting themselves into someone else's shoes? And when our capacity to do our job productively and soon, of grabbing our job from the claws of automation, hinges on the hypothetical wear (and tear!) of those shoes, shouldn't we be eternally trying on a new pair?

Permission to be Human

As I was saying at the start of this chapter, there is no permission for any of this to be front of mind in most companies these days, except for the digital elite, where the permission is the number-one preoccupation.

In most places, if we are honest, spending time thinking, learning, questioning the purpose, examining trust, learning and contemplating moral values, working on ourselves to be better listeners and carers, doing any of our inner homework all seems so awfully self-indulgent and somewhat naughty to the average office worker as a result of the decades of drilling the opposite that it's easy to use as a good excuse for not doing it. It is as if the enterprise tells us, 'If you're going to breathe, meditate, think or feel, you need to do so on your own time buddy, at work you're only paid to show up, punch numbers and look semi-alive in meetings.'

That isn't what everyone 'hears' though.

'Consummate professionals' AKA 'smart grown-ups' at the top have always spent a lot more time doing the self-improvement work and being interested in these topics as they realized the need and the value, but this appetite and space for mindful betterment have traditionally never trickled down the ranks of the organization. Executives with individual coaches, flexible working schedules, decision autonomy, their Yoga teachers and their therapists aren't uncommon, but companies are awfully good at making it sound as if being a better version of yourself is only the apanage of the management layer and a luxury that can't or shouldn't be democratized.

Most times this is because it's a step too far removed from the current status quo to see how creating a focus on people topics that revolve around the emotions of individuals and the dynamic of teams can be introduced into the 'no emotions allowed' frozen tundra of most companies.

Should HR or any other well-intentioned exec or department do the legwork of finding proof points to bring back to the business to secure this permission to be human, they would be able to bring anything from Miao Qian's 'Leader Emotional Intelligence and Subordinate Job Satisfaction' from 2016 to even how Momm, Liu, Wihler, Kholin and Menges found that 'Emotions Recognition Indirectly Predicts Annual Income' in 2015, alongside a bevy of other Gallup and Forester studies over the year, showing the effects of reduced Human Debt in terms of happier, more engaged employees treated with respect.

The 'business case' for building Empathy, EQ, Purpose and Passion to build Psychologically Safe – and therefore high-performing – teams is patently clear and it all starts with allowing humanity and emotions back in the workplace with open arms.

The companies who have done so – Netflix, Google, Zappos – they all have had to overcome preconceived ideas of their workforce, who, coming from places where even saying the word 'emotion' was dangerous, had to learn to trust again and understand their humanity is now wanted and welcomed.

The work to affirm and reaffirm the permission to be human is likely to be extensive in most places and not a one-time project but a constant preoccupation at the organization level before we can hope to have changed people's minds about how being 'professional' is not contradictory to being 'human'.

The 'People Practice'

Presuming they'd want to and that they 'buy' this 'permission to be human', we assume everyone has the skill set to be a good leader and take care of their teams. We assume wrong. This anonymous play on words holds uncomfortable amounts of truth:

> This is a story about four people named Everybody, Somebody, Anybody and Nobody. There was an important job to be done and Everybody was asked to do it. Everybody was sure Somebody would do it. Anybody could have done it, but Nobody did it. Somebody got angry about that because it was Everybody's job. Everybody thought Anybody could do it but Nobody realized that Everybody wouldn't do it. It ended up that Everybody blamed Somebody when Nobody did what Anybody could have done.

The big job at hand, and it is one for *all* of us, including the numbers guys and the hardened programmer guys and the battle-scarred ops and security guys, is to increase our own EQ and obsess about the team, not because it's a nice thing to have, but because it's a mandatory element of success. To recognize and improve our own emotional state and that of our people. To create well-being by being open and enabling others to open up. To reaffirm direction and purpose by holding transparency and inspiration dear. To keep learning and incite curiosity in our team. To seek, to create and innovate. To not cringe around nebulous, fluffy stuff. To excite. To carry. To ignite. To focus. To demand. To understand. To push and pull. To feel and let feel. To be intensely, comfortably and safely human.

And they should 'want to' because, whatever used to be the 'day job', it is no longer that as soon as someone is meant to be a leader, be it a CEO or the line manager of two. None of the initial set of skills that an individual had previously been hired for is even remotely of any importance as compared to understanding that their number one priority now is to avail themselves of the permission to be human, focus on their own EQ and start constructing their 'people practice'.

Most times this will consist of understanding some principles such as the importance of Psychological Safety and that of obsessing over the well-being of each and every individual as the manner in which a team leader decides to deliver on these, and what collection of tools and habits they implement to satisfy it can and should be a matter of personal choice. In other words, how often they keep in touch with their people, what they keep an eye on from the components of Psychological Safety in their teams and the interventions they put in place to improve performance by affecting behaviour are less important than the practice of incorporating all those into the day-to-day to the detriment of what used to be their conventional hard-skills-based job description.

Beyond the Team

From an individual perspective, recognizing the importance of EQ, empathy and anything else we call 'soft skills' for your own development is paramount in terms of future-proofing one's employment. If we want to remain competitive in the job market for the remainder of our careers, there will be no escaping investing in the above.

Doing the work will not be comfortable but it will be undoubtedly valuable. Getting in the gym midway through life after a youth spent on good times filled with takeaways and pints is never easy or joyous. It's painful and demoralizing and so uncomfortable it makes you question the meaning of life on an hourly basis but it's undoubtedly necessary for survival.

There's no contest that getting our bodies healthy is hygiene and thankfully, the same acceptance is starting to apply to having our minds healthy as well, and finally, the same work needs to be invested in bettering our EQ to be a better team leader and a better employee.

From an organizational perspective, the way to both find 'talent' and train EQ must be thought of. In some companies, this is well embedded at a basal, DNA, cultural level, but in most, it requires a huge shift in mentality, both to seek it and to learn to develop it and demonstrate permission.

In terms of finding readily-EQed individuals, this can be almost impossible. There are few schools out there that do anything at all to prepare future professionals and future leaders in particular for the task at hand by honing their Emotional Intelligence – certainly no six-month course in empathy or even a week-long seminar in interpreting emotional states of yourself and others that I've ever heard of. As a result, recruitment is utterly failing in selecting talented individuals on the matter. 'Being good with people' or having 'people skills' is a nebulous nice-to-have afterthought on job specs everywhere and with such low entry standards and a complete focus on the matter that would at least enable people to develop, there is little progress on the way.

Reclaiming our humanity in the workplace will take sustained effort. To learn how to listen to our emotions in lieu of ignoring them, to remember it's OK and desirable to open-heartedly listen to the voices of others, to give ourselves permission to have reactions and emotions and be a better team member or leader for it. Most importantly, to feel you have space, resources and permission to work on yourself, all of that is as uncomfortable as any sudden betterment work.

The beauty of doing work on ourselves work-wise – learning, increasing our EQ, growing our capacity for empathy, starting to listen to our intuition and just overall being better at being human at work – is that everyone wins once it happens. Starting with the undeserving, short-sighted, P&L-driven enterprise as productivity goes up, but above all, the employees who are then starting on the true self-value-creation work, where they make themselves invaluably irreplaceable by either machines or the slackers who didn't put in the hours to work on being human.

CHAPTER SEVEN

What Happens Next and the Post-Pandemic World of Work

- The 2020 Pandemic
- Remote vs Flexible (Where vs How)
- Designing the New Reality Together
- The Effects of the Sudden Shift to Remote
- Remote and the Work/Life Balance
- Productivity and Performance in the VUCA Digital World During a Global Recession
- The Post-Pandemic World of Work
- What's Next for Work and Teams?

The 2020 Pandemic

The COVID-19 (or coronavirus) pandemic needs no introduction to those of us reading this as it is perhaps the biggest historical event we will ever have to live through. Having reportedly originated in Wuhan in December 2019, by July 2020 it had infected 10 million people and swept through the population of 188 countries resulting in over 500,000 deaths.

Economically, the initial effects of the pandemic reverberated stronger than any other event of its kind due to the protective governmental lockdowns imposed all over the world and the way they reflected in changing work behaviours and then in the inevitable period of deep economic recession that followed.

To remain focused on the levers of change, this chapter is an analysis of the workforce segments which remained employed at the end of those initial trials and tribulations and were, therefore, the teams considered fortunate even if the spectre of the millions that weren't so lucky and became unemployed remained ever-present and reflected in the way they performed.

The effects of the pandemic on the world of work are maybe best summarized by an iconic meme that flooded social media in the first half of 2020, which looked like a mini-survey where the question was 'Who led the digital transformation of your company?' and the options provided were a) The CEO; b) The CTO; c) COVID-19.

The reason why this proved as popular as it was is that anyone exposed to the terms of 'digital transformation' over the years knew that a solid reform of the ways of work was long overdue to accommodate the speed of technology and the demands of the consumer, yet the progress up until the virus crisis was maddeningly slow, whereas once Working From Home (WFH) became mandated by the governmental lockdowns around the world, it all changed overnight.

The same incumbent companies who had spent considerable amounts of effort and money on running risk audits and feasibility studies regarding the tools and processes needed to move towards remote work in light of how they could see the monetary and productivity benefits that the early adopters were achieving, and had either shelved the findings and postponed any action or even concluded it to be impossible, were now forced to do it anyhow.

The pandemic was a time of monumental shifts. Some potentially unconnected, such as the Black Lives Matter protests of June 2020 following the police's killing of George Floyd in Minneapolis, but many others, such as the larger appetite for social and economic reform regarding most issues, including racism and discrimination and climate change, could well be traced to how it constituted a time of collective pause and reboot. Nonetheless, the work arena is the domain where the pandemic has left the most significant and lasting change.

Before 2020, for years most companies had flirted with the concepts of flexible working and remote working and the relationship between the two but despite lip service, the overall feeling remained that business was best (or 'exclusively') done in person. Being able to look into someone's eyes and shake their hand either in a day-to-day meeting, a sales opportunity, or in the networking section of an event had long been regarded as the only truly valuable type of interaction that ought to speed up relationship creation and therefore give us the results we needed.

Equally, being in the same room was seen as paramount to most teams working together on joint projects and despite the rhetoric and the many studies that came out in recent years, it was often evident that while the nature of work no longer demanded it (or really, even permitted it), our ingrained perception of what is 'valuable' still relied largely on the physicality and the proximity.

The research in support of online meetings (arguably the ones based on regularity, common purpose, empathy and the perennial presence of the much-debated video interaction) being as good as a live meeting was starting to emerge, but it was still relatively obscure and even if the statistical data would unequivocally prove it, the underlying feeling at the start of the pandemic for most professionals, who had spent tens of years interacting differently, was that online communication in all its forms was just an inferior means of relating with both business prospects and colleagues.

By the end of 2020 video had become the accepted norm for most interactions, both internal and external, in the workplace. This ushered in a whole set of interesting queries regarding the nature and manner of communication, and opened up some subjects that had previously been overlooked around the physical projection of self (for example, wearing a tie and tennis shorts became commonplace, as did the understanding that some meetings were 'internal-AKA-make-up-free', etc). New rules regarding turn-taking became a natural extension of the environment. Maybe the most valuable consequence of this greater understanding towards the remote distribution of teams has been towards how, in the subsequent hybrid model, many companies insisted on the rule of 'if one is remote then ALL are remote'. This means that if one team member is not in the room and is dialling in virtually, even if everyone else is available in person they ought to all still dial in from their machines to equalize the playing field and allow for true dialogue. This eliminated one of the main impediments in getting distributed teams to have a strong team dynamic previously, because having some people on the periphery, unsuccessfully attempting to participate in the team dialogue, is always disastrous.

At the beginning of the pandemic crisis, conferences and events still regarded content and knowledge dissemination and creation as secondary to the networking side of things (and with select exceptions such as events that allow innovative design-based spaces, the value of the corridor-bump was highly exaggerated, but rarely questioned) and organizations everywhere struggled with the practicalities of cross-departmental 'Spotify-like' teams that had to be created cross geographies and these inabilities collectively were some of the biggest barriers to adopting the new ways of work and creating Agile, Lean or DevOps teams.

A few weeks into the pandemic, most Silicon Valley giants were quick to declare their hand regarding remote work, with Twitter and Square being among the first to make optional remote working the default. Cost-wise, preliminary studies showed that closing offices was counterintuitively not, in fact, going to mean a huge cost reduction when companies needed to augment home working instead in terms of kitting out home offices, retraining and tooling their remote workforce while still maintaining enough satellite offices to allow them physical spaces to come together, should they need it (the hybrid model) but some companies saw the talent opportunities in the shift.

When it emerged that 50 per cent of Facebook's workforce could permanently shift to remote working in the next 5–10 years, CEO Mark Zuckerberg told employees in May 2020: 'This is probably overdue. Over the past few decades, economic growth in the US has been quite concentrated, with major companies often hiring in a handful of metropolitan areas. That means we've been missing out on a lot of talented people just because they happen to live outside a major hub.'

Alongside the practicalities, a more important side effect was the sudden opening in the dialogue regarding people at work brought about by the sudden shift to remote. Issues that had previously been treated as inconsequential and were never considered priority, such as the mental health of individuals and the teams' degree of engagement, all of sudden came sharply into focus when the workforce was no longer under watchful eyes and when everything had changed.

Remote vs Flexible (Where vs How)

One of the most common misconceptions that impeded this dialogue was that the concepts of 'remote work', 'working from home' and 'flexible working' are one and the same. Not the case. While the first two may be synonymous in the pandemic context (but not necessarily outside of it), 'remote' and 'flexible' are in no way interchangeable. In fact, the remote character is but one of the aspects of flexible and firmly contained in the concept.

Flexible working refers to work that is performed differently than traditional on-site or office work, and it refers to both the location and the manner of said work. Not exclusively discussing either one or the other, the location and the process are both contained in the topic.

Included in it, concepts such as part-time work, term work (during school terms), job sharing, output-based working (one of the most interesting concepts that many companies will have to pay attention to in the coming years), compressed hours (such as the experiments on the four-day working week in New Zealand in 2018 that showed a 20 per cent increase in productivity) and the most interesting of them all – flexitime, which is the concept that allows employees to choose when to begin and end work within certain set limits that are mutually agreed with the employer.

Each of the variations in the type of work mentioned above come with substantial amounts of research that support their efficiency and their ability to increase productivity by staggering amounts, starting at 30 per cent in most surveys. Broken down into why, the main reason is a huge increase in employee satisfaction, engagement and therefore performance, but also the fact that they reduce attrition and sick days that were previously overwhelmingly connected to work-related stress, anxiety or depression. Nonetheless, in the context of the pandemic, the only change discussed and enforced when COVID-19 changed the world had been in relation to the location of work exclusively. In other words, none of the necessary discovery, research, design and negotiation that ought to have happened went into figuring out any of the other variations on the set model of office. This amounted to throwing ex-office workers off the deep end with no real training in how to translate their work to WFH, and no real advice on how to avoid its many pitfalls.

Chief among them, a feeling of continuous availability towards the household and work became highly taxing and made many feel inadequate no matter what they tried and how much more they worked to satisfy both parties. In the absence of any clearly set, intentional personal boundaries, they quickly reached burnout levels without much of a platform to express it due to the situation and against a background of ever-increasing lack of job security.

Once again, those workers who already had a remote work practice pre-pandemic were favoured in the lockdown context as they had previously been able to develop their work process to take into account a multitude of factors to ensure they remain productive and many had, in fact, a flexible working practice as dictated by experience. Most of those who were suddenly remote, though, were given no guidance in terms of creating their own schedules and trying to observe their own patterns to be sustainable in working from home. They instead simply had to clear a space in their house, from which they started being pulled into a never-ending succession of meetings and Zoom calls, topped off with endless email chains and confusion. Home schooling was added to the schedule of many, thereby further complicating their situation.

This just about worked for the short term as enterprise and workers alike believed the situation to be temporary, but as the weeks extended into months, it became clear for everyone involved that it could no longer be treated as an extreme measure but as a way of life. As such, a couple of months into forced lockdown, the first questions around sustainability and with them, of individual limits and physical and mental constraints, surfaced and an honest conversation started emerging online. Unfortunately, this coincided with a discourse about a potential 'return to the office' – before the dust seemed to settle around a hybrid model of the future – and, with the emergence of news about the extreme recession which followed, it made many of the honest conversations around the 'why' and the 'how' of flexible work once more become confined around the 'where' and an even more poignant and ever-terrifying 'if'.

When the enormous potential scale of the recession became clear in the second part of 2020, few people were willing to speak about their own limits and demand respect and care from an organization when they were overwhelmed with gratitude that they even had a job. When you spend your entire time working double time from a paralyzing fear of being disposable, you don't demand the thinking necessary to find what are the best times and ways in which you'll be at your most productive, on the contrary. Added to this, for most households where there were single parents or even two parents with full-time jobs and children, the workload was indescribably heavy when it became clear that the lockdown was not in place for a week or two, but instead, ended up expanding over many months in some cases.

At first, childcare and home schooling were surprisingly little discussed in any meaningful fashion, beyond a flurry of memes and the occasional opinion piece bemoaning some humorous situation, but it stands to reason that they would have had a greater collective hardship effect than we imagined at the time, and certainly added to the overall issues with burnout and mental health – and therefore productivity – in the long run. As time passed, the concern became more vivid.

Faced with the added pressure of housework and home schooling, many parents found themselves overcompensating if they were lucky enough to have a flexible work arrangement, by working into (or starting in) the wee hours. Which of course increased the risk of burnout sharply, in particular as most teams had been left to their own devices with no clear communication, no policy and no guidance in most enterprises. It wasn't until the summer of 2020 that some of these started to emerge and that the dust started to settle on the models of the 'new normal'.

Empirically, we all noticed that high-performers were likely suffering the most as they went from excelling at their professional roles to being subpar in their role as a teacher, with rampant levels of impostor syndrome when they had to sneak Google searches under the table while appearing even remotely authoritative. In addition, the usual 'working mum guilt' was now extended to parents of any gender (although it's likely that if anyone were to check, more women were taking on the home-schooling workload than men during the pandemic, regardless of their own work situations) as they became increasingly exhausted and felt like they were playing catch-up, battling incipient forms of both 'survival guilt' and 'impostor syndrome' as a teacher and as a worker.

Designing the New Reality Together

At various points in 2020, it became clear for companies that wanted success that the future of work should undoubtedly start with a co-creation and design session, where everyone talks openly about what works for them in the context of achieving high performance. That wasn't a dialogue that existed before the COVID-19 crisis and due to how the transition to remote happened – forced, sudden and by mandate, not by design – most struggled to collaborate in this defining moment.

Despite how surveys such as 'People and the Bottom Line' (2018, Institute For Employment Studies & The Work Foundation or 'People And The Bottomline' or 'The Future of Work: Jobs and Skills In 2030' (2014, UKCES) had all suggested that flexible working needed to be investigated and carefully designed for higher collaboration and better innovation results, the main assumption we had collectively challenged pre-pandemic had been reduced to merely the utility of having individual offices inside the office building and even there, it seemed we had had one big moment of questioning followed by the wrong assumption – open-plan offices rule! – and then no correction once that had been debunked scientifically. Study after study, such as Ethan S. Bernstein and Stephen Turban's Harvard-commissioned 'The Impact of "Open" Workspaces on Human Collaboration' and others, had clearly shown that open-plan offices create toxic workplaces, uncollaborative workers hated them and they brought down productivity.

In every other area, on any other coordinate of work in the office, the assumptions abounded, and the open dialogue needed to remove bias and misconception was completely absent.

In a research paper from the Federal Reserve Bank of Atlanta, employees reported they would like 40 per cent of their working days to be WFH, whereas polling their employers revealed they assumed that appetite to be at 20 per cent so they were planning for that proportion.

It is worth pointing out an interesting phenomenon – for every example of policy and new ways of work bravery that emerged in the early days of the pandemic, there was also a corresponding seemingly cautionary take from the top management. As an example, while Microsoft was one of the first companies to announce remote working almost as soon as COVID-19 hit, in April of 2020, CEO Satya Nadella told *The New York Times*, '[W]hat I miss is when you walk into a physical meeting, you are talking to the person that is next to you, you're able to connect with them for the two minutes before and after.'

The origin of the apparent dissonance between the public declarations and the executive's rhetoric is not necessarily a signal that they are 'saying one thing and thinking or doing another' for PR reasons but rather the fact that remote working translated in very different ways at an individual level, with every type of personal preference and personality type represented from those who immediately loved it to those who hated it, and that the executives themselves were experiencing it in their own individual fashion and then projected that stance on their entire workforce.

Once this became clear, many rushed to map personality types to preferences regarding the location of work and make generalizations based on what they thought held true.

Perhaps the most important advice, however, is for leaders to recognize that remote working will affect each member of staff differently, including themselves. It is therefore crucial that managers recognize their own styles of working as to not impose their preferred work patterns onto employees. In turn, if employees understand how they work to the best of their ability, they are better equipped to cope with remote working. By understanding what strategies work for them, how they can best switch off, avoid information overload, set boundaries and find a form of work-life balance that suits them, they can reduce their stress levels, which will in turn help to combat the rise in stress during this difficult time.

J. Hackston, Head of Thought Leadership at The Myers-Briggs Company

To avoid such glaring generalizations, all we can still do in every enterprise, in every company irrespective of size, is to ask. To genuinely poll our employees in the most open-ended of ways to find out where they stand on the spectrum described above and then work out the best ways to cater to all those eventualities.

The other great misconception in the discussion on remote and flexible work was that these considerations should only be relevant for technology-driven companies whereas during the pandemic this hasn't appeared to be the case. Take these findings from 'The Future of Work: Work from Home Preparedness and Firm Resilience During the COVID-19 Pandemic Study' (2 June 2020, John (Jianqiu) Bai, Northeastern University, D'Amore-McKim School of Business, Wang Jin, Massachusetts Institute of Technology (MIT), Sebastian Steffen, MIT Sloan School of Management, Chi Wan, University of Massachusetts Boston):

Companies with high WFH index values have higher stock returns, lower return volatility, and better financial performance during the pandemic. Contrary to conventional wisdom, our results hold primarily in non-high-tech industries.

In the years following the pandemic, to succeed with the new reality of remote and flexible working, the need remains in every industry for robust dialogue with the employee and to find effective ways to truly co-create the 'how' of work in lieu of executives' personal feelings or outdated generalizations.

The Effects of the Sudden Shift to Remote

Much of the chances of eventual success any enterprise had during the pandemic hinged largely on the teams' previous levels of Psychological Safety, how tight they already were, how resilient, how in-built courage was and whether they already had a culture of speaking up. So, for the teams that were scoring high, this period, even if it brought about a highly unsettling sudden move to remote, proved to be reaffirming and strengthening.

And then there were those teams that may not have been as strong on Psychological Safety, but were well versed in remote and by luck also had a secure economic position and therefore some degree of job security. They were also fortunate enough to have had a highly EQed leader, who quickly honed their people practice. These teams had a good chance to hold on tight to each other and build in Psychological Safety even if in some cases they didn't even know its name.

The rest were in a place between fear and paralysis, between doing their best in the new eerie environment and with the ask they understood was asked of them, while operating under extreme uncertainty and avoiding rocking the boat – therefore, not speaking up and impression managing like never before on and off video calls, trying desperately to appear competent and in control. Consequently never raising opposing viewpoints or daring to admit any failure or question any decision. And therefore dropping what little Psychological Safety magic they may have had to begin with. A drop that would then start to show in performance.

Even teams that were already remote had not escaped the extreme nature of the lockdown and were not sailing breezily through it, chiefly as the nature of their WFH efforts before isolation had been fundamentally different than they were in lockdown.

'The situation in which we are all working remote is not a normal situation,' said Kieran Snyder, CEO of Textio, a Seattle startup that uses AI to augment writing. 'Everybody's carrying so much more stress. If it's a difference between choosing to work at home today, but then you still head to the gym, you head to the grocery store, you go see your friends at night for dinner, [it's] really different than what's happening right now where everyone's trapped in their homes.'

Since this extreme situation caused by the pandemic constituted many employees' first experience of remote, it may well have resulted in making them less enthusiastic about WFH in general, whereas those who had already done it before recognized that the negative aspects were largely connected to the 'cabin fever' and 'lack of freedom', not remote working in itself.

Across the board, there was evident suffering in terms of mental health all through the isolation period and through the extreme shift in work habits. From the very beginning of the pandemic, studies (such as Brooks, Webster, Smith et al., February 2020) reported a bevy of negative psychological effects, from anger to anxiety and confusion to signs of post-traumatic stress disorder (PTSD) emerging in everyone living through these difficult times.

As we saw in 'What Psychological Safety is *Not*' (*see also* p. 102), there is a serious distinction between the mental health and well-being of the individual and the term of Psychological Safety as it refers to the desired behaviours of high-performing teams, but the conflation of the terms has become naturally more pronounced during the pandemic crisis when the lack of perceived safety at an individual level becomes clear and unbearable to all.

While they cannot be completely separated – the team is after all a collection of individuals and if each and every one of them is suffering to a degree or other from a mental health point of view, it stands to reason that their interaction cannot help but reflect that and suffer as well. They are ill-served by being shoved in the same ideological bucket and would be much better helped by forensic and clear distinction.

The mental health of each and every person living through the pandemic was affected to one degree or another, yes, and what we need to do is recognize that, discuss it and provide support as communities, employers and as our own selves. Short of offering every employee emotional support through a coach or therapist, which was neither economically viable nor really an evident moral imperative as the situation unfolded, there was little that companies could have done to have prevented the mental health epidemic to follow other than maybe to use their team leaders to fulfil that role where possible.

Nonetheless, at an individual level, honing resilience techniques and practising self-care was extremely necessary and useful and many team leaders worth their People Practice salt would have recognized this and spent time making sure some of these ideas were in place for their team members with the help of the many touching offers of free help from coaches and mental health practitioners as they adjusted to the challenging new normal.

Where that happened, it was, for the most part, the result of self-improvement drives that remained at team or personal level and they were rarely supported, guided or organized by the enterprise in the pandemic. Some organizations did eventually respond by appointing chief mental health officers but it was typically a reaction that happened months into the pandemic and after the collective damage was arguably done.

For our part at PeopleNotTech, we sat down with a sense of 'we have to do something' at the beginning of the crisis and as part of a COVID-19 response aimed largely at those who were asked to work from home suddenly, we opened up access to our software for free for a period, offered mini-EQ trainings for leaders and more importantly, we built a 'Stay Connected' package of questions designed to measure nothing but to reaffirm to the team that there is a commonality in the horrendous experience they were traversing.

We asked team members to tell us about their pain points: 'Do you hate having to use video?', 'I feel disconnected from the rest of the team', 'I work twice as much now', 'I feel like I'm on a never-ending Zoom carousel', 'I feel like I can never take a sick day while WFH', etc., but we also gently outlined suggestions and positives with occasional affirmations such as 'I can see my kids every time I get a coffee', 'Home-cooked lunch every day FTW!', 'I am enjoying the lack of commute', 'I don't always have to wear pants in meetings' and so on. The questions and affirmations were all included to soothe and assuage, not to measure anything.

We also wrote this 'Open Letter to the Team Leaders of Newly Remote Teams' addressed to anyone in a position of leadership:

Dear Team Leader,

It doesn't matter if you run a corporation or a department, a software development team or a start-up, a division or small team of any kind, if you 'line manage' – what a hateful term that is! – and have had your people move to remote working in light of this crisis, then this one is for you.

It's a terrible time for everyone but for you, it's been blindingly hard. And not the work in itself. That's the least of your problems. You found you did very little of that unless it has been to pick up what you thought was slack from some of your people that haven't settled into this new reality fast enough.

No one knows exactly what you're facing but yourself.

Maybe you are cc-ed in frightful chains about firings – scenario planning, disaster modelling, business continuity plans and so forth – that make your blood curl and fill you with dread.

Maybe you just really miss the day-to-day structure you were accustomed to.

Maybe you wish you still had the school run excuse.

Maybe you're struggling with the home set-up just like everyone else – tech that's not working as it should, corners in the house that work for emails but are a nightmare for video calls, VPNs [virtual private networks] that fail, wobbly internet connections, the suddenly mandated strange project management or communication software you were sent home with, and your team facing the same things so you have to cheerlead, not commiserate.

Maybe you're stunned to discover you now have to factor in housework or this dreaded new role of a school teacher that gives you impostor syndrome hives in front of the kids as well.

Maybe you find you have less mental space to think of work even if there are so many more hours to execute.

Maybe you feel always on the back-foot, dropping balls, overwhelmed, always catching up, never ahead of the game and eternally behind.

Maybe you feel completely unqualified to deal with people from afar when it was hard enough in person, where you could smile or high five or hold a door open, whereas now you have to probe, face being potentially intrusive and spend a massive amount of your time asking and speaking and doing none of what you used to think was your 'day job'. Make no mistake about it, while our work tool and others like it, go a long way towards alleviating some of that discomfort by helping you keep an eye on the team's pulse, it doesn't replace your relentless and very deeply human curiosity about your people.

Here's the thing though – it's OK.

It's OK to be scared – deeply and intensely, this is the most effed-up thing either of us will ever have to live through and we just really need to do the latter.

It's OK to be paralyzed by sheer worry.

It's OK to feel unprepared to deal with these humans who look at you as a leader/parent when you were barely adulting before this all happened.

It's OK to feel like your 'actual job' is slipping.

It's OK to organize – or ask the company to organize – a same-level, cross-departmental manager/team-lead support group – at the very least a Slack channel so you post tips to each other or feel you have a place to have a moan. Ask us about some of the ones we helped set up with our clients.

It's OK to trust your people – everything good that you've ever thought of your teammates is probably true and it will come in to play now. You'll witness them being flexible, courageous and pick up the balls you fear they're dropping.

It's OK not to be productive week #1 or really, even week #3. Take your time to find your rhythm and define flexible work as it best plays out for you. This is the new normal, settle in.

It's OK to think of how you feel and put 'self-care' in place. You're not a 'key worker' for the nation, but you're the 'key worker' for your team and your family and if you won't stop and process and find equilibrium, they'll feel it.

It's OK to be resentful of how much more is being asked of you now all of a sudden, all the courage, the inspiration and the stability.

It's OK to pry. It's more than 'OK' – it's needed.

It's OK to share with your team that you feel that way – just not incessantly as a negativity-fest but occasionally as a sign of honesty and because you trust them with it. It's OK to be vulnerable, that's where the courage lives. It's OK to be human.

It's tough. It feels like all roles are a sham. The work one, the household contributor one and even the parenting one. Your entire job description changed overnight to being an astute and wise people shaman and doing so digitally, a facilitator extraordinaire, an exceptional empath, an experienced counsellor, a knowledgeable and reassuring pedagogue and an inspiring leader at a Steve-Jobs-on-a-good-day level.

This will get better. It's already ever so slightly easier than it was last week. It will keep improving. You'll emerge out of this having aced this new job description and with a whole set of new superhuman abilities. Breathe and get help. From your people, from software, from friends and family. We will all emerge out of this undoubtedly stronger, we just have to hold on tight and focus on our team and think of the mountains we can move once this is all over.

The response we had was overwhelming, with thousands of people resonating intensely and telling us that in an act of reciprocal recognition that helped us all move forward. Similarly, organizations that showed intense care and empathy towards their workers during the pandemic may not have proven able to have eliminated the negative consequences of a major drop in productivity and the disastrous effects on the mental health of the individual but they have mitigated some of this risk and will prove to have invested in a better future.

Remote and the Work/Life Balance

When it comes to the heralded term of work/life balance, maybe the most interesting opinion of them all comes from Amazon's Jeff Bezos, who famously doesn't believe in one at all: 'I get asked about work/life balance all the time. And my view is, that's a debilitating phrase because it implies there's a strict trade-off.' Instead of viewing work and life as a balancing act, Bezos said that it's more productive to view them as two integrated parts: 'It actually is a circle. It's not a balance. This work/life harmony thing is what I try to teach young employees and actually senior executives at Amazon too. But especially the people coming in.' He went on to describe how he intermingles work tasks with home tasks and leisure tasks in a rhythm he found to work best for him.

If the effects of the pandemic in 2020 should have taught us as professionals and individual contributors anything, it is that it's undoubtedly worth spending time thinking about how we structure our online interactions and our work. More than ever, to stay sane and remain productive and competitive in the long run, we had to recognize that we had to be compassionate not only towards others but ourselves, that we don't all work the same way and we all have different but equally important limits.

Limits we should know and understand and then take the time to communicate with each other.

Of course, not everyone has the luxury to pick and choose what they engage with work-wise, for how long and when, and for some of us, it often seemed like a never-ending carousel of meetings and the more of those that were above and beyond our natural limits, the more exacerbated our feelings of despondency and anxiety became, and the more negative our outlook proved.

What the more consummate professionals who could afford it had done was to take stock of their abilities honestly and observe when they were hitting the 'too much' limit. Once clear, they took the time and dared to tell their teams and team leaders what they found to be their natural rhythm and mental and emotional availability in terms of interaction and as a result, what they could comfortably cope with.

Some leaders listened and spent time co-creating truly flexible working environments that strived to harmonize what they had learned from these professionals, with the client or delivery constraints of their particular team, allowing individual work to happen unrestricted by time while collaborative and teamwork happened at the times agreed upon in common.

Not all leaders realized they should – or were able to – accommodate this type of deep insight into their people's individual work styles, but nonetheless, the act of having communicated it had already taken some of the edges off the mental discomfort.

A large majority of remote workers either never felt they had 'permission' to observe their true limits, never took the time to recognize them, or they didn't feel it was constructive to 'rock the boat' of the already strained business by communicating them, but more likely, were stopped from doing so by abject fear of recession and job loss and as a result, they simply never spoke up about them.

A handful of visionary team leaders have communicated a need for their newly remote employees to be self-reflective and invest in self-care and they have underlined to them that ignoring personal limits is unsustainable and borderline irresponsible long term. They took the time to focus on a sustained campaign of having one-on-ones with each team member, they asked in the common meetings, they provoked the right conversations.

Ultimately, they discussed this in Team Re-Launches together with a culture canvas and as part of the interaction contracting around what tools and processes best work to define their particular team's flexible working in the remote context. They reinforced that there is value in the introspection and in the honesty of the communication and that it is necessary to remain competitive.

They encouraged people to spend time realizing where their overload threshold was. Every employee has a particular amount of online interaction (in particular, video interaction) that they can comfortably and productively engage with, and anything above this amount is really nothing more than presenteeism or a box-ticking exercise with zero engagement value.

An exercise of asking everyone to define and communicate what their 'too much' consisted of was unbelievably helpful to some of these leaders, who were truly interested in building healthy working habits in the heavily digital environment in the midst of the terrifying outside conditions of the crisis.

Even where this happened, and where employees communicated their limits and the team redesigned and re-contracted interactions to accommodate for them, with clear flexible working permission, the lesson was that it still came down to the individual employee to then demonstrate their own ability to time manage, autonomously perform and work on their individual productivity hacks and own growth and well-being practices.

The ones who understood this put in place clear and well-meaning, well-structured schedules they intended to follow to keep themselves sane and functional and help them get the much-needed sense of structure within the freedom of the remote and flexible work context created within the team.

Initially, most of these schedules featured the same delineation between work and home life and declared no work will be done after a certain hour or at the weekend, but during the months of lockdown, those borders blended when people realized we can sneak in an email in the middle of the child working on a home-schooling task, or that it's easier to banter on the Slack channel while on the balcony watching the world go by at lunch. But for the more performance-oriented, despite work slipping in the Bezos model above, they still took their breaks when they needed to, and remained focused on their golden hours when they were most productive.

That in itself is the key revelation behind flexible working at an individual level and the only antidote to burnout – which is that we each have a natural rhythm to our moments of inspiration and that we deserve a right to accommodate for it and do our best work – in as far as those moments are possible without direct interaction with others. Because no matter what we do, we all want to do our best work and we can all clearly see there are times when we are razor-sharp in focus, full of great ideas and productive and those are the times when we should cram more quality work into an hour than in a whole week devoid of these moments. If we do so, in a rhythm that is natural to our own mental well-being, we can avoid running ourselves into the ground, overloading and eventually suffering.

Making room for these individual human circumstances and various rhythms should, therefore, be a serious preoccupation of any company post-pandemic and post-recession. John Gaunt, Chief Human Resources Officer, Synechron, shares: 'For employees working from home, multi-tasking would mean caring for elder parents with health conditions, looking after a toddler, or even domestic chores along with the usual office duties.

'Employers, thus, need to watch out for several signs that employees may show such as increased anger or irritability, lack of motivation, procrastination, persistent sadness, excessive worrying or anxiety, poor sleep patterns, lack of creativity or innovation, negative or pessimistic thoughts, increase in substance use/abuse or even reckless behaviour.'

Some of the factors that played a part in an employee's attitude towards working from home during the pandemic were:

- Nature of the work – what percentage is individual contribution versus what percentage needs collaboration;
- Access to necessary technology tools and sufficient communication;
- Ability to show results and outcomes clearly;
- Home situation – those who added home schooling now had two jobs, one of which they found themselves to be rather bad at, with studies suggesting this was particularly taxing for high-performers;
- Previous experience of remote;
- Existent levels of resilience;
- Company's attitude towards flexible working and self-determination, both at the individual and team level;
- Own capacity for volume and productivity – and a willingness to understand one's own limits and communicate them;
- Personality – introverts versus extroverts reacted differently to the ability to work from their homes;

- Level of management support – whether they had a middle manager panicking about the loss of control or a leader who was focused on their People Practice, supportive and a servant leader;
- Individual's time management and self-motivation skills;
- Perception of 'permission to think of own limits at this time' – arguably connected to seniority as the more well-established a professional is, the more likely they feel their value enables them to demand a respectful and bespoke work environment that fits their individual needs;
- Previous levels of Psychological Safety in the team;
- Existent levels of EQ – reading others' emotions and being able to express your own online *is* harder in the absence of proximity and context.

From one's machine and while not shaking hands, we had to be much more emotionally intelligent, much sharper, more connected, more focused on the team dynamic, more on-task and less concerned with the ceremony of live business interaction.

When we had to read someone's state of mind from a few emails, a Slack thread or a video call, we suddenly found ourselves having to pay more intent attention and having to employ a lot more empathy than ever before, and when we had to drop out of a meeting when our toddler followed the 30th 'Mummy!' or 'Daddy!' signal with a description of an acute need – most of an urgent (and often disgusting!) nature – we did end up rethinking the concept of 'work/life balance' as we knew it and focused on what counts – the work to be done and the humans we did it with, irrespective of how and where we did it within limits that allowed us to speak up and feel safe.

Irrespective of the exact particulars of the 'where' and 'how' of the future of work, this remains the net gain of the pandemic. The proof of concept of remote and the proof of concept of flexibility with its applications to each individual, who will, from hereon, always have to think in terms of their particular limits and abilities so this will become a ubiquitous skill of the future.

All of the individual growth practices regarding work, EQ and a focus on people will become a sine qua non condition of being a professional, in a largely hybrid future in which office-only work will be a distant memory, so each of us ought to invest in getting in the mental shape and the self-respect space where we deeply and firmly understand what the best way of working is for us.

Productivity and Performance in the VUCA Digital World During a Global Recession

It's hard to say exactly how bad the ensuing global economic recession will turn out to be. The projections are terrifying and point towards one of the worst economic times in history for some countries and the biggest since the Great Depression, but the reality is that irrespective of how severe it proves, the recession adds a further level of an extreme layer to the already existent nature of VUCA in a new digital world.

For organizations amid some form of transformation towards digital, where Agile wasn't at DNA level yet when the pandemic ushered in the new ways of work, there were no guarantees. Some – arguably those who were close enough – managed to ride the wave and use new processes to reinforce an already clear and foundational mentality change. Others, who were far from having laid the initial foundations, struggled as their people – leadership included – now even more stressed, relentlessly tried to return to the 'familiar' set point of waterfall practices and political games.

With the exception of the segment that the 'Accelerate: State of DevOps' report classifies as 'elite performers' – those who were digitally native and already nearly fully 'remote', and who therefore had a strong foundation of a culture of Psychological Safety for every team, meaning that they were already people-obsessed and best poised for this new reality – everyone else struggled to retain their gains in a WoT For WoW (Way of Thinking for Way of Working) mindset. Some even 'gave up' and rolled out very sequential ways of work for the remote reality.

By the time you read this, it is entirely conceivable that the companies who had done nothing to reduce the Human Debt fell prey to their own lack of resilience and conviction of opinion and are not even still around. Even the elite performers and the nimble start-ups struggled.

There are multiple reasons to fear for Psychological Safety in a recession as immature businesses will deprioritize it and misjudge its importance as a survival mechanism at a time when our people may be feeling most shaky, most fearful and most inadequate. With burnout and impression management rampant as it will prove to be the case in the midst of the recession, it is really even more important that we continue to make it a firm priority in the years where we rebuild after the pandemic.

Here's what I fear: that the forced circumstances of our crisis will appear to have been manageable for hundreds of thousands of remote teams who have – rightfully – remained remote after the lockdown was lifted, whereas, in fact, the extreme drop in Psychological Safety they will eventually exhibit will prove to have been more detrimental to their performance than we can begin to imagine.

In other words, that by not having found ways to design and implement a true 'People Practice' in time, with no regard towards the ideas behind designing an intentional flexible working policy that takes into account a necessary work/life balance and finds the best ways to interact to minimize negative mental health effects, we have damaged pre-existent levels of positive team dynamics in teams irreversibly, and we have failed to instil them in new ones, and that this damage will result in productivity drops that will be not only crippling for some companies, but as severe as to prove recession-enhancing overall for years to come.

For anyone understanding the tight correlation between Psychological Safety and productivity, this is not a far-reaching fear.

If we return to the definition of Psychological Safety: the shared belief that the team is safe for interpersonal risk-taking, a common ability to always speak up and be vulnerable and open with each other, and a lack of impression management in a team that feels like a family – let's critically evaluate who may have had this during this crisis. The answer while not exact in data is common sense: very few if any.

Some did, the previously mentioned already-remote teams that had a chance to have become well versed with the intricacies of digital collaboration in 'times of peace' were highly Psychologically Safe and resilient and doubled down on the mental well-being of the individual and of the team during the pandemic with astute leadership which focused on increasing EQ and spent even more time than usual on their People Practice. Needless to say, these examples were scarce. For the rest, the shock of the transition, the overwhelming lack of physical safety, the isolation, the increased level of difficulty of home life in quarantine superimposed and have all piled on top of a generalized sense of anxiety and sheer fear for one's employment and therefore has given rise to the negative fear-based behaviours that prevent Psychological Safety.

With impression management being defined as the fear of appearing incompetent, ignorant, negative, disruptive or intrusive in a workgroup situation, disastrous amounts of that set of behaviours have slipped into the work-life of most teams during the pandemic. The first two of these, tightly coupled with our generalized impostor syndrome, have been exacerbated as no one wanted to appear not able, or not knowing at a time like this, but the last ones – a fear of appearing negative or disruptive and, above all, a fear of appearing intrusive – would have motivated many a moment when team members would stop themselves from being their authentic self even further and prevented them from genuinely relating.

Take the fear of intrusion – even in well-established and skilfully remote teams, the habit of asking deeply human questions and the ability to share deeply human emotions with the rest of the group was hardly commonplace before the crisis as the EQ of various teams varied greatly, and its existence was never a historical prerequisite in the workplace.

During the COVID-19 crisis months, the need to relate became infinitely more stringent for all teams in light of the pandemic and those who were unable to quickly find ways to open up deeply and connect intensely out of a fear of looking like they pry, because of this underdeveloped team EQ, missed the opportunity to draw on the only soothing energy available: the power of recognizing a shared reality. In other words, those teams who couldn't find the reserves of courage to 'get personal' missed a major trick in becoming compassionate by recognizing the commonality of suffering, which then reflected in their performance levels as it denied them the opportunity to move as a cohesive unit instead of a collection of isolated and anxious individuals.

When this laid on top of sheer fear of job loss, it is little wonder it generated extreme impression management and few teams, if any, recall having heard any dissenting voices, any questions raised, any constructive disagreements and any open speaking-up behaviours during the pandemic.

While speaking up, being open and authentic and avoiding impression management are the sine qua non conditions to productivity and high performance, a temporary suspension of these for the few months of this tragedy may arguably not have seemed fatal to most teams – except for those where big mistakes have silently happened because no one was willing to point them out – but by the same token, a few months is a long time for habit formation and as a result, many of these teams learned this new group behaviour of not being open, which has then sabotaged any hope of success long term.

For many, Psychological Safety suffered so severely, the effects on the team in the absence of intervention will sadly unveil themselves in dismal results and faltering KPIs for years to come, which is why these should really be the years when we reduce the Human Debt and start with (re-)establishing healthy team behaviours and solid People Practices to reverse the ravaging effects of the pandemic.

The Post-Pandemic World of Work

If the discourse on what happens next was initially very black and white, as 2020 unfolded and some countries and their economies emerged out of lockdown, it became apparent the future of work in terms of location was rarely clear-cut and few places had made the transition to fully and exclusively remote working or on the contrary, executed a mandatory and complete return to the office.

For most companies where remote work was a possibility at all, 2020 was the end of the either/or policy in terms of location and the beginning of a new 'Hybrid Era', where part of the work happens WFH and part in the office.

Some argued for this formula on the premise of the idea that true collaboration is tightly linked to accidental encounters such as the ability to 'bump into each other in the hallways' or to 'congregate around the watercooler' informally, or to be in the same room for any collaborative activities that were formal and that if we don't facilitate spaces for these encounters, we would damage collaboration.

Nonetheless, many companies with a sufficiently keen and curious eye observed the behaviour of their employees during the COVID-19 crisis and found that they were more open and collaborative online despite what they regarded as conventional wisdom previously.

Aaron Levie, Chief Executive of Box, a cloud software maker which in 2020 announced their company will be taking the hybrid route, reported that remote working had actually increased innovation at his company. Instead of generating ideas with small groups in conference rooms, or when people happen to run into one another, he said, the company is having conversations with larger and more diverse groups on Slack. He reported that in a new project they noticed this happening: 'We've taken what would have been a five- to 10-person project to a 300-person idea generation machine, with people who never would have participated in this project, even interns. It might have been the equivalent of 20 meetings in conference rooms when in reality, a Slack channel with a few good ideas might make up for all the meetings.'

So the rationale behind the hybrid model goes beyond facilitating collaboration and instead takes into account individual preferences of some employees who crave the human interaction while allowing others to eschew it where possible.

Some of the organizations we interviewed and worked with during the pandemic had a series of these goals on their radar if not, in the fortunate cases, all of them:

- Hybrid as the norm;
- Deeply understand and respect the idea of individual limits and flexible working as well as individual preferences regarding the location;
- Use technology confidently;
- Question and rethink every so often;
- Reduce Human Debt – take the time to build around genuine care;
- Put new protective and enabling policies in place after close co-creation with the employees themselves.

This last one is the least common and yet it is very important. When organizations applied genuine interest, observed with an open mind and asked the right, invested and open-ended questions, and when they eventually found themselves designing a new work policy (note: not a 'remote work policy'), they often found that the key factor to keep in mind is that they will need to lay down truly protective measures.

Being protective of their employees' well-being was a very new stance for most workplaces and if it hadn't been for the huge amount of debate around the effect on the mental health of employees being effectively the next pandemic that ought to be feared, this would have maybe never been the case. However, in the post-2020 world, companies had to shift from the punitive and coercive nature of policies that characterized work in the past to an era where these policies came out of genuine care and respect, not as a moral imperative, but as an economic one.

These policies chiefly revolved around replacing the way they had previously dictated participation to how they now enabled it. They found that the best protection against burnout and lack of engagement was to be honestly invested in the deep people practice work and to start at debating 'remote' versus 'flexible' and discuss outcomes-based work by redefining the interaction in ways that work for each team individually.

The places that wanted to remain competitive post-Covid and navigate the recession allowed for great team autonomy and often started to demonstrate this by asking them to perform regular Team Launches and Re-Launches to include contracting exercises around interactions.

How many meetings? When shouldn't we have any to cushion individual work time? How shall we communicate in between? Which ones are mandatory? When are we most productive? What types of collaborative work do we need to do? Are we being forensic about the need for the meeting in the first place? Do we all agree on the tools? Do they help? Are we helping each other? What do we expect of each other? What should we avoid? How do we do effective conflict? When and how do we get to team build? Are we thriving? What can we change? What haven't we examined and we could so that we do better as a team?

All of those and many more are questions that typically took teams no longer than a couple of hours to answer online and could, therefore, be answered again at a later point a few weeks later, as they tested processes and learnt more about the work styles that most enable them to be highly performant. The organization should then simply figure out the best ways to harmonize the points of interaction between these bubble-level ways of work and those of other teams they need to interact with, to ensure they can collaborate when needed.

An example of these policies in place to protect is the principle that spread like wildfire in 2020 of 'One remote means all remote', which meant that all meetings were to remain digital and be conducted online if as little as one team member was not present. This took the place of the previous practice, which often involved remote members of distributed teams being left half-forgotten on poor-quality calls while those physically in the room conducted a meeting. Another example comes from Seattle-based Uplevel, who started by ensuring their employees settled into remote work by delivering their desk possessions to their home at the start of the pandemic and then sending a care package containing plants, puzzles, snacks and office supplies, but then further formalized the care towards their well-being by adopting a set of policies to be mindful of their work rhythm, such as meetings being barred from 12–13:30 to ensure everyone had time for a lunch break, keeping at least 10 minutes between Zoom meetings and keeping Fridays open for teams playing games online and expensing a lunch delivery.

Some of the teams we worked with during the pandemic even went so far as to create a distinction between 'active' meetings and 'passive' or 'listening' meetings and encouraged their teams to state what type the next meeting was. Obviously, most of the meetings that are one-on-one will fall into the first category, but they simply encouraged teammates to only schedule as many of those as they think they can honestly handle, and feel free not to pick up a call or accept every meeting invite. They also let them know it's OK to use any of the channels and answer something by text or email instead of a call, etc. and in general, allowed them to think of any strategies that would make it easier and more sustainable for them.

For group and team-level meetings, allowing people to engage as much or as little as needed – where the need always included the imperative of 'conversational turn-taking' to ensure everyone is heard – and be forensic about employing EQ to try and read their reactions while they engaged was very useful.

Crucially, dropping the 'video-always-on' requirement also proved significant for some companies. While at first, it may have been much more necessary to have video on to get everyone comfortable with its regular usage in the absence of face-to-face, the reality is that it is an undeniably overbearing demand to some employees and the resentment of having to do it can negatively impede on the meeting to the point where it defeats the very object of supposedly creating more closeness. If teams work on understanding individual limits and communicating them first and find ways to accommodate those in the way they interact, then video should come in naturally on its own, as a result of the sense of closeness and comfort created, not be demanded, mandated and policed by management or policy.

No matter when you are reading this and no matter how you work, where, and for how long and with what results, it's never too late to create a habit of doing Team Re-Launches, where everything is once more up in the air and re-examined. Doing so is probably one of the best investments in your People Practice you can make in this hybrid and ever-changing VUCA work reality and the best defence against succumbing to the speed of change and institutionalized and outdated practices that will ultimately put you at risk economically, as it gives everyone the space to reconnect, reaffirm and recreate a sense of co-creation every so often, thus contributing to improving all the components of Psychological Safety.

What's Next for Work and Teams?

It's undeniable that there are amazing lessons to be taken to heart that have emerged from the *annus horribilis* that 2020 proved to be, starting with the amazing community expressions of compassion, to the heroic acts of some, all the way to how this would have brought about lasting changes in how we work and whether we understand the value of humans at work. The winners of the future will be those willing and able to work tirelessly to reduce their Human Debt openly with care and respect and while questioning everything. The 'why' and the 'how' of what they do. Over and again.

One of the tech giants that has readily embraced the remote working challenge, both for themselves as they announced their employees can remain remote post-Covid where possible, and for others, seeing how they had a vested interest in providing enabling software to the market through their 'Teams' solutions, was Microsoft.

Sam Guckenheimer, Azure Product Owner at Microsoft, said they are conducting 15 studies on the future of work and that in their view the world of work as it was will never return but instead, post-pandemic, 'We will have Strivers who will blame the pandemic, value prediction over the outcome, want to restore the status quo, whereas the Thrivers will hit refresh, value learning over prediction, get stronger under stress, invest in core, divest in context, embrace DevOps for Agility, work in Remote and Hybrid settings, Adapt on the Edge of Chaos.'

Some of the smartest companies that wanted to take the growth opportunities the crisis presented put some serious thought into questioning everything and tried a culture-reset design sprint. Just as the planet was getting a chance to breathe, they saw the opportunity to give the office a chance to shake the effects of damaging posturing, politics, unquestioned convention and lack of empathy. They regarded it as a collective exercise in humanity, where they had to all keep close, pull together and relentlessly focus on their EQ, eternally trying to decipher the mood, needs and feelings of their fellow teammates, and then intensely and demonstrably care razor-focused on a new human lens. They whipped out a canvas across the enterprise and got everyone involved online through a variety of collaboration tools in redesigning what they stand for and what they want to see happening. These are the topics most had come up with:

- **Respect and Decency** – 'Reaffirm basic human values we can all get behind, such as "We are all humans and we will not be horrible a-holes to each other, no matter what". This includes anything from bullying to discrimination and lack of empathy and compassion. This makes us be diverse and inclusive and lets us look at each other open-heartedly to see our value';
- **Define and Measure True Value** – 'Understand the impact of our individual and team work and quantify outcomes that matter in lieu of the wrong measures as the foundation for achieving truly flexible work';
- **No More Command and Control** – 'Find quick ways to help managers become servant leaders with truly autonomous teams – Micromanagement never helped anyone, in this day and age, to run fast. We need to count on every player and empower them to be their best selves';

- **Explore Trust and Grow Pride** – 'Point out our value as a group and as individuals, remind everyone why we believe in each other and how awesome we are and work on keeping that pride as part of the WHY';
- **Do Away with Presenteeism** – 'We won't monitor things or measure anyone on acts of presence but acts of value. We must find ways to reward true emotional investment and discourage just being around with no real participation';
- **Work on the Permission to be Human** – 'Our people don't trust they have our permission to be their authentic human selves with emotions and thoughts in the workplace and our leaders are not modelling courage, passion and openness either – we must change both and do away with impression management and the fear of looking unprofessional';
- **Un-ban Emotions** – 'Ask everyone to understand we now place EQ as one of the most important attributes anyone can bring to this work and help them grow it, while helping team leaders transition from thinking of their "people practice" as an afterthought to realizing it's their main job if they manage teams';
- **Get Serious about the Permission to Fail** – 'We need to elevate the basics of experimentation from an implicit nod to an explicit and desirable outcome. We have to start celebrating failure as an act of courage and innovation before we can demand the latter. Also, if we realign around flexibility, we'll be more resilient should anything like this happen again';
- **Open an Honest New Dialogue** – 'We will replace the annual surveys no one cared about or took seriously anyhow with some mechanism to keep our eyes on the pulse and ask questions all the time. We need to show we value most completely open and frequent feedback and there should be no fear of repercussion';

- **Take Well-Being Seriously** – 'Not only mental well-being and organizational well-being (which we should spend a lot more time on), but re-focus their own well-being and growth as individuals – we need to show we truly care as a company and are hell-bent to get them to the best version of themselves'.

And of course, the most important of them all:

- **Focus on Team Magic** – 'We must obsess about the team and their Psychological Safety, from becoming religious about speaking up to eliminating impression management to keeping an eye on each of the components of Psychological Safety and affecting the ones that slip with people-centric interventions by ever more EQed team leaders'.

The positive responses in this trying time all drew on an existent thirst for emotion that we all collectively had in our respective workplaces. An acute need for compassion and humanity we had tried to do without. So really, when it comes to the components of Psychological Safety, we have all shown courage and flexibility and that will build resilience. We have all learned intensely, more than we have done in years, and understood that we need to continuously do so some more.

We all realized empathy is both needed and permitted – an indescribable shift from its previous ideological confinement to 'the little table of fluffy stuff' – and that it is OK to be human. Now if we can resolutely focus on speaking up, on being intently open and over-communicating and on the happiness, if we can remain obsessed with the team and protect our work-bubble, then we can stop impression managing and let go of some of the fear we're conquering so we stand a good chance of staying – or even becoming – Psychologically Safe and therefore high-performing teams.

The Silicon Valley darlings and the digitally native success stories won't suffer from this. This could be just the time when their cultural competitive advantage that relies on no office but ways of truly making things happen will see them completely annihilate the competition.

For the rest of us, the stakes are high. A relentless focus on increasing EQ. A sustained effort to catch and stop impression management at all levels. An obsession with the team that leaves the organization rhetoric behind and hones in on Leadership 2.0, Agile/DevOps, a People Practice and Psychological Safety for everyone. These are the only tools that will let us compete by creating cultures of goodwilled, trusting and trusted humans in family-like, high-performing teams who work in ever-changing new ways that make them happy. That is the only path to reducing our Human Debt – and reduce it, we must. Urgently. I put it to us that anything else, anything less, would be disastrous.

Appendix

Interview with Gene Kim, award-winning CTO, researcher and author

Can you remember when you first heard the term 'psychological safety'?

Yes, it must have been around 2013, after the Phoenix Project came out and it was in the DevOps community. There was so much talk about blameless post-mortems, as being done by Etsy, and Google has a similar term called the PIR (post-incident review) often said in the same breath as blameless post-incident review and it was the big 'A-ha!' moment for me. I mean at first I thought 'oh, this is just about being nice to each other' which is absolutely not the case, as is demonstrated by Dr Amy Edmondson, but you know still I did not initially understand until I heard a talk by Randy Shoup. He was the Chief Architect for eBay. He was a VP of engineering for Stitch Fix, for WeWork and he was also with Google as a Director of Engineering, and he said: 'Engineers love stories about disasters – even if it's about themselves', and 'the most important thing is to be able to create the conditions where people can actually share what happened'.

He said that they would have blameless most post-mortems for every customer-impacting incident, and people would always wait for the publication of those because whenever there was a big disaster it was very exciting to read. Then one week there was a very peculiar situation when he was in charge of the Google app engine team. They ran out of customer-impacting incidents to talk about, so they did it for team impacts – things that didn't affect the customer, but impacted the team. Then they ran out of those so they talked about near misses. For example, of the seven safeguards they put in place to prevent a particular team-impacting incident from happening, six of them failed: so what can they do about that? And so the result was this ever-increasing safe sharing environment.

This example actually made it into *The DevOps Handbook* but for me it was one of my 'a-ha' moments on the power of feeling psychologically safe. You can't do that – talk about things that almost went wrong, about accidents that almost happened – without psychological safety.

Why do you think that the concept of Impression Management as the negative set of behaviours that stops us from speaking up is not more widely spread?

That's a great question. When you first mentioned impression management to me, it immediately caught my attention. It was one of the more startling things I've heard in the past couple of years. I had never heard of it. I like it just because it resonates with my own personal experience so much. I recognize these behaviours in the thoughts of senior leaders the evening before a high-stakes meeting. How much of it was actual preparation for the work material, versus worrying about who spoke to whom, how they would represent themselves, etc. It wouldn't surprise me if Impression Management is kind of the missing tool that we may need to make a clear connection. If I understand the literature right, this is a very visible manifestation of what happens when there is an absence of psychological safety, and these fear-based behaviours kick in. Maybe closely linking that with the five dysfunctions of a team would be useful, but my suspicion is that it will become an important tool.

What examples can you think of when it comes to Impression Management?

There are some environments where you can be your true authentic self as a leader, but there are some environments where it is more difficult, even in the most non-judgemental way – say in the political realm, which is very complex, or in the military where the most senior leaders really cannot actually say what they think all the time because of particular alliances or relationships with civilian populations. I would be interested in understanding these environments where 'radical candour' wouldn't work and where impression management would take place. And if that's an independent variable there, what would be the deep-ended variables that would affect it?

So as you've probably read I have an obsession that we must stop talking about 'organization' and 'culture' because we run the risk of doing so in a sterile, action-less way. Would you say people should rather focus on making team dynamics better or attempt to change the organization?

So my own belief is – something I've learned from Steve Spear that is very personal in his view – in 'dominant architecture' and 'structure and dynamics'. 'Structure' is how you organize teams in the organization, who's allowed to talk to who, and what are the interfaces between the teams. And 'dynamics' are almost entirely a function of the structure. So 'dynamics' means who gets feedback? How quickly? 'Dynamics' are weak signals that are amplified – like when you have a safety culture; a blameless, innovative culture, then signals spread wide and are amplified by top leadership; whereas if you have a culture of fear the signals are suppressed or extinguished entirely. This can be seen as a very 'mechanistic' view of the world but I find that it can explain a lot. And if the question is: 'Is it more important to shuffle the teams around on the org charts?', which we know is incredibly ineffective, in particular because in technology we don't understand how teams interact with each other, we can't seem to get them to couple so they keep working independently, etc – or 'Is it more important to work on the dynamic within the team not the dynamic between the teams in the organization?', I think focusing on both the dynamic within the team and the dynamic between teams is supremely important as that reveals how we can maximize communication. Within a team it should be a given that they feel safe and can communicate effectively, or they cannot achieve their goals, but then again teams don't work alone in isolation, so we have to think what is an effective dynamic. Is it trust? Is it how they talk? Maybe they don't even talk at all, maybe that is entirely mechanized through electronic interfaces in the future and that's the answer. So in short – within a team? Critical. And at times when you need integration and cooperation, then also critical.

So are you saying if the definition of an organization is the mesh of nodes of communication between teams that already have healthy team dynamics, then we should work on that?

Right. And there are some conditions in which the entire structure is wrong. I mean if there are global calls where everyone has to listen in and hope they get the critical information, and if they doze off at the wrong time then mayhem ensues, well then that's wrong. Teams of thousands of people? What dynamic is that? Or when you have a small thing that depends on multiple teams. That's also structure, and it's wrong, but it all does hinge on dynamics, internal and external.

One last question – what are some examples of organizations that have the least amount of 'Human Debt™', as I call it?

Yes, your term 'Human Debt™' – it's very startling to me because when I read it, it immediately resonated that there is a gap. Sometimes someone uses a term and you think immediately 'oh yes, that's a thing, right?' So I've been studying high performing technology organizations for about 21 years. These organizations have the best performance, the best operational stability and reliability, the best possible security and compliance. Looking back, the DevOps movement has let me see that these organizations are the ones who also have the best integration between these functional domains: product, development, QA, operations and security. Not only do they have the best integration of it, they also have the best holistic treatment of the most important element: the customer. And to quantify that, it's also a matter of 'Are they paying down technical debt?', 'Are they delivering features at a speed and quality required by customers and business needs?' And it wouldn't surprise me at all if they wouldn't be the same organizations that we would find have the lowest level of Human Debt as well.

So the elite performers in the State of DevOps Report?

Yes, in the report if you look at the BFD [the Big Fulsome Diagram] on how the technology correlates with the organizational and psychological parts, you may have to squint to see it but there are hints of it and the evidence to support the thesis that they are the ones doing well on the human side of things. Project Aristotle in itself suggests that. So I would be stunned if it wasn't these same high performers that have the least amount of Human Debt.

Glossary

Agile – In software development, Agile approaches develop requirements and solutions through the collaborative effort of self-organizing and cross-functional teams and their customers of end users. It advocates adaptive planning, evolutionary development, early delivery and continual improvement, and encourages flexible responses to change. The term was popularized by the *Manifesto for Agile Software Development*. The values and principles espoused in this manifesto were derived from and underpin a broad range of software development frameworks, including Scrum and Kanban.

CI/CD – CI/CD generally refers to the combined practices of continuous integration and either continuous delivery or continuous deployment and is viewed as the precursor to 'DevOps'.

Culture Canvas – The Culture Design Canvas is a strategic tool for designing new workplace cultures or mapping existing ones. It is a visual chart to understand current state and define the future by describing the purpose and values, strategic priorities, emotional culture, decision making, team rituals and rules.

Culture/Organizational Culture – Organizational Culture is defined as the underlying beliefs, assumptions, values and ways of interacting that contribute to the unique social and psychological environment of an organization. Simply stated, organizational culture is 'the way things are done around here' (Deal & Kennedy, 2000).

DevOps – DevOps is the combination of cultural philosophies, practices and tools that increase an organization's ability to deliver applications and services at high velocity, evolving and improving products at a faster pace than organizations using traditional software development and infrastructure management processes.

EQ – EQ stands for Emotional Quotient or Emotional Intelligence and it is the equivalent of IQ (Intelligence Quotient) when it comes to emotions. It is the capability of individuals to recognize their own emotions and those of others, discern between different feelings and label them appropriately, use emotional information to guide thinking and behaviour and manage and/or adjust emotions to adapt to environments or achieve one's goals. It was popularized as a term by the author and emotions scholar Daniel Coleman in 1995.

Google's Project Aristotle – 'Project Aristotle' is the name used by Google in their 2012 study, which set out to understand what makes their teams effective. They investigated vast amounts of data over four years and 180 teams and consistently only found correlation to five key characteristics despite monitoring hundreds of others. These were Psychological Safety, Dependability, Structure and Clarity, Meaning and Impact.

Group Dynamic – Group Dynamics is a system of behaviours and psychological processes occurring within a social group (intragroup dynamics), or between social groups (intergroup dynamics).

Group Norm/Behaviour – 'Group norms are the informal rules that groups adopt to regulate and regularise group members' behaviour' (Feldman, 1984).

Human Centred Design – is an approach to problem solving, commonly used in design and management frameworks that develops solutions to problems by involving the human perspective in all steps of the problem-solving process.

'Human Debt' – Human Debt™ – is the equivalent of 'Technical Debt' but for HR. It refers to the concept according to which organizations of various sizes have neglected the actions that would have been morally desirable and economically wise to be taken regarding making their employees happy. Whenever they have cut corners, ignored important concepts such as 'engagement' and 'satisfaction', 'respect' and 'care' or other ones connected to their 'well-being' by branding them as 'fluffy' and deprioritized them. Where they have not measured productivity and performance, organizations have developed a backlog of actions and mindset changes that reflects in a workforce that is not engaged and passionate and is not being treated as a value and being given permission to be authentically human and effective. This state of affairs is holding them back from being able to fully avail themselves of the speed and promise of technology and the new ways of working.

Impression Management – Impression Management is the negative side of the positive 'speaking up' team behaviour norm outlined in **Psychological Safety** below and refers to the set of motivations that cause a team member not to openly offer their input. These are fear-based and they refer to times when someone in a team hasn't spoken up because they were afraid of looking incompetent, ignorant, negative, intrusive or disruptive. If a team member impression manages in that they choose to remain silent for fear of consequences, the overall Psychological Safety of the team is diminished.

Jira, Trello, Slack, Kanban Boards, Backlogs – Software tools and techniques used in Agile new ways of work and project management.

Organizational Design – Organizational Design is a step-by-step methodology which identifies dysfunctional aspects of workflow, procedures, structures and systems, realigns them to fit current business realities/goals and then develops plans to implement the new changes. The process focuses on improving both the technical and people side of the business.

Psychological Safety – Psychological Safety is a team behaviour observed and studied by academics and business alike in the context of work. The concept is a group-level behaviour and refers to the dynamic of a team. It can be defined as a shared belief that the team is safe for interpersonal risk taking and that team members can employ their selves without fear of negative consequences for their image, status or career. While 'trust' is considered a precursor to the concept, they are not equivalent although some call it 'trust at team level'. When teams have high Psychological Safety, they report that they feel 'like family' and that it feels like they are 'making magic together'. The main positive and desirable behaviour norm in Psychologically Safe teams is that of 'speaking up', where team members always openly and without fear offer their opinions, criticize and contribute. The scientist that has dedicated her career to the concept and contributed the most robust body of evidence to it is Professor Dr Amy Edmondson of Harvard.

Scrum Team Launches – One of the biggest levers to a successful Scrum implementation are Team Launches, which are workshops for teams in the forming phase where they come together and decide on a common framework from the values they share, the language they agree on, all the way to interaction contracting in the way they decide they will work together, with what tools and through what medium, etc.

Servant Leadership – Servant leadership is a leadership philosophy in which an individual interacts with others – either in a management or fellow employee capacity – with the aim of achieving authority and inspiring leadership that promotes well-being rather than power. This occurs in a decentralized organizational structure. Servant leadership involves the individual demonstrating the characteristics of empathy, listening, stewardship and commitment to personal growth towards others. Servant leadership is considered the opposite of the 'command and control' management philosophy that refers to dictating and checking, not inspiring and leading.

Spotify Model – The Spotify model is a people-driven, autonomous framework for scaling Agile while emphasizing the importance of culture and network. This methodology uses Squads, Tribes, Chapters and Guilds – the foundation of which is the Squad, which acts like a Scrum team (see **Scrum Team Launches** above).

Teaming – The concept of 'teaming' has been coined by the same Professor Dr Amy Edmondson and can be defined as 'teamwork on the fly'. It applies to groups of virtual strangers who must become an 'instant team' as they have to solve a common task and is a common instance in the medical field or in emergency situations.

VUCA – VUCA is an acronym that stands for 'volatility', 'uncertainty', 'complexity' and 'ambiguity' that was first used in 1987 and based on the world-renowned leadership theories of Warren Bennis and Burt Nanus. It was the response of the US Army War College to the collapse of the USSR in the early 1990s. Suddenly, there was no longer the only enemy, resulting in new ways of seeing and reacting. In the early 2000s, it has entered the realm of business leadership and strategy and denotes the unpredictability of our current circumstances that call for unprecedented ideas and flexible mindsets.

Ways of Work (WoW)/Future of Work – Umbrella terms that define all the methods, techniques, processes, mindsets and philosophies that denote the changes in the working environment in the past 20–30 years in the digital age. They refer to where the work is performed (office-based, remote work such as working from home (WFH) or hybrid) and to how the work is performed (Agile new ways of work, Lean, experimental, etc.).

Reading and References

Ashcroft, P., Brown, S. & Jones, G. (2019), *The Curious Advantage: The Greatest Driver of Value in the Digital Age*, Laïki Publishing.

Barnard, J. (1998), '*What Works in Rewarding Problem-Solving Teams?*', Compensation and Benefits Management.

Bock, L. (2016), *Work Rules!: Insights from Inside Google That Will Transform How You Live and Lead*, John Murray.

Brown, B. (2018), *Dare to Lead: Brave Work. Tough Conversations. Whole Hearts*, Vermilion.

Clark, T.R. (2020), *The 4 Stages of Psychological Safety: Defining the Path to Inclusion and Innovation*, Berrett-Koehler Publishers.

Collins, J. (2001), *Good to Great: Why Some Companies Make the Leap – and Others Don't*, New York: HarperCollins.

Covey, S.M.R. with Merrill, R.R. (2008), *The Speed of Trust: The One Thing That Changes Everything*, Simon & Schuster.

Coyle, D. (2019), *The Culture Code: The Secrets of Highly Successful Groups*, Random House Business.

Devonshire, S. (2018), *Superfast: Lead at Speed*, John Murray Learning.

Edmondson, A.C. (1999), 'Psychological Safety and Learning Behavior in Work Teams', *Administrative Science Quarterly*, Harvard Business School, June 1999.

Edmondson, A.C. (2012), *Teaming: How Organizations Learn, Innovate, and Compete in the Knowledge Economy*, Harvard Business School.

Edmondson, A.C. (2018), *The Fearless Organization: Creating Psychological Safety in the Workplace for Learning, Innovation, and Growth*, Wiley.

Edmondson, A.C. & Lei, Z. (2014), 'Psychological Safety: The History, Renaissance, and Future of an Interpersonal Construct'. *Annual Review Organizational Psychology and Organizational Behavior*, Harvard Business School.

Ferris, K. (2020), '*Unleash the Resiliator Within*': Resilience: A Handbook for Leaders, Karen Ferris.

Fladerer, J-P. & Kurzmann, E. (2019), *The Wisdom of the Many: How to Create Self-Organisation and How to Use Collective Intelligence in Companies and in Society – From Management to ManagemANT*, Books On Demand.

Gibbs, J. & Gibson, C. (2006), 'Unpacking the Concept of Virtuality: The Effects of Geographic Dispersion, Electronic Dependence, Dynamic Structure, and National Diversity on Team Innovation', *Administrative Science Quarterly*, Johnson Graduate School, Cornell University.

Glaser, J.E. (2014), *Conversational Intelligence: How Great Leaders Build Trust and Get Extraordinary Results*, Brookline: Bibliomotion, Inc.

Goffman, E. (1956), *The Presentation of Self in Everyday Life*, Doubleday.

Goleman, D., Boyatzis, R. & McKee, A. (2002), *Primal Leadership: Realizing the Power of Emotional Intelligence*, Boston: Harvard Business School Press.

Goman, C., Ph.D. (2011), *The Silent Language of Leaders: How Body Language Can Help – Or Hurt – How You Lead*, Jossey-Bass Publishing.

Grodnitzky, G.R., PhD (2014), *Culture Trumps Everything: The Unexpected Truth About the Ways Environment Changes Biology, Psychology, and Behavior*, Mountainfrog Publishing.

Harter, J., Schmidt, F. & Killham, E. (2003), *Employee Engagement, Satisfaction, and Business-Unit-Level Outcomes: A Meta-Analysis*, The Gallup Organization.

Hawkins, P. (2011), *Leadership Team Coaching: Developing Collective Transformational Leadership*, Kogan Page.

Helfand, H. (2019), *Dynamic Reteaming: The Art and Wisdom of Changing Teams*, O'Reilly Media, Inc.

Hoegl, M. & Gemuenden, H.G. (2001), 'Teamwork Quality and the Success of Innovative Projects: A Theoretical Concept and Empirical Evidence', Review.

Junger, S. (2017), *Tribe: On Homecoming and Belonging*, Fourth Estate.

Kahneman, D. (2011), *Thinking, Fast and Slow*, New York: Farrar, Straus and Giroux.

Kasperowski, R. (2015), *The Core Protocols: A Guide To Greatness*, With Great People Publications.

— (2019), 'High-Performance Teams: The Foundations', lulu.com

Kim, G. (2019), *The Unicorn Project: A Novel about Digital Disruption, Redshirts, and Overthrowing the Ancient Powerful Order*, IT Revolution Press.

Kim, G. & Behr, K. (2018), *The Phoenix Project: A Novel About IT, DevOps, and Helping Your Business Win*, Trade Select.

Kim, G., Debois P., et al. (2016), *The DevOps Handbook: How to Create World-Class Agility, Reliability, and Security in Technology Organizations,* Trade Select.

Koslowski, S. & Bell, B. (2001) *Work Groups and Teams in Organizations,* Cornell University IRL School.

Leary, M.R. & Kowalski, R. (1990), *Impression Management: A Literature Review And Two Components Model,* Psychological Bulletin.

Lemoine, J. & Blum, T. (2019), *Servant Leadership, Leader Gender, and Team Gender Role: Testing a Female Advantage in a Cascading Model of Performance,* Wiley Online Library – Personnel Psychology.

Lencioni, P. (1998), *The Five Temptations of a CEO: A Leadership Fable,* Jossey-Bass.

— (2002), *The Five Dysfunctions of a Team: A Leadership Fable,* John Wiley & Sons.

LinkedIn (2016), *"Purpose at Work" Global Report,* Imperative & LinkedIn.

Logan, D., King, J. & Fischer-Wright, H. (2008), *Tribal Leadership: Leveraging Natural Groups to Build a Thriving Organization,* HarperCollins.

Maslow, A. (1943) *A Theory of Human Motivation,* Psychological Review.

Mayer, R., Davis, J.H. & Schoorman, D. (1995), 'An Integrative Model of Organizational Trust', Academy of Management.

McChrystal, General S., Collins, T., Silverman, D. & Fussell, C. (2015), *Team of Teams: New Rules of Engagement for a Complex World,* Penguin.

McCord, P. (2018), *Powerful: Building a Culture of Freedom and Responsibility,* Missionday.

Moss Kanter, R. (1987), *The Attack on Pay,* Harvard Business Review.

Putman, L. (2015), *Workplace Wellness That Works: 10 Steps to Infuse Well-Being and Vitality into Any Organization,* John Wiley & Sons.

Reiss, H., MD et al. (2018), *The Empathy Effect: 7 Neuroscience-Based Keys for Transforming the Way We Live, Love, Work, and Connect Across Differences,* Sounds True.

Royce, W. (1970), *Managing the Development of Large Software Systems*

Schmidt, E. & Rosenberg, J. (2015), *How Google Works,* John Murray.

Scott, S. (2002), *Fierce Conversations: Achieving Success in Work and in Life, One Conversation at a Time,* Piatkus.

Sinek, S. (2011), *Start With Why: How Great Leaders Inspire Everyone To Take Action,* Penguin.

— (2017), *Leaders Eat Last: Why Some Teams Pull Together and Others Don't*, Penguin.

Snow, S. (2018), *Dream Teams: Working Together Without Falling Apart*, Piatkus.

Ulusoy, N., Moelders, C. & Fischer, S. (2016), *A Matter of Psychological Safety: Commitment and Mental Health in Turkish Immigrant Employees in Germany*, Journal of Cross-Cultural Psychology.

Willink, J. & Babin. L. (2015), *Extreme Ownership: How U.S. Navy Seals Lead and Win*, St. Martin's Press.

Zenger, J., Folkman, J. (2019) *The 3 Elements of Trust*, Harvard Business Review.

(2017, 2018, 2019) *State of the Global Workplace Report*, Gallup.

(2020) *Cigna 2020 Loneliness Index*, Cigna.

Acknowledgements

If what this book postulates resonates with you, make sure you read anything there is to read coming from the mind of the main scholar of the topic – Professor Dr Amy Edmondson. Please read all her books and articles and see her TED Talk. When it comes to Psychological Safety, doing all of the necessary research is vital.

Needless to say, Gene Kim's books are also a must and if you follow him for a bit, you'll soon see why I regard him as one of the few living and breathing examples of a deep, inquisitive and truly Agile heart.

I am genuinely blessed with an amazing team at PeopleNotTech: our CTO Rikard Ottosson, a stunningly brilliant – and thankfully, funny! – tech mind has always been my rock, our incredible team whisperer Ffion Jones is my daily-awe-and-learning-opportunity. All the other wonderful people in our team that we were lucky enough to collect for our bubble make the software that changes so many lives for the better possible and our story a page-turner. They keep me honest in the fight to eradicate this Human Debt every day.

Index

Note: page numbers in **bold** refer to diagrams.